THE CONFLICTS BETWEEN LABOR AND ENVIRONMENTALISM IN THE FEDERAL REPUBLIC OF GERMANY AND THE UNITED STATES

The Conflicts Between Labor and Environmentalism in the Federal Republic of Germany and the United States

HEINRICH SIEGMANN

St. Martin's Press   New York

#12105020

R-89

Library of Congress Cataloging in Publication Data

Siegmann, Heinrich.
  The conflicts between labor and environmentalism in the
Federal Republic of Germany and the United States.

  Bibliography: p.
  1. Labor policy--Germany (West)   2. Labor policy--
United States.   3. Environmental policy--Germany (West)
4. Environmental policy--United States.   I. Title.
HD8451.S56 1985   331.12'0943   85-10004

ISBN 0-312-16236-7

Contents

Preface

In one way or another, many individuals and institutions have contributed to this book. I wish to thank all of them. In particular, I should like to thank the Wissenschaftszentrum Berlin (WZB) and the director of its International Institute for Comparative Social Research, Professor Karl W. Deutsch, for a doctoral fellowship and other forms of support. I feel equally indebted to Professors George Rathjens and Suzanne Berger from the Department of Political Science at the Massachusetts Institute of Technology, U.S.A. Serving on my Ph.D. thesis committee, they contributed invaluably to form and substance of what should eventually lead to this book. The International Institute for Environment and Society at the WZB encouraged and supported me to update the thesis into a book. Newell Mack from Harvard suggested the voting analysis discussed in Chapter 3. The Center for European Studies at Harvard, the WZB and the Deutsche Forschungsgemeinschaft in Bonn provided travel grants. Researching the LER in the United States, I benefitted greatly from the assistance and hospitality of the Center for International Studies at MIT, the Washington Office of the United Steelworkers Union, the Urban Environment Conference in Washington, and Ric Doery. Of course, I am solely responsible for whatever biases, errors or shortcomings this book might contain.

1 Introduction

This book studies the relationship between organized labor and environmental organizations in the United States and the Federal Republic of Germany (FRG) since the mid–1960s. Given the political agenda of this period, energy issues play an important role in this inquiry. As a whole, labor and environmentalists in both countries have widely disagreed on pertinent employment, environmental and energy related issues. Often, their disagreements have appeared to be so profound that the conflicts between the two movements have come to be viewed as natural and inevitable. On the other hand, contrary views have asserted that labor and environmentalists could cooperate –to the advantage of both sides– if they only followed their "true" interests. The main question, which this book will address, is whether and under what conditions the labor–environmentalist conflicts indeed are inevitable; or whether, and how, the two movements COULD cooperate more. To avoid misunderstandings, the question whether they SHOULD cooperate is not the central issue.

I will briefly present some considerations why this topic was chosen. Unemployment and the degradation of the natural environment have become severe, persistent, and possibly worsening problems for most industrialized Western societies. At times, energy, unemployment or environmental protection have been judged by Western publics the most important problems facing their country. While energy and the environment might have lost some of their political saliency for the time being, they are certainly issues to stay. Energy, employment and environmental protection concerns have become recognized as being closely interrelated, but there has remained wide disagreement as to the nature of their interdependence. In a nutshell, dichotomous, integrated and trade–off positions have been distinguished. Traditionally, more employment and a cleaner natural environment were believed to be mutually exclusive. The opposite view has claimed that environmentally protective measures and strategies are particularly labor intensive. The middle position sees a trade–off between both goals, i.e. environmental protection on balance creates employment,

1

yet job losses due to protective measures at particular locations and points in time can not be avoided. Over time, the evidence and social awareness have grown that a way-out of the conflict between the economy and ecology (Simonis, 1983) exists, and that jobs can be secured without pollution given proper economic strategies are applied (Binswanger, et al, 1983).

Energy has probably been the most important issue area bearing on the labor-environmentalist relationship (LER). Energy ranked high on the political agenda, was a central issue in the debate on employment and the environment, and has on many occasions been the reason for direct labor-environmentalist interaction. Energy growth projections, energy mixes, energy prices, governmental policies with respect to energy at times have polarized Western societies (e.g. Lehner, 1979a:45). The California Energy Commission noted "the existence of an energy policy stalemate based upon competing views of energy needs, centralization and preferred technologies" (1979 Biennial Report:7). Lindberg (1977:19) warned:

> We cannot predict the precise patterns that will exist from country to country or in the industrialized world as a whole, but lagging growth rates, high levels of unemployment and frequent bouts of inflation will eventually bring about either a reorientation of the existing energy policy trajectory or the imposition of authoritarian or quasi- authoritarian measures to suppress the protests of the unemployed and those who will see their incomes steadily eroded.

While the importance of energy is undisputed, there is wide disagreement as to how energy choices influence the economy and society. Since the LER has become a salient issue, long-held consensuses have been questioned if not reversed. To name just a few changes: Economic growth per se has come under serious scrutiny. Nuclear energy once believed to be "too cheap to meter" and to be the ultimate answer to mankind's energy needs has turned into a catalyst for broad-based and fundamental criticism of modern industrialized societies. The elasticity of economic and energy growth long believed to be close to one has definitely dropped now to lower values but profound disagreements remain as to where the optimum lies. The approach to the energy issue as basically a supply problem has been challenged by demand oriented views.

These and other breakdowns of consensus have made the perceived interdependencies between energy, employment, and the natural environment, in general, and the LER, in particular, highly political. In both countries studied, the labor movement has already been, and the environmental movement has become an important political actor. Without the acceptance or at least concurrence by labor and environmentalist organizations, policies and programs aiming at increasing employment levels and affecting environmental quality have been difficult to formulate and implement. Environmentalists were accused of blocking tens of billions of dollars worth of investments (e.g. FR, 21.3.1978 and 23.3.1978; in Tofaute, 1978) accompanied by losses or delays of possibly hundreds of thousands of jobs while labor unions have decisively supported projects with allegedly devastating environmental consequences. Indeed, the conflicts with labor and environmental organizations in opposite camps have been seen as politically destabilizing.

> And now environmental politics have polarized this country. Fundamental issues are locked in confrontation; constant antagonisms paralyze the development and enjoyment of natural resources. Balance, compromise and understanding seem to have been arbitrarily banished, as if they had no role in economic and

ecological futures. (AFL—CIO Building and Construction Trades Department Conference, 1979:45)

Similarly, the German Federation of Labor Unions ("DGB") argued that the polarization between labor and environmentalists with respect to nuclear energy has "prevented the evolution of the broad consensus absolutely necessary in a democratic society for a decision of fateful importance" (DGB, 5.4.1977). More generally, the labor—environmentalist conflicts may be taken as instances of the "crisis of governability" alleged by Crozier, Huntington (1975), Kelleher(1981) and others.

> The fundamental issues involve the nature and goals of the post—industrial welfare state, the choices to be made between the requirements of external security and those of domestic welfare, prosperity and distributive justice. The crisis has been precipitated by the end of the remarkable period of post—war economic growth, the increased degree of Western interdependence and resource vulnerability, and increasing political assertion of individual economic and social rights. Thus, at a time when the basic issues on national political agendas are beyond national resolution, governments fave increasingly fragmented and mobilized groups, each demanding solutions carefully responsive to its interests or guaranteeing it a veto in problems of direct concern. To ignore these groups is to court electoral peril; to accede to all is impossible in era of constrained resources. (Kelleher, 1981)

Of course, the LER is not only political in terms of its effects on politics, it is also affected by politics. The party system, the electoral system, the state—economy relationship, the mode of interest intermediation of a country, the policy—making process all come to bear on interest groups and their ways of political interaction.

The political nature of the LER suggests a comparative approach for studying it. Political, cultural, economic and ideological characteristics possibly affecting the LER can best be determined by looking at more than one country. "By comparing our system with another we can recognize legal rules and social institutions which shape the special character of our system" (Summers, 1979:257). As will become apparent, the LER in the US and the FRG, respectively, has been different in important ways.

1.1 Conflict and Cooperation

This work seeks to describe and explain the relationship between organized labor and environmentalism in the two countries under study. Throughout most of this text, the two ideal—type outcomes or manifestations of the LER will be labelled "conflict" and "cooperation". In reality, of course, the LER encompasses a whole spectrum of forms of dissent and consensus. While it seems unnecessary to develop something like a taxonomy of the labor—environmentalist conflict — cooperation dimension, it might be useful to state specifically what "the LER" encompasses in practice.

The most sensational form of conflict probably are violent physical clashes between unionists and environmentalists. Such clashes conceivably occur at picket lines or during site occupations. They will tend to be the more intensive, the more people on both sides are involved and the heavier the fighting. Such conflicts have been rare. More frequent have been conflicts such as demonstrations and counterdemonstrations where at times large numbers of people committed much time and effort to support their cause. Less intense forms of conflict are diverging lobbying activities, affiliations, and

statements and views on programs and policies. Somewhere in the middle
of a conflict— cooperation spectrum is the exchange of views between
the two movements in formal and informal channels. Their views may, on
balance, tend to coincide or diverge, respectively. But compared to
another option in the middle of the spectrum, i.e. no contacts
whatsoever, an exchange of even divergent positions seems slightly on
the cooperative side. To agree on what one disagrees is probably more
cooperative than to entirely ignore each other.

The forms of cooperation are somewhat of a mirror image of the
degrees of conflict. Similar views —yet short of active endorsements—
on goals, policies or activities of the other movement may lead to
active cooperation. More intense forms of cooperation are active
endorsements of positions of the other group, campaigning or lobbying
in behalf of the policies or candidates of the other group, or lobbying
and campaigning jointly with the other group. An even higher degree of
cooperation is reached when both movements participate in or sponsor
common activities such as boycotts, rallies, petition drives,
alliances, coalitions or networks. The intensity grows, of course, the
more each side commits people and resources and the more permanent the
organizational structures are. Thus, instances of conflict and
cooperation can be expected to vary in duration, geographic scale,
intensity and the forms of activities one engages in. An examination
of the LER, therefore, must be concerned not only with the positions on
issues of the major actors but also with the forms of activities, the
intensity of commitments, and the forms of political organization.

Any discussion of the LER becoming more cooperative or conflictual
must ask what the two movements each might have to gain and lose,
respectively, from cooperation: Who gets —or loses— what, when and how?
Several theoretical considerations suggest that labor—environmentalist
cooperation can be mutually beneficial. The perspective of labor could
be the following: Environmentalism in the long term has gained in
popularity whereas union influence has stagnated if not declined. In
the US, labor as a political force has lost influence since the late
1950s, as membership decline, lost legislative battles, and fewer
successful unionization elections indicate. In the FRG, labor is
stronger but has also faced erosions of its political clout.
Environmentalism in both countries has come a long way to shed narrow
particularistic interests and has turned to look at employment not as a
peripheral issue but one crucial to any long term comprehensive
environmental perspective. Environmentalism in the US has become an
important member of "the more broadly based coalition" which Piore
(1978:4) considered necessary for labor to enter into in order to
prevail in some of its most critical political battles. In the FRG,
Seitenzahl (1976:89), similarly, advocated increased connections and
changing coalitions between labor and other organizations: "The
cleavage must be bridged confining [environmentalist] citizen groups to
problems in the 'reproductive sector' while one seeks to locate unions
solely in the 'productive sector'". Such areas could be occupational
safety and health, employment security, housing and urban development,
consumer issues, energy pricing, etc.

The environmentalist perspective, on the other hand, suggests
advantages from cooperation as well. Environmentalism as a political
movement is still young and could benefit from labor as an experienced,
accepted, and respected political force by drawing on its political,
financial, and organizational resources. More cooperation could raise
the awareness among the two respective constituencies and the general
public of the interdependencies of energy, environmental and economic
policies. Labor— environmentalist cooperation in the energy field
could entail the promotion of energy sources which are both employment
intensive and environmentally benign.

One must, of course, not expect that labor will favor employment
intensive energy options by default. After all, workers are also
consumers and —except for those benefitting directly from
labor—intensive energy— might be more interested that energy be cheap,

4

safe and reliable than that it be labor- intensive. On the other hand, environmentalists can point to the fact that on the micro level, energy intensity has increased and labor intensity has decreased -and at least some causality might be assumed. That a company selects the energy-labor mix that suits its interests best is, of course, a rational and legitimate behavior. However, what is rational on the micro level may be quite irrational and costly for society as a whole. Thus, it is quite conceivable that parts of both environmentalism and labor should seek to create the political environment (in terms of taxes, subsidies, regulations, inter-agency consultation, etc) which would promote employment- intensive and environmentally benign energy sources and usage. In the past, employment considerations, indeed, played only a small role in national energy planning. In general, a labor-environmentalist rapprochement would likely strengthen the "anti-conservative" political forces in both countries, most notably as a counterweight to business power.

What might increased labor-environmentalist cooperation possibly cost each movement? First, each movement might lose members who disagree for economic, political and ideological reasons with increased cooperation. Second, increased cooperation might be perceived to result in policies in the short or long term disadvantageous to the whole or some parts of the two movements.

Under the first category might fall disgruntled members who oppose the other movement for ideological reasons. As we will see, the membership of the National Wildlife Federation, or of building and construction unions are such possible candidates. Further, officials in the unions and work councils with entrenched political affiliations might not agree to work with environmentalists. Tensions if not secessions within the organizations will be likely consequences.

Second, parts of either movement might perceive employment and environmental protection as basically dichotomous. One example would be to pose the choice as one between either higher wages or improved environmental protection in order to improve productivity. Overall, labor-environmentalist rapprochement would imply to those groups sharing this view that they would have to "pay" by earning less or by being exposed to a more degraded environment, respectively. Further, changing energy policies as a result of labor-environmentalist rapprochement might exacerbate the probable conflicts especially within the labor movement. Even if shifts toward more environmentally benign energy production and usage will result in the net increase of employment that environmentalists and many US unions (as well as independent studies) have predicted, the kind and mix of the new employment will certainly be different from the old. Supply oriented energy policies, for instance, have meant construction jobs using heavy machinery distinctly different from the more manual construction work that a more conservation oriented energy strategy would entail. Not only might extensive retraining for the effected workers be needed but -from a union perspective- perhaps more importantly, union jurisdictions would have to be redefined. McConnell (1967:306f) argued that a change in the constituency foundation of any organization is profoundly disruptive, especially to the security of the leadership. Applied to organized labor, "powerful fiefdoms" (Herding and Sabel, 1979) not uncommon in many unions might face serious challenges.

Any profound change of work patterns is bound also to effect wage patterns in ways which will often mean less pay. The building and construction industry, for example, which will be one of the first affected by policy changes as a result of labor-environmentalist cooperation, has the highest earning differentials between union and non-union workers in the US. All these possible conflicts within and among unions might weaken the labor movement as a whole and thus weaken the chances for cooperation with environmentalism.

In sum, the possible benefits of a joint labor- environmentalist strategy deriving from the combination of their forces must be balanced especially against the possible cost of increased internal divisions

5

mostly within the labor movement.

1.2 Explaining the LER

In order to seek an answer to the central question of this study, i.e. "Is the LER necessarily conflictual or is cooperation possible?", the relevant influences on the LER must be identified and examined. The first explanation that comes to mind has at its center the economic interests of the two main actors. As long as these interests are different, there will be conflict; the more compatible they are, the likelier will there be cooperation. Explaining manifest political differences merely by differences of economic interests, however, would be a bit trivial and only raise the new question of which factors determine these interests.

What, then, might be the pertinent influences on the LER that ought to be examined? I will approach this question from two angles. The first is interest group theory; the second what (European) political science today calls peace and conflict research. The discussion of interest groups is obviously related to this topic since labor and environmentalists are interest groups. Recent research on interest group politics suggests that the examination of socioeconomic and market factors by themselves is insufficient to explain the intermediation of interests today (Berger, 1981:65). Rather, variables such as national historical experience, the role of the state, and the instabilities inherent in representational systems ought to be additionally examined. Second, the area of peace and conflict research, although primarily concerned with the nation–state level, appears applicable to deal with cooperation and conflict at the subnational level. Karl Deutsch et al. (1957) examined the process of integration and disintegration of what they called security communities. The Deutsch group made the following definitions:

> A SECURITY–COMMUNITY is a group of people which has become "integrated". By INTEGRATION we mean the attainment, within a territory, of a "sense of community" and of institutions and practices strong enough and widespread enough to assure, for a "long" time, dependable expectations of "peaceful change" among its population. By SENSE OF COMMUNITY we mean a belief on the part of individuals in a group that they have come to agreement on at least this one point: that common social problems must and can be resolved by processes of "peaceful change". By PEACEFUL CHANGE we mean the resolution of social problems, normally by institutionalized procedures, without resort to large–scale physical force (p.5).

Applying these concepts to the LER, cooperation between organized labor and environmentalism, then, can be thought of as the attainment of a "sense of community" and of institutions and practices strong enough and widespread enough to assure for some time the pursuit of interests held in common. Like the sense of community found relevant for the integration of nations, a cooperative labor–environmentalist relationship can be expected to be "a matter of mutual sympathy and loyalties; of 'we–feeling', trust, and mutual consideration; of partial identification in terms of self–images and interests; of mutually successful predictions of behavior, and of cooperative action in accordance with it –in short, a matter of a perpetual dynamic process of mutual attention, communication, perception of needs, and of responsiveness in the process of decision making" (p.36). Without this kind of relationship, conflict must be expected.

Thus, the beliefs of individuals organized in groups, the institutions they have formed, the practices they have adopted, the processes by which they rank decisions, their historical experiences, the ways their institutions are integrated in the polity are all possible influences on the LER. The presence or absence, respectively, of certain factors possibly explains a conflictual or cooperative relationship. This study will analyze the saliency of five explanations for the LER: (1) The perception of a built-in contradiction between employment and environmental protection goals necessitates conflicts between labor and environmentalism; (2) differences in demographic and socioeconomic composition of the two movements prevent cooperation; (3) internal, organizational will formation and decision making processes favor the persistence of conflicts; (4) existing political/ institutional features in the two countries prevent increased labor-environmentalist cooperation; and (5) cleavages of values, ideologies and world views going far beyond those of the first explanation prevent changes of the LER. These explanations are complementary rather than mutually exclusive, and are introduced in the following.

The first explanation notes the absence of a sense of community between labor and environmentalism due to perceptions of a built-in contradiction between efforts to protect the environment and to assure employment. In this view, new jobs often can be created only at the cost of environmental deterioration while —on the other hand— environmental protection measures tend to threaten existing and future employment. Economic growth is seen as a pre-condition to create and secure employment while inevitably infringing on the natural environment. Increased energy production, in this view, is necessary to maintain economic growth. Economic prosperity is believed to be the best prerequisite to pay for anti-pollution measures. Therefore, particularly at times of economic crises, conflicts between labor and environmentalism are seen as natural and inevitable.

In the coming years, structural economic problems must be expected to persist in most industrial countries: Unemployment will remain high, keeping down inflation will be difficult, government budgets will be severely constrained, productivity will need boosts, environmentalal cleanup will be expensive. These developments, in this view, will tend to increase the cleavages between labor and environmental interests and likely mean intensified labor- environmentalist conflicts.

Second, labor-environmentalist conflicts are explained by the different demographic and socio-economic bases of the two movements. Organized labor consisting of a large share of blue-collar workers is pitted against the predominantly middle-class environmental movement. The average environmentalist, the argument goes, is better educated, has a higher income, works in higher-valued jobs, and is younger than the average union member. These differences, in this view, have exacerbated the conflicts between workers and environmentalists. The attitudes toward employment and environmental goals are believed to be decisively determined by one's social base and, thus, have been significantly different.

Third, internal will formation and decision making procedures within the two movements have been cited as possible sources of conflicts. This argument has been applied to the relationship between leadership and membership within an organization as well as to the relations among member organizations within a federation. Conflicts prevail, in this view, if the respective memberships favored different relations to the other movement than its leadership pursued, while its opportunities to actually challenge the leadership or its policies are limited. This argument has been particularly applied to unions since being a member in an environmental organization is much more voluntaristic than union membership. A lack of internal democracy, of course, could also have prevented higher conflict levels between the two movements. Further, different degrees of centralization within, in particular, the labor movements have possibly affected the nature of an individual union's or its subordinate bodies' relationship with other organized interests. The more a union or a labor federation is centralized, the more will its constituent bodies be limited in taking positions or courses of action on their own. In this view, unions and environmental organizations have been in conflict because limits to internal decision making procedures prevented more environmentally concerned views and factions in the union movement to prevail.

The fourth explanation focuses on political features in the two countries. Different political affiliations and access opportunities to political institutions of labor and environmentalism, in particular, may have contributed to the conflicts or, at least, have prevented more cooperation. It is conceivable, this argument goes, that their conflicts were exacerbated because one movement had close ties to the government apparatus, a party or the legislature but the other had not. If the two movements have affiliations of different strength, let's say, to political parties, then party cleavages may easily also cause conflicts between the two movements. The length of time a movement has been present on the political scene, furthermore, probably has influenced the movement's political access and affiliations in important ways. Here, the differences between labor and environmentalism, of course, are substantial. Further, if one movement has access to the political process and the other does not, then the consequent lack of opportunities or incentives (often provided by government fora) to meet, to exchange views, or to agree on what to disagree, likely reduces chances of cooperation.

The fifth explanation focuses on cleavages of ideologies, values, world-views or historical experiences underlying the LER. This explanation may be put forth in three ways. One way is to look at the labor-environmentalist conflicts as following a left-right dimension. Given the socio- economic differences of the two movements, labor is seen as functioning as the protector of the economic underdogs seeking to gain more economic equity. Environmentalists, on the other hand, are depicted as the defenders of the economic status-quo who –being higher up on the economic ladder– are inclined and can afford to protect their environment, their "private idyl".

A second version of this explanation argues that the labor-environmentalist conflict basically is one between "old" and "new" politics. According to Inglehart (1977 and 1979), those engaging in "old" politics tend to view the world in "materialist" terms and emphasize representation- based political activities. "New" politics, on the other hand, are governed by "post- materialist" values and entail direct (rather than representational) political activities. Labor, in this view, perceives the employment/ environment problem basically as one aligned along a socio- economic left-right dimension while environmentalism approaches it in "new politics" or lifestyle terms. Thus, from this perspective, labor-environmentalist conflicts are rooted not merely in differences over policy but are centered in the more normative question of how present and future generations may want to organize their physical and political environmental.

The third version of the ideology explanation is concerned with a movement's ideological propensity to cooperate or disagree with other interest groups. One would expect that the more particularistic an organization's scope of concerns, the more difficult will it probably be to enter into agreements or coalitions with other political actors. Also, the closer a movement perceives its integration into the political system, the more hostile will it tend to feel toward interests (still) outside of the system. Central in this explanation is an organization's perception of what comprises a favorable state-economy relationship and where does the organization fit into it. If, to give a probable example, organized labor and environmentalism both would see business or government policies as adversary to employment and environmental protection, then the perceptions of a common enemy could possibly be a strong bond and entail future common activities. On the other hand, if –as many argue– labor has become more or less interlocked with the energy industry and government (with respect to energy matters) and guided by similar basic worldviews while environmentalism politically and ideologically stands on the fringes, then the labor—environmentalist conflicts might conceivably be explained by such a factor—of—order/ countervailing power dichotomy. 12

Hill (1978:10) proposed to break down vague generalizations into actual mechanisms and weigh the importance of one factor against another (not necessarily quantitatively) rather than trying to find one single explanatory theory. He considered such an approach more realistic than hoping to build theory from the results of "endless specific hypotheses tested against the whole mass of available data". I will also follow such a course of action. Regarding the LER, each explanation probably has applied somewhat. How relevant are they relative to each other and over time? What are the conditions under which conflicts have prevailed? When did the two movements cooperate? What may the future bear? The bulk of this volume will seek answer to these questions by discussing these explanations one by one.

I will make the following arguments:

1. The perception of a dichotomy between assuring employment and protecting the natural environment with respect to energy policies by the labor unions but not the environmental movement was a major reason for the labor—environmentalist conflicts in the past (i.e. Explanation 1 applied).

2. The composition of the labor and environmental movements (Explanation 2) differed considerably but it is questionable that these differences have translated into clearly conflictual attitudes and behavior. Existing processes of internal will formation and decision making (Explanation 3), political/ institutional factors (Explanation 4), and ideological and historical backgrounds (Explanation 5) all contributed to the conflicts prevalent in the past.

3. The perception of a built-in dichotomy has been losing ground to the view that environmental protection and employment can co-exist, and that a more cooperative LER is feasible in principle. Overall, labor unionists and environmentalists over time have cooperated more. However, important differences have existed (1) between the general conditions pertinent to the LER in the FRG and the US, respectively, and (2) among the labor unions in the US.

4. In the FRG, the labor movement is well integrated politically which the environmental movement is not. This has prevented significant changes of the LER, if it is measured by official policies and formal contacts. Inofficial ties between union membership and environmental groups, on the other hand, have increased. "New Politics" sentiments predominate the politically active in the environmental movement but also gain ground among labor membership. The centralized structure of German labor buffers obvious cleavages and likely exacerbates latent ones between union membership and leadership. The advent of ecological parties may increase labor— environmentalist tensions in the short term but improve the LER in the long run. Compared to the US, "high-level" politics bear particularly strong on the LER.

5. In the US, the perception of similar interests, in general, between parts of labor and environmentalism has been growing. As a whole, the LER in the US has been better, more divers and less static than in the FRG. With respect to energy issues, cleavages among labor unions have been substantial. Cooperation between environmentalism and several large unions in the service and industrial sectors has increased while the building and construction LER has remained predominantly conflictual. Improvements of the LER in the US were linked both to changing perceptions of the interdependencies among employment, environmental protection and energy; and to the outwardly "hostile" politics of the Reagan administration. This process, in turn, was

encouraged or facilitated by the decentralized structure of American organized labor (compared to the German situation), the lower degree of corporatism in US society, the Presidential system in the US (as opposed to the German Parliamentary one), and the more pronounced countervailing power role of important parts of US labor with respect to issues pertinent to the LER.

1.3 Outline and Methodological Remarks

The book follows the chain of thinking outlined so far. Chapter 2 will present some background information pertinent to the LER. It introduces the main labor unions and environmental groups active in energy matters in the two countries. Subsequently, it gives a run-down of the most important events of the LER and of the major arguments used by both sides with respect to energy and environmental policies for both countries. This chapter seeks to answer the question "What is the LER?" while the subsequent chapters discuss why the LER was the way it was.

A conceptual difficulty permeating this work ought to be raised here. In a topic as broad as this, how does one distinguish between descriptive and analytical information? Chapter 2 is clearly meant to describe the LER. But Chapters 3 to 7 while intended as an analytical response to the question "Why was the LER the way it was?", are also descriptive in response to questions like "What is the membership composition of environmentalism?" or "What is the decision making structure of German labor?". In each of these chapters, I can see no way of avoiding considerable amounts of information that are descriptive in the latter sense in order to be analytical in the former.

Chapters 3 to 7, hence, will discuss the explanations for the LER introduced above. In Chapter 3, I will examine the view that the LER has been conflictual because employment and environmental goals pose a built–in dichotomy. I will study how the general public, labor and environmentalists have traded–off concerns regarding employment and the natural environment. Particularly, I will be concerned with the political response to the employment/ environmental protection strains at times of economic difficulties. For the US, this chapter includes a bivariate statistical analysis studying the correlations of a LER indicator with unemployment and unionization rates.

Chapter 4 studies the alleged influence of the different membership compositions of the two movements on the LER. It analyzes the demographic and socio– economic composition of the two movements, the shifts thereof, and examines in what way membership characteristics have affected pertinent membership attitudes –and, thus, possibly the organizations' policies. This chapter relies on a secondary analysis of public opinion and membership survey results.

Chapter 5 is concerned with the possible impact of intra–union will formation and decision making on the LER. It asks whether there is a concordance between union democracy and the readiness to work with other interest groups. It studies the external and internal constraints unions underly which might preclude the democratic processes heralded by Western polities. Subsequently, union electoral procedures, proceedings at union conventions, the role of the union press, interest intermediation between leadership, membership and work councils are examined on how they have affected union policy making in particular with respect to energy and the environment.

The impact on the LER of two characteristics of the political systems in the FRG and the US is discussed in Chapter 6. This chapter looks at the different opportunities granted by the US Presidential system and the German Parliamentary system to interest groups which seek to influence legislative decisions, elections, and to participate in government fora for interest articulation and aggregation. It seeks to show how the strong interlocked relationship of parts of labor with government bodies and/or industry have contributed to the impression that important unions in the energy field have become a factor of order while environmentalism has functioned as a countervailing power. Further, it compares the political weights of the two movements in the two countries and discusses how differences in organizational and conflict potentials have affected the LER. Finally, the impact of two recent developments in the two countries are discussed. In the FRG, the consolidation of the environmental movement into the Green party means both new strains and new opportunities for the LER. In the US, the Reagan administration has significantly changed the political environment bearing on the LER.

Chapter 7 closes off the analysis of the labor–environmentalist conflicts by looking at the impact on the LER of the organizations' different heritage, ideologies and worldviews. It traces how US business unionism and German social partnership have affected labor's relationships to government and private interests; and how labor's heritage and ideology have made it possible to assume the factor of order role alleged in Chapter 6. This chapter further seeks to answer the question to what extent the perception of business as a common adversary of the two movements has affected the LER.

The final chapter summarizes the validity of each explanation and discusses under which circumstances which explanations were the most appropriate ones. Moreover, several questions that have not been answered are raised. The book concludes with a, somewhat speculative, outlook for labor and environmentalism, and thus the LER, in both countries.

2 The Evolution of the LER in the FRG and the US

2.1 Labor and Environmentalism in the FRG: The Main Actors

The labor movement in Germany, with its origins in the 19th century, had become a considerable political force when the Nazis came to power, forbidding and eradicating organized labor activities. After WWII, labor was reconstituted under the umbrella of the Deutscher Gewerkschaftsbund (DGB) —the Federation of German Labor Unions. The DGB consists of 17 individual unions with a total of about eight million members. Outside of the DGB, several associations represent another 1.5 M members of the labor force. Close to 40% of the work force belongs to a union. Unlike in the US, union membership in the FRG has been increasing in the long run both in terms of absolute numbers and percentage share of the labor force. This book will exclusively deal with DGB unions, since they comprise the vast majority of organized labor and are commonly —also with respect to environmental and energy issues— equated with the "labor union movement".

The most important unions relevant for the LER are listed in Table 2.1. The largest union is the Industrial Union of Metal Workers (IGM) with about 2.7 M members, followed by the Union for Public Services, Transportation and Traffic (OTV – 1.1 M members). Both unions have a substantial stake in energy related issues. The IGM jurisdiction includes workers and employees in component manufacturing for power plants and energy-intensive industries. The OTV organizes among others the workers and employees of electric utilities totalling 120,000 people. A third union with a heavy stake in energy and environmental politics is the Industrial Union of Mining and Energy (IGBE). Most of its members are coal miners. Affected by the construction of energy facilities is the Industrial Union for Construction, Stones and Earth (IGBSE). Also important for the LER is the Chemical, Paper and Ceramics Workers Union (IGCPK). It represents 650,000 members in some of the most heavily polluting industries. Several smaller unions have received less attention in the environmental and energy debate but have often adopted positions contrary to the DGB and the major unions.

12

Union	Membership 1983	Reasons for Consideration
Industrial Union of Metal Workers (Industriegewerkschaft Metall - "IGM")	2,536,000	largest, most influential union in the DGB; represents auto, steel, power plant component manufacturing, etc.
Union for Public Services and Transportation (Gewerkschaft öffentliche Dienste, Transport und Verkehr - ÖTV)	1,174,000	second largest union; represents workers in public utilities; important participant in nuclear energy disputes
Industrial Union for Mining and Energy (Industriegewerkschaft Bergbau und Energie - IGBE)	366,000	long-standing involvement in coal politics; supporter of expansion of fossile and nuclear power
Industrial Union for Construction, Stone and Earth (Industriegewerkschaft Bau, Steine, Erden - IGBSE)	523,000	has important stake in (large) construction projects
Industrial Union for Chemicals, Paper and Cheramics (Industriegewerkschaft Chemie, Papier, Keramik - IGCPK)	635,000	involved in issues like asbestos, toxic chemicals, ocean dumping

Table 2-1 : German Unions Involved in Environmental and Energy Politics

The unions in the DGB are fairly independent of the umbrella organization. They have financial authority, are national in scope, and are autonomous in collective bargaining ("Tarifautonomie"). The main functions of the DGB are to represent labor's political interests, to coordinate their activities, to be a forum for jurisdictional disputes, and to reduce organizational costs by assuming tasks which would otherwise be done by several unions less efficiently. The DGB has played an important role in energy and environmental policy development.

The environmental movement in the FRG is much more diversified than the labor movement. According to Watts (1979:171), it consists of "all groups, from nature protection groups, local citizen groups, support groups for alternative technology to all those alternative groups striving for environmental goals". Three basic groupings make up the German environmental movement. They are the nature protection and conservation groups, environmental citizen action groups, and electoral environmental parties and lists. Most nature protection and conservation organizations started at the turn of the century as part of an international conservation movement while citizen action groups ("Buergerinitiativen") and a few environmental organizations began to form in the late 1960s in response to environmental pollution. The nature groups and some of the modern environmental organizations operate on a regional or national scale, meet regularly, have a formal organization and a large dues-paying, passive membership reached by regular, magazine-type publications. The alternative or citizen groups movement, on the other hand, is a loosely connected network of local groups which have been convened on an ad-hoc basis with a small but active membership, with a high membership fluctuation and a minimum of formal structure. According to Watts (1979:171), the main ideological difference between nature and citizen groups lies in the fact that the former "in principle accepts the industrial state while the latter tends to critically reject it".

The nature protection and conservation organizations combine 2-3 M members but have kept a low profile in energy and environmental politics. Two notable exceptions are the Federation for Environmental and Nature Protection in Germany (Bund Umwelt- und Naturschutz Deutschland — BUND) —an organization that had rapidly grown to more than 40,000 members within a few years time after its formation in the early 1970s (Natur & Umwelt, 4/77:15); and, more recently, the German section of Greenpeace.

Estimates of the number of active citizen groups and their membership in the FRG have varied considerably. In 1977 when their influence peaked, estimates ranged from 3-4000 groups and 1.5 M members to 50,000 groups. The Federal Ministry of Interior, presumably the most reliable source, estimated in 1976 that 15,000 groups were formed in the last few years. Among those were presumably 3-4000 environmental citizen groups totalling more than 1.2 M registered members (Andritzky,et al., 1978:36). The best known alliance of citizen groups and probably the environmental spokesman in the nation became the Federation of Citizen Groups for Environmental Protection (Bund Buergerinitiativen Umweltschutz — BBU). Formed by 15 local groups in 1972, it consisted in 1977 of more than 900 environmental citizen groups representing 300,000 members that are allegedly capable of reaching more than 15 M citizens (Zeit, 25.2.1977:2). The citizen groups were by far more politically active than the established organizations. However, while still forming the "base" of the environmental movement, the citizen groups have vacated the top spot as environmental spokespersons for the Green party.

Since 1978, parts of the environmental movement have entered electoral contests with growing success. By the end of 1981, ecological parties or lists had been elected to numerous city halls and into three state parliaments. However, they had missed the 5 quorum in several other states, in the 1979 elections to the European Parliament and in the 1980 federal elections nor in several state elections. Only three years later, the Greens have become established as a political force of their own. They were elected to the German and European Parliament and to most state legislatures. In many city halls and in one state, they have entered into formal or informal coalitions with the SPD. They have replaced the FDP as the third party in the country. If this trend continues, it seems only a question of time until the Greens hold government positions on the state level.

2.2 The Main Events and Arguments Pertinent to the LER in the FRG

Protection of the natural environment became a political concern around 1970 in the FRG. By that date, the terms "Umweltschutz" (environmental protection) and "Lebensqualitaet" (quality of life) became widely used, coinciding with the beginning of the SPD-led national government. Not accidentally, although erroneously, the coinage of the term "Lebensqualitaet" has been frequently ascribed to the new Chancellor Willy Brandt. First environmental citizen groups began to form and the first environmental protection laws were debated. In 1972, the DGB published a document titled 'Guiding Thoughts on Environmental Protection', and the IGM sponsored a major conference on 'Quality of Life, Employment and Economic Growth'.

By the mid-1970s, the complexities involved in attaining environmental quality had become apparent. The oil price crisis had introduced the topic of resource scarcity to the unexpecting public. In 1974, the country went into a recession. Energy became a political issue and the federal government passed its first energy program. The DGB published its 'Environmental Program' which as a statement of intents is still authoritative today. Also, the first political tensions between employment and environmental protection interests surfaced. In the perception of the public and within labor, the requirements of economic growth clashed more and more with environmental protection goals. The LER was becoming an issue.

Hans-Helmut Wustenhagen, at the time spokesman for the BBU and for several years probably the most renowned environmental leader, for example, declared in 1974 "that everything now depends upon whether there will be an alliance with the labor unions. If, however, we cannot reach an alliance with the unions, then the future will look bleak" ("Konkret" 4,1974:22, in Alemann, Mambrey, 1980:246). The newly stated DGB position, indeed implied willingness to cooperate with environmental groups. Thesis 4 in the DGB Environmental Program depicts environmental protection and its realization as dependent on political power. It sees industry interested in low production costs pitted against those directly and indirectly affected by production processes endangering the environment. Thesis 31 asserts that people affected by pollution will have to surpass considerable obstacles in deciding about and protecting their environment (DGB Umweltprogramm, 1974).

In practice, however, labor-environmentalist cooperation was not a serious possibility. In labor's views, environmental politics isolated as they were faced slim chances of success. Rather, the argument went, these groups groups needed close ties to the struggle of wage earners and their unions for co-determination at work and in the economy. The installation of Economic and Social Councils, in which the labor movement would be represented and which have been an old labor union demand, would allow to integrate environmental concerns with those of the work force.

2.2.1 Open Conflicts on Nuclear Energy: 1975-1977

Despite generally growing environmental awareness and sharpening local environmental conflicts, the environmental movement was not of national political influence until the mid-70s —if it could rightly be

15

called a "movement" at all. Rather, it was what Deutsch and Rokkan (Lerner, Gorden 1969:36) might have called "the mobilization of the periphery" that established the environmental movement as a political entity and the LER as a politically salient issue. In 1975, local and regional citizen action groups opposing a nuclear power plant near the village of Wyhl in southwestern Germany resorted to occupations of the planned construction site. This resulted in skirmishes with the police, attained national media coverage, and led to a construction stop which is still in effect. The environmental movement visibly had proven its clout for the first time. In late 1976, a large demonstration, this time in northern Germany opposing the nuclear power plant to be constructed near the village of Brokdorf again received national attention and made the LER a political issue of national significance. The Brokdorf protests triggered a counterdemonstration of 7000 employees of the Kraftwerk Union, the largest German manufacturer of power plants (WdA, 3.12.76:2). During 1977, more protests were mounted against several nuclear energy facilities and coal-fired power plant projects. Most notable were: a second and this time "peaceful" demonstration near Brokdorf; a demonstration and the construction of an "anti-atom village" against a nuclear plant near Grohnde which resulted in numerous injuries; a demonstration against the breeder reactor under construction in Kalkar; protests against the site selection process for the integrated reprocessing and waste disposal center in the state of Lower Saxony which finally selected the Gorleben site; the abandonment of a coal-fired project in Berlin; and the "sell-out" of a citizen group in Bergkamen which waived its objections against a coal-fired plant in return for a large sum to be paid by the utility to the members of the group. By 1978, virtually a moratorium for new nuclear plant construction existed and the focus of environmental protests temporarily shifted to other issues.

The DGB responded to the flurry of anti-nuclear protests by issuing in April of 1977 a first official statement cautiously in favor of nuclear energy. It expressed much stronger support for the German nuclear program in November in a revised statement (see Chapters 3 and 5 for more details). Numerous unions adopted resolutions favoring the expansion of nuclear energy usage under certain conditions. Further, coal miners demonstrated against the Bergkamen pay-off (WdA,13.5.77:8). Most newsworthy, in November 1977, a rally attended by 40,000 trade unionists was held in Dortmund where the leaders of all unions with a major stake in energy issues demanded the uncurbed construction of coal and nuclear power plants. The labor-environmentalist conflicts had reached a climax.

The positions taken in public by leaders of the two movements were assymetrical. The environmental spokesmen were interested in cooperation with the unions but were disappointed with labor's pro-nuclear reactions. Labor, on the other hand, was reluctant to accept the citizen groups based environmental movement as a legitimate and viable political force. It appeared to wait for the citizen groups to die away and thus relieve labor from having to deal with them.

Commenting on the conflict in Wyhl, i.e. prior to the first DGB statement, Wolfgang Sternstein (1976) -a BBU leader- criticized labor that it lacked a public stance on nuclear energy. In general, he claimed, the unions had adopted a position of "optimism toward progress ("Fortschrittsoptimismus") and growth fetishism" (p.84). He apparently had hoped that labor would oppose nuclear energy: "If the international labor union movement should decide to wage a struggle against the international nuclear industry in the interest of mankind, then that might indeed be a historical turning-point of world-wide significance" (p.85). No wonder that the BBU was extremely critical of the labor union demonstration for coal and nuclear plant construction in Dortmund which the BBU claimed served "exclusively the economic and profit interests of the nuclear industry" (SZ, 12.11.77:2). By its unambiguous affirmation of nuclear energy, the BBU argued, the DGB had succumbed to the "atom lobby", and had created "an unpleasant and unnecessary front" against the environmental citizen groups. The BBU pointed out that, after all, particularly labor unionists were quite active in the citizen groups. Yet, the environmental movement also acknowledged that it was difficult for labor unions to identify citizen groups as partners of cooperation. Hans-Gunther Schumacher (1978), member of the executive board of the BBU, argued that labor unions being mass organizations were inert finding it difficult to change priorities, especially if a basic consensus was lacking on which direction they should go. He further conceded that the middle-class base of the citizen groups made it difficult to understand labor union concerns. (These thoughts correspond to Explanations 3 and 2 forwarded in Chapter 1, and will be taken up in Chapters 5 and 4.)

Labor's main target of criticism in the environmental movement was the citizen groups, while the traditional nature protection organizations were mostly ignored. Several themes emerged. One major theme concerned the ability and legitimacy of environmental groups to represent the public will. In general, the citizen action groups were described as violators of or, at least, intruders in the established political order. The DGB weekly 'World of Labor' (Welt der Arbeit —"WdA") rejected the frequently made argument that the citizen groups have been a result of the lack of communication between political parties and citizens. While parties should try to correspond to the public will, the paper argued, citizens should try to become active within and through the political parties. If the citizen groups seek to struggle against majority interests, then they will inevitably come into conflict with laws and the constitutional order. Only if they obey the rules of democracy, then they can play a useful role in the extra-parliamentary realm (WdA, 14.1.77:4).

Similarly the IGM, the most influential union in the country, expressed support for improved citizen participation in site selection and planning since open disputes over disagreements were the best way to arrive at the proper decisions. The union also stressed the citizen groups' rights to peaceful demonstrations. But it explicitly rejected a partnership with the BBU (Metall, 5/77:11, 7/77:2, 10/77:3, 20/77:2). Eugen Loderer, the president of the IGM, warned:

> We value critical initiatives of citizens. But they must not rise to become a substitute for political parties. Above all, they lack firm democratic structures. Their decision making process is not transparent. If these forces even try to push through violently as a small minority what the force of their arguments can not achieve, then we will no longer accept them good-humoredly. It is necessary that the parties again fill the vacuum that they have let evolve. (Rechenschaftsbericht zum Gewerkschaftstag der IG Metall, 1977)

The chemical workers union resolved at its 1975 national convention that

> models like citizen groups ... are examples that citizens are willing and capable of participating in decisions affecting them. But they must not seek to substitute parliamentary democracy by "grass-root mobilization" nor parliamentary control by direct democracy ("Imperatives Mandat",HS).
>
> The formation of opinion and political will outside of parliament must, however, be geared at maintaining, vitalizing and expanding parliamentary democracy. Within this framework, there is also a wide area for trade union activities —not as "appendices" to anonymous or politically directed initiatives nor with them in "action coalitions" but as an independent and

17

self—reliant force. (GMH, 1976:313f)

The OTV president Kluncker stated in his 'Theses on Nuclear Energy' that the unions will not tolerate being misused like a Trojan horse by some small groups who agitate against nuclear energy or who say environmental protection but mean to question any state authority (otv—magazin (6/79:3).

The second theme of criticism voiced by labor regarding environmental citizen groups contended that there are different interests because of the different socio— economic bases of the respective memberships. As will be discussed in detail in Chapter 4, labor depicted environmentalists as belonging to the more affluent segments of society who live in the suburbs and thus could afford to be concerned about the environment. Labor union members, on the other hand, lived in a less privileged situation. They had to be concerned with securing employment and making economic ends meet which left them with less time and fewer motives to worry about a clean natural environment [1]. Environmental leaders, in turn, rejected this argument as a defamation intended to denounce a cumbersome critic.

A third line of argument rejected the environmental groups as an amalgam of idealists, elitists, and naive innocents, which have frequently even been subverted by "radicals". A DGB district in the Ruhr area asserted a desire to return to pre—industrial life when a citizen group sought to prevent the drilling of mine and air conditioning shafts for an underground coal mine in a recreation area. Since German environmental laws belonged to the strictest in the world, the argument went, the "anti—groups" had no reason for "environmental hysteria". The citizen groups were depicted as prefering a life with outhouses and jungle drums to power plants, cars, roads, sanitation facilities and telephones (WdA, 17.9.76:8).

Moreover, several unions depicted citizens with environmental idealism and lack of political experience as easy prey for communist and terrorist subversives. An OTV official in the district where the Brokdorf plant is located claimed that communist groups with hardly any workers among them had ideologically infiltrated a federation of citizen groups active in his district. Stressing the social responsibility of environmental protection, he suggested that the citizen groups were not part of a social movement and some would not even merit the term "citizen" (WdA, 25.3.77:4). The IGBE went even further in its rejection of the environmental citizen groups. While its president Adolf Schmidt who is also a high ranking SPD official and member of the Bundestag, was initially resigned to living with the citizen groups "since we once brought them to life as electoral supporters", the IGBE journal saw them later on the same level as terrorist murderers:

> The question of the constitutional order is too important to be left aside. There is also no reason for being careless. Violent attacks on the constitutional order have not decreased but increased. They do not merely include the cowardly murders of Drenkmann, Buback, Ponto (public figures killed by terrorist groups,HS) and many others. They also include those violent actions and site occupations that we experience with respect to securing our energy supplies. (Einheit, 15.8.77)

Moreover, the IGBE depicted the nuclear opponents as myopic uninformed communists protesting under red flags. They were advised, therefore, to get better information on the Soviet Union where many nuclear power plants had already been operating. Many protestors would forget their concerns about a nuclear power plant if it only bore a red star, the paper sarcastically stated (Einheit, 1.5.79:2, 15.5.79:1).

18

2.2.2 1977-1982: Less Open Battles But Conflicts Remain

After the high point of the labor-environmentalist rift in the fall of 1977, the open conflicts quieted down and the LER became more subtle. Several developments are noteworthy.

The citizen groups continued to mount highly visible campaigns. I will briefly list the most important events. At the end of March of 1979, the so-called Gorleben-hearing on the suitability of Gorleben as the German reprocessing and waste disposal site coincided with the Three-Mile-Island reactor accident in the US. It gave much additional publicity to the "Gorleben-Treck" originally planned to put pressure on the Gorleben hearing. Fifty to one hundred thousand demonstrators gathered in Hannover and probably influenced Lower Saxony's decision to postpone indefinitely construction of a reprocessing plant "due to political infeasibility" while Gorleben's suitability as a waste disposal site continued to be explored. In the fall of that year, Bonn saw the largest demonstration in its history sofar when 100,000 to 150,000 convened a protest against the German nuclear program and in support of a reorientation of environmental policies. In 1980, the Gorleben site was occupied by several thousand nuclear opponents for more than a month, until the occupants as well as the media present at the site were finally removed by the police. In early 1981, a crowd of 100,000 demonstrated against the actual beginning of the construction of the Brokdorf nuclear power plant which again was accompanied by heavy clashes with police. Moreover, the extension of the airport in Frankfurt became a focal environmental issue. In 1980 and 1981, tens of thousands repeatedly protested in numerous ways against the extension. Finally, "dying forests" at an increasing speed and scale climbed rapidly toward the top of the environmental agenda. The issue mobilized even political conservatives and contributed markedly to the growing strength of the Greens, since the issue was clearly of national scope and thus was felt to be beyond the grasp of citizen groups.

The ascent of an environmental party was important for the LER in several ways. It indicated, of course, that environmentalism could be organized on a more permanent basis. It forced labor to rethink its assumption that environmentalism needed not to be reckoned with since it was a passing fad. Moreover, ecological electoral groups competed mostly with SPD votes. Because of the strong ties between the SPD and labor unions, they affected the political environment of SPD and labor leaders directly. Further, given the German federalist system, the fragility of the governing SPD/FDP coalition, the slim majorities of the party or parties in power in several states, the closeness of the FDP to the 5% vote margin in several states, and deep cleavages within the SPD, the Greens turned into a political factor of national importance far beyond the environmental agenda (c.f. Chapter 6 for more details).

The environmental movement itself was becoming a broader social movement. Not only did it trigger the rise of ecological parties, it also provided an example and link-up for other extra- parliamentary concerns. What started out as environmental citizen groups often also became involved in urban development and housing, transportation issues, civil liberties (against police brutality, for more public participation, for better computer privacy laws, etc.), women's rights, or peace and disarmament issues. On the other hand, citizen groups initially formed in response to these issues often also shared environmentalist concerns. Many of the groups' most active members were also labor unionists and often SPD members. In addition, parts of the media expressed sympathies for the "alternative" movement and disapproved of the seemingly unchecked use of state power. Indeed, a new national daily newspaper originated from what became to be called the "alternative scene".

The broadening and link-up of environmentalism made it difficult for the labor movement to rationalize a clear conflict of interest. Rejecting environmentalism as the particularistic interests of wealthy elitists, dreamers or communists as labor leaders had done earlier became less credible. On the other hand, the union leadership did not renege on earlier—stated formal positions. Thus, the erosion of general societal consensus was paralleled by deepening internal splits within labor and the SPD.

Within the labor movement, pro—environmental sentiments grew. Several smaller unions adopted critical positions with respect to nuclear power. In most unions, substantial minorities rejected the official leadership positions toward nuclear energy and environmental protection policies (see Chapter 5). Further, while the officially adopted positions of the DGB and the large unions continued to support the further construction of nuclear power plants, reprocessing facilities and a demonstration breeder reactor, and the continued exploration of Gorleben's suitability as a waste—disposal site, the unions no longer pushed these projects. In fact, most unions including the DGB began to advocate energy saving and environmental protection as employment—creating measures (see Chapter 3). Also, labor union publications repeatedly criticized the often rude use of state power against protestors. Further, public opinion surveys revealed that labor union members had at least as pro—environmental attitudes as the general public —which were generally high (see Chapter 4). Moreover, local initiatives of critical unionists formed. For example, in more than forty cities, union members from all unions disagreeing with official leadership positions on nuclear energy formed local initiatives which became a loosely connected national network called "Aktionskreis Leben" (AKL). The AKL established numerous local ties with environmental organizations and probably (although hard to measure) influenced the internal will formation and decision making of the unions. Most visibly, it organized an anti— nuclear demonstration in Berlin attended by 10—20000 participants. Further, in the Frankfurt airport extension controversy, union members at the nearby Opel auto plant belonged to the main opponents of the project. Finally, the railroad workers union entered into a form alliance with environmental organizations —the first time that has happened— opposing the construction of a large waterway connecting the Rhine and Danube rivers.

It would be a mistake to conclude from these examples that the LER in the FRG had become cooperative. Labor leadership continued to distrust the environmental movement and wanted to have little to do with it. But demonstrations like the one in Dortmund in 1977 became impossible. The internal tensions within the unions, and not only in response to energy and environmental policies, grew considerably. More divergent views were articulated and informal cooperation between "deviant" groups in the labor movement, environmentalists and other causes started.

2.2.3. Since 1982: Opposition Triggers Propositions

The change of government in Bonn enhanced the rapprochement of labor and environmentalism already under way. The SPD, no longer the party in power, and the Greens, elected to the Bundestag for the first time, both became opposition parties on the federal level. While being in opposition at times facilitates competition, since the lack of responsibility for implementation tends to lead to a spiralling of demands, on balance the opposition to major government actions usually led the SPD and the Greens to take stands on the same side of an issue. SPD chairman Willy Brandt once remarked that regardless of short term fluctuations, those to the right of the SPD were the minority in the country. Because nobody seriously expects the SPD to win an absolute majority nor the Greens to disappear from the parliamentary scene, Brandt's assessment acknowledges that both parties depend on each other in the long run.

The change in Bonn aided the labor—environmentalist rapprochement in several ways. It enabled the SPD and labor to shift their positions on important issues closer to those of the Greens. These issues were not restricted to environmental protection but also covered crucial areas on the national agenda such as economic policy, security policy (and most notably here the question whether or not to deploy American Intermediate Range Missiles in the country), collective bargaining (especially for the 35-hour work-week), civil liberties, or social policy. Secondly, electoral shifts to the Greens and the goal of the SPD to make up the loss of power in Bonn by maintaining or strengthening its position at the state and local levels fostered cooperation between environmentalist and labor interests. Most spectacular so far was an agreement in the state of Hessia where the Greens supported an SPD government in return for major policy concessions. However, the main point here is not the substantive policy results, but the fact that such a formal agreement was reached at all, and that this model will likely be repeated elsewhere; thus, such cooperation will be institutionalized.

Besides this profound turn on the political party scene, other developments have improved the climate for the LER. Public awareness of the degradation of the natural environment has grown to the point where environmental policies have become extremely politically sensitive. Moreover, (structural) unemployment levels have remained so high that labor has come to recognize environmental protection as one, if not the area with a very high potential for creating new jobs (c.f. Chapter 3). In addition, energy issues, which were the major source of disagreements in the past, have lost a good deal of their political saliency. Therefore, both major former stumbling blocks for the LER were removed and common goals have become visible. The LER by no means has become cordial, but in terms of politics, institutions and shared interests, both sides have become much more compatible within a short period of time.

2.3 The Major Political Groups in the Two Movements in the US

The US labor movement has its roots in the late 19th century. In the late 1880s, mostly craft unions formed the American Federation of Labor (AFL), which was the main representative of organized labor until the 1930s. The New Deal brought a rapid expansion in number and legitimacy for labor. In the mid 1930s, the Congress of Industrial Organizations (CIO) was formed as the umbrella organization for the rapidly growing industrial unions. Until 1955, AFL and CIO coexisted, sometimes in heavy competition for membership and organizational jurisdictions. They then merged into the AFL-CIO which up to the present has made up most of US organized labor. For 1978, the US Statistical Abstract (1982/83:408) listed 174 unions with a total membership of 21.8 M. Among those, 108 unions with 17 M members were affilated with the AFL-CIO. Contrary to the FRG, union membership in the US has remained at roughly constant levels throughout the 1970s but has dropped in the 1980s. Its relative share of the work-force has decreased from more than 30% at its peak to less than 20%. Its political influence has also declined (c.f. Chapter 6).

Many of AFL-CIO's political activities occur through its Committee on Political Education (COPE). It publishes annual ratings of all members of the US Senate and House based on how they voted on selected issues important to labor. COPE also supports electoral candidates on all political levels.

I will focus on the politics of the AFL-CIO and eight individual unions toward energy and the environmental movement. The unions have been former affiliates of both AFL and CIO. Table 2.2 lists the unions considered. Except for the Teamsters [2] and the Food and the Commercial Workers , the largest unions in 1980 are included. Most are directly affected by energy construction, operations and legislation. AFSCME has been included since it is a white collar union and since it

21

Union	1980 member- in 1ooo	Reasons for Consideration
United Auto Workers (UAW)	1,357	*Member in several environmental alliances; industry affected by environmental (car emissions) and energy (fuel efficiency) politics
United Steelworkers of America (USWA)	1,238	*Heavily affected by air and water pollution controls
International Brotherhood of Electrical Workers (IBEW)	1,041	*Very pro-nuclear, pro-development; conflicts with environmentalism
International Association of Machinists (IAM)	754	*Very involved in energy politics; outspoken contra the 'corporate state'
American Federation of State, County and Municipal Employees (AFSCME)	1,098	*Fast growing, service sector union
International Union of Operating Engineers (IUOE)	423	*Construction union; pro-growth; Disagreements with environmentalism prevailing
United Mine Workers (UMW)	245	*Strongly affected by environmental and energy politics
Oil, Chemical and Atomic Workers (OCAW)	154	*Actively pro-environmental and pro-nuclear; affected by toxics

Source: US Statistical Abstract, 1982/3

Table 2-2 : US Unions Considered Most Pertinent for the LER

is very fast growing. The UAW, USWA, and IAM are particulary known for strongly supporting environmental legislation and have repeatedly been allied with environmental organizations. The IBEW and IUOE have been the most distant from the positions of the environmentalists.

As in the FRG, the environmental movement in the US consists of permanent national organizations and ad—hoc local groups. Most of the members of the national organizations limit their activities to paying dues in support of the various environmental activities of the organization while the local organizations have usually been formed in response to a specific local or regional environmental issue involving direct citizen action. But unlike in the FRG and notable exceptions notwithstanding, the national organizations have been politically the more important ones. Of no importance have been attempts to form environmental parties.

Odom Fanning (1975:214) estimated that approximately 40,000 'environmental' organizations represent 20 M environmentalists. They included as a hard core the 5.5 M people who belonged to or contributed to 19 "primary" environmental conservation organizations. A more recent survey of the environmental lobby in Washington identified the 14 groups listed in Table 2.3. I will particularly often refer to five groups. The Sierra Club and FOE are lobbying organizations and have frequently cooperated with labor unions. They are distinguished from the non—lobbying ones like NWF in that the latter establish contacts with legislators only upon invitation. The NWF has been chosen because of its large membership and because its ties to labor have been limited. The Urban Environment Conference (UEC) has served as a "unique Washington meeting ground" of environmental, labor and minority groups (Labor, Environmentalists & Minorities ... Together, 1979). It has convened representatives of these organizations for lobbying advocacy and education.

Unique in the environmental movement is the League of Conservation Voters (LCV). It acts like the political arm of the environmental movement in the Capital corresponding to labor's COPE. It rates the voting records of each member of Congress on selected issues and supports, or opposes, congressional and gubernatorial candidates. In Chapter 3, LCV's and COPE's Congressional ratings will be compared.

Local and regional environmental groups formed or operating in response to an energy issue have been numerous but politically much less visible than the citizen groups in the FRG. They are also much harder to analyze since they lack an umbrella organization like the German BBU.

2.4 A Synopsis of the LER in the United States

2.4.1 From the Mid—60s to the 1973 Oil Embargo:
Lack of Disagreements but Little Cooperation

In the second half of the 1960s, individuals and groups concerned about the protection of the natural environment became increasingly organized. At the same time, influential parts within the labor movement began to address environmental pollution and quality of life issues. In a first phase lasting from the mid—60s to the 1973 oil embargo, few direct disagreements caused serious labor—environmentalist conflicts. In these years, the complexities surrounding environmental protection perhaps were less apparent than later on —a fact that possibly fostered agreements. Looking back, the AFL—CIO hailed some cooperative efforts with certain environmentalists: "the labor movement has maintained and strengthened its longstanding commitment to a clean environment for America. It has broadened to areas of agreement and often joined action in cooperation with responsible environmental organizations" (Federationist, Oct.79:7).

At the forefront of labor—environmentalist cooperation were UAW and USWA. Since a cooperative LER contradicts conventional wisdom, I will

23

Group	1982 Budget (millions)	Members (1000s)	
Mass Organizations			
National Wildlife Federation (NWF)	$ 37.1	4,2oo	Mainly hunters and fishermen; broke recently from traditional conservative posture
National Audubon Society	22.2	47o	
Sierra Club	13.o	311	Most activist big group
Litigators			
Natural Resources Defense Council (NRDC)	4.5	4o	Founded by lawyers; lobbies and litigates
Environmental Defense Fund (EDF)	2.8	5o	Scientific and economic analysis for litigating and lobbying
Generalists			
Friends of the Earth	1.3	3o	Aggressively anti-nuclear
Environmental Policy Center	1.1		Has most registered environmental lobbyists
Politicos			
League of Conservation Voters	.9	3o	The green lobby's PAC
Specialists			
The Wilderness Society	3.6	68	Focus on public-lands
Defenders of Wildlife	2.3	56	Endangered Species
Solar Lobby	1.o	53	Promotes Renewable Energy
The Izaak Walton League	1.3	5o	Water and Public Lands
National Parks & Conservation Association	1.3	35	Establishes local citizen groups to support parks
Environmental Action	.7	25	Sponsored Earth Day; annual "filfthy five" campaign

Source: FORTUNE, October 4, 1982: 139

Table 2-3: The Major Environmental Groups in the US

quote several statements stressing cooperation at some length. As early as 1965 when environmental concerns had just begun to be voiced, the UAW testified that it had attempted to provide leadership in all aspects of community life

> outside as well as inside the auto plants. For many years, the UAW has lent its weight to campaigns for neighborhood conservation, urban renewal, beautification of the city and the country, and restauration of water resources. (Testimony submitted by International Union, UAW, at Federal Pollution Control Enforcement Conference on Detroit River— Lake Erie Pollution, Detroit,MI, 17.6.65:1)

Stronger than perhaps all other unions, the UAW has stressed the need for rooting environmental efforts in a solid local base. In 1965, it convened for the 'United Action for Clean Water Conference' a thousand delegates from 8 Great Lakes states and Canada along with representatives from conservation clubs, civic organizations, all levels of government, and recreation organizations. UAW President Walther P.Reuther hoped that the conference would be the

> beginning of a massive mobilization of citizens; the beginning of a popular crusade not only for clean water, but for cleaning up the atmosphere, the highways, the junkyards and the slums and for creating a total living environment worthy of free men (UAW, 6.11.1965:2).

First of all, Reuther argued, an aroused citizenship was needed.

> There are literally millions of allies in this struggle. Where are they? They are your neighbors; they go to the same churches that you go to, they live in the same communities, they belong to the same organizations. Go back to your neighborhood, stimulate interest in this problem; then out of that try to form groups in your communities, try to tie these together in terms of a community organization and state organization so that we can begin to develop the leverage of an aroused people, who understand the problem, who sense the urgency and the importance of this matter, and who will move this nation toward a solution. (op.cit.:10)

In the following years, the UAW joined numerous citizen group coalitions on a variety of issues, and has been harshly critical of the lack of openness of public agencies:

> [This meeting] is called a public hearing but yet the agenda excludes the public. [Why is] this charade called a public hearing? ... Is this so-called public hearing a display aimed at quieting the public furor? (Statement of James P. O'Keeffe, International Representative serving the UAW before the Federal Water Pollution Control Administration, 27.6.1969).

Also in 1969, the Steelworkers Union (USWA) was the first union to conduct a national environmental conference on air pollution for 250 local union steelworkers signalling the union's strong interest in comprehensive clean air legislation.

At the turn to the 1970s, several environmental laws with far—reaching consequences had been passed by Congress with considerable input from labor and environmental groups. The National Environmental Policy Act (NEPA) of 1969 made it a responsibility of the federal government to assess the environmental impacts of projects involving federal action. The Environmental Impact Statements (EIS) requirement became an important instrument for environmental intervenors providing for public review of many projects and actions. In 1970, the Earth Day symbolized the final break—through of environmental concerns in the US and labor and environmentalists celebrated it jointly. The Occupational Safety and Health Act (OSHA) was passed; the Environmental Protection Agency (EPA) was established; and rather stringent Clean Air Amendments were passed. These acts were supported by both labor and environmentalists, and might not have been passed without one or the other. Sheldon Samuels, the Director of Occupational Safety and Health in the AFL—CIO, explained to me that labor had sought OSH legislation since 1949 but that it was the environmental movement which gave OSHA its shape and substance since it created the needed political climate (Interview, 24.2.1981). The Clean Air Amendments, in turn, were strongly backed by the UAW and USWA. In the next year, the Super Sonic Transport (SST) was abandoned in a struggle that pitted labor and environmentalists against one another. In 1972, both labor and environmentalists supported passage of the Water Pollution Control Act amendments which included a provision enabling EPA to investigate publicly environmental blackmail allegations.

2.4.2 1973 to the Late 1970s: Conflicts Mostly on Energy Issues

A second phase of the LER began at around 1973 when the linkages and trade—offs of environmental protection with respect to other interests became more and more apparent. The UAW had already admonished environmentalists to seek the support of other interests in society.

> The environmental movement has been too slow to grasp the social and economic aspects of the environmental issue which the movement has so effectively brought to national attention. Non—labor members of that movement have done yeoman's service in creating an awareness of environmental policies. But in failing to come to grips with the politics of the environment, they have exposed themselves, as well as the working men and women who should be their strongest allies, to the trap being set for them by corporate polluters.
> The challenge of environmental degradation is also too important to be left to environmentalists, because without support from the American people as a whole, especially from workers and the urban poor or near—poor who are pollution's worst casualties, the environmentalists will be fighting a lost cause. They are the bearers of bad news, and industry is already moving to discredit them as extremists. The new scapegoats, in fact, may well be not those who are most actively polluting the nation and the planet, but those who are sounding the alarm. (Leonard Woodcock, UAW president, Sierra Club Bulletin, Dec.71:15)

The LER conflicts subsequently increased —especially as a result of energy shortages becoming a political issue and the formation of an oppostion movement to nuclear energy. The Calvert Cliff decision of the Supreme Court of 1972 (requiring the Atomic Energy Commission to obey NEPA EIS regulations) became a decisive legal asset for the anti-nuclear segment of the environmental movement. In the next two years, the Alaska pipeline project was a major source of conflict for the LER, as was the extension of the Price-Anderson nuclear insurance legislation in 1975. Various anti-nuclear groups held their first national conference in 1974 (Nelkin, 1978). Further, labor and environmental organizations were deeply divided over the continuation of the Clinch River breeder program. On the other hand, they were repeatedly allied in favor of tighter tax laws for oil companies and strict strip mining legislation.

In the 1976 to 1978 period, the labor-environmentalist conflicts became sharpest as a result of the peaking of the public debate on nuclear energy. In 1976, environmental oppostion groups sought the passage of anti-nuclear referenda in several states. In 1977 and 1978, large demonstrations against the nuclear power plant to be constructed in Seabrook, N.H.; the Rocky Flats nuclear weapons plant near Denver, CO; and the nuclear fuels reprocessing facility in Barnwell, S.C., further gave the nuclear energy controversy national attention. In response to these protests, the unions assumed a more active role and mobilized for the defense of their jobs. In 1976, the AFL-CIO conference on 'Nuclear Energy and America's Energy Needs' concluded that "rapid development of nuclear power is a 'must' without which the nation's economy would falter" (quoted in Logan, Nelkin, 1980:6). Organized labor joined forces with utility companies to defeat the anti-nuclear propositions in California and other states. Further, construction workers demonstrated in favor of the Seabrook power plant. In 1978, the AFL-CIO Building and Construction Trades Department negotiated the National Nuclear Construction Stabilization Agreement with contractors in order to speed up construction of nuclear power plants.

Not all but the vast majority of the AFL-CIO unions, and among them most ardently the building and construction unions, were supporters of nuclear power plant construction. However, by no means all environmental organizations had been nuclear energy opponents. Many environmentalists were supporters of this energy source, because they considered it more environmentally benign than coal. Yet, in the course of an increasingly conflictual nuclear power debate, all national environmental organizations adopted critical views. Since the views of the environmentalist side on nuclear power are similar and well-known (e.g. Nelkin, 1978; Logan, Nelkin, 1980) but those of the unions under consideration fairly diverse, I turn now to a brief outline of the positions of the unions considered here.

The IBEW has been one of the staunchest supporters of nuclear energy and belonged to the harshest critics within labor of environmentalism. Starting in 1973, the IBEW Journal has run a series under the headline "Are Nuclear Power Plants Needed? Yes". Each article usually ended with the credo:

> The IBEW continues to support the expansion of the nuclear industry. It is IBEW's opinion that nuclear power is safe, reliable, environmentally acceptable, and the best economic way to meet the power needs of the consumers of the nation.

In the mid-70s, these views were shared by many in labor —including those unions that had cooperated with environmental organizations on other issues. However, the relationship to the environmental movement in response to the differences regarding nuclear power varied considerably.

The IBEW labelled nuclear opponents generically as obstructionists, defined by IBEW president Charles H. Pillard as "...a group of people who call themselves environmentalists but who are really nothing more than obstructionists against progress in this modern world" (IBEW Journal, Nov.78:22). While the union supported the clean air, clean water and occupational safety and health acts —"that's something we don't disagree about"— the conflict with environmentalists on nuclear energy overshadowed possible common interests (interview with Mr. Dickinson, IBEW Research Department, 25.2.1981). The union has made no attempts to persuade environmentalists of the necessity and safety of nuclear energy —and neither have environmentalists seriously tried the opposite (Interviews Brock Evans, Sierra Club; Dickinson, IBEW). Indeed, the only places the IBEW and environmental representatives possibly had direct contacts in the nuclear power controversy might have been local hearings —but, of course, as adversaries.

The International Union of Operating Engineers has also been critical of environmentalism but has cooperated in some issue areas. The union, for example, fought environmentalist opposition to coal—fired power plants that were designed to comply with all existing environmental requirements (such as the use of low—sulfur coal and a closed—loop scrubber system). This sort of environmentalists, the union argued, betrays a lack of understanding for the need of "a balanced position between the environment and the economy" (OE, April 1978:10). The union has encouraged Coalitions of Concerned Citizens (CCCs) all over the country as grass—root efforts to promote highway construction or as intervenors in pollution disputes. The activitites of the CCCs in which the IUOE has sought to keep a low profile have led to confrontations with environmentalists (Interview with Ted Reed, IUOE Research Director, 25.2.81). On the other hand, the IUOE has worked with Environmentalists For Full Employment (EFFE) promoting solar energy and conservation as a means of creating employment in the inner city (ibid.). It supported Seabrook which, the "Operating Engineer" argued, has encompassed all of the key issues in the controversy on nuclear power. The union saw the fate of that plant being inextricably linked to the fate of nuclear energy in the US. In addition, the union argued,

Of even more significance, however, are the underlying implications for society. The demonstrators who took part in the 1977 occupation are not merely opposed to nuclear energy; they are opposed to the very way in which most people live their lives. Therefore, what is really at issue is the lifestyle the majority of our people will follow in the coming decades (OE, Jan.1979:4).

The only major union that rejected nuclear power from the beginning was the United Mine Workers union (UMW). In the late 1970s, several other unions began to oppose nuclear energy as well. The UMW thus adopted a position diametrically opposed to that of the German coal miners' union which belonged to the strongest supporters of the German nuclear power program. Yet, the ties between the UMW and the environmental movement have been weak.

The largest union in the US, the Teamsters, strongly supported nuclear energy. The second largest, the UAW, also supported it in principle, but with reservations. In 1959 already, UAW president Walter P. Reuther led the AFL—CIO to file the first suit in the country to stop construction of a nuclear facility, the Fermi I breeder reactor. They sued because 3 M people, including 500,000 UAW members, lived within a 30 mile radius of the reactor. The union endorsed President Carter's decision in 1977 to indefinitely defer all further breeder reactor developments. Similarly, the Steelworkers supported nuclear energy in principle but opposed specific nuclear projects and policies such as the Clinch River breeder reactor. District 31 of the USWA, representing 130,000 members, in 1978 passed a resolution against Indiana's Bailly nuclear power plant, and two locals intervened against the project. Overall within UAW and USWA, considerable differences of opinion on the nuclear power issue existed, and both unions preferred to remain silent. Their ambivalence with respect to nuclear energy, however, did not preclude cooperation with environmentalists on other issues.

The Oil, Chemical and Atomic Workers (OCAW) union was in a particularly sensitive situation. Representing about 20,000 atomic workers, i.e. 10% of its membership, naturally it has supported nuclear power in principle. On the other hand, it has opposed the Clinch River breeder reactor. It has also pushed hard for stringent safety standards for industrial chemicals and for radioactive materials in civilian and military uses. Further, it has advocated stronger enforcement of standards (for instance by changing jurisdiction over health and safety from the NRC to OSHA), and unfettered research on the linkages between exposure levels and health effects. In 1973, the OCAW in fact called a strike against Shell Oil over workers' safety. On all those issues, the union's positions have concorded with those of environmental groups –and cooperation, indeed, has occured. Most notably perhaps was the support given by eleven national environmental groups to the strike against Shell Oil.

2.4.3 Late 1970s to 1981:
Cooperation on the Rise But Old Conflicts Remain

While prior to about 1976, individual labor and environmental organizations have cooperated at many occasions in a piecemeal way, the third phase of the LER saw attempts to cooperate deliberately on a longer–term basis.

The cooperation involved only parts of the two movements. On the environmental side, for example, the largest organization in terms of membership –the NWF– was barely involved. On the part of labor, only about a dozen national unions cooperated actively while most unions remained reserved, if not hostile, toward labor–environmentalist coalitions. However, several of the largest unions in the country such as the UAW, USWA, IAM or AFSCME belonged to those cooperating.

The groups sharing in cooperative efforts did not agree on everything. But usually, they could agree on what to disagree, and then deal only with non–contentious issue areas. This pragmatic approach permitted both sides to leave aside the nuclear power issue at the beginning of this phase (which, as we have seen, coincided with the height of the nuclear power controversy), and allowed to establish some mutual trust and confidence.

A key event for that phase was the "Black Lake Conference" held at the Reuther UAW education center in 1976. A national conference to define current issues relating to jobs and the environment, it sought "to develop specific ways for unions, environmental groups and community organizations to work together for environmental quality and economic justice" (Background paper for Black Lake conference). Initiated by the UAW and financially supported by an EPA grant, it brought more than 300 individuals from the 3 constituencies together for the first time. Although there was no single, tangible, spectacular result of the conference, the "spirit of Black Lake" spawned a multitude of joint labor–environmentalist activities throughout the country.

At the national, state and local level, unions and environmentalist joined in numerous coalitions usually also including other interest groups. Several important cooperative efforts are listed in Table 2–4. The major issue areas were occupational safety and health, environmental protection, energy and employment, and community and urban affairs. Establishing ties between the various constituencies was a central objective of these efforts. Table 2–4 indeed shows that linkages between these events exist both in terms of the groups frequently involved and in terms of a genealogy of cooperative structures. The Black Lake Conference strongly influenced the work of EFFE and was the impetus for the Regional Workshops Programs (RWPs). The UEC coordinated the RWPs and aided in the formation of the

Group/Program/ Conference	Groups Involved	Issues	Activities	Year formed	Initiated by	Comments
Black Lake Conference	all major environmental organizations; 9 international unions; community groups (300 individuals)	cooperation and coalition building on OS&H, environmental protection, energy, employment	share information on problems with respect to jobs-environment; develop skills for organizing at home; develop positions; begin building networks	1976	UAW	funded in part by EPA
Urban Environment Conference (UEC)	alliance of national labor, environment and minority organizations	1) Protect on-the-job and community health 2) Energy, transportation, civil rights, employment	lobbying advocacy education coalition building	1971	Senator Philip A. Hart	aided in coalition building of: C/LEC, Women for Environmental Health, National Coalition of Disease Prevention and Environmental Health, Progressive Alliance worked with: SANE, National Clean Air Coalition
Regional Workshop Program I and II (RWP)	local organizations; in 1978/79: 367 local co-sponsoring organizations, Workshops attended by 1615 individuals from labor 57%, environmentalists 24%, community 19%	toxic substances at the workplace and in the community jobs, environment and community, environment and economy	assistance in organizing workshops (funding, technical) RWP I&II: 24 workshops	1977	outgrowth of Black Lake Conf.	funded by EPA coordinated by UEC
Environmentalists for Full Employment (EFFE)	coalition of more than 100 environmental and community-based groups	to promote a full employment economy in a clean and healthy environment	inform on employment potential of public work projects and corporate projects, products and services; clearinghouse forged labor-environmentalist alliances Congressional lobbying and testimony	1975	individual environmentalists	involved in Black Lake Conf; initiated Labor Committee for Safe Energy and Full Employment; assembled National Panel on Energy and Employment Policy; funded in part by DOE

Table 2-4: The Major Labor-Environmentalist Coalitions in the US

Continued .....

Group/Program/ Conference	Groups Involved	Issues	Activities	Year form- ed	Initiated by	Comments
Citizen/Labor Energy Coalition (C/LEC)	more than 200 groups: unions, public interest, senior citizens, church, environmentalists, minority, community, including: IAM, AFSCME, UAW, Sheet Metal Workers, USWA, OCAW, Environmental Policy Center	energy policy; energy pricing, employment impacts, environmental impacts, structure of energy industry; against utility winter shut-offs; against natural gas price deregulation; for improved residential conservation service plans; for utility support for weatherization and solar; lifeline standards for gas prices; state oil tax campaign	built on national, regional, local level; organized regional conferences; built state and local coalitions that develop action and legislative programs	1978	IAM by UEC	
Labor Committee for Safe Energy	UMW, UAW, IAM, SEIU, Graphic Arts Union, Chemical Workers, Furniture Workers, Woodworks, Longshoremen & Warehousemen, Coalition of Labor Union Women	anti-nuclear, pro-coal; support energy conservation and renewable sources; against environmental blackmail and energy monopolies; for more democratic control over energy development and use	organized National Labor Conference for Safe Energy and Full Employment (857 unionists and 150 environmentalists participated); March on Harrisburgh	1980	EFFE; Individual unionists	conference was picketed by IBEW; Building and Construction Unions mobilized against March on Harrisburgh
OSHA and Environmental Network	AFL-CIO Industrial Unions Department, UBC, Sierra Club, Wilderness Society, FOE, statewide groups from labor and environmentalists	preserve OSH and environmental (especially, Clean Air) laws; improve effectiveness of laws and rules	focus on 12 key states, in each of which activities are coordinated by one labor and environmental organization; organize political action campaigns	1981	AFL-CIO IUD	formed in response to Schweicker OSHA amendments
City Care Conference	"representatives of nearly every racial, geographic and interest group" 75 organizations, 750 individuals	neighborhood environmental enterprises and jobs; housing and health conditions; energy for cities; transportation; parks and recreation; waste and recycling	plenary and core group sessions; workshops; topical and regional caucuses; follow-up activities by CITY CARE Action Committee	1979	National Urban League, Sierra Club, UEC	6 federal funding sources; NUL and Sierra Club each have made the Urban Environment a top priority

Table 2-4: The Labor-Environmentalist Coalitions in the US

Citizens/ Labor Energy Coalition. EFFE participated at the Black Lake Conference and was instrumental in forming the Labor Committee for Safe Energy and Full Employment. Each of these cooperative activities, in turn, effected labor—environmentalist joint ventures at the regional, state, or local levels.

In the late 1970s, environmental groups and most AFL—CIO unions continued to be divided over general energy policy directions or the so-called 'bottle bills' while they agreed on specific environmental protection, energy taxation, or occupational safety and health issues. Deep cleavages arose between building and construction unions, on the one hand, and industrial and public employees unions on the other. The 1977 Clean Air amendments, as a case in point, were strongly endorsed by the Steelworkers and rejected by the Operating Engineers (IUOE). Increasingly, the direct linkage of energy politics and employment was recognized. Further, IAM, UAW, the Sierra Club, EFFE, the National Urban League and others wanted to include into energy planning "Employment Impact Statement" requirements patterned after the Environmental Impact Statements. Environmental organizations supported legislation very dear to labor such as OSHA related bills, the Humphrey— Hawkins full employment bill and Labor Law Reform. In 1977, the Sierra Club Legal Defense Fund filed a friend-of- the-court brief before the Supreme Court in defense of OSHA regulations. The Club worked with many labor unions to obtain passage of the Toxic Substances Control Act. It also supported the full employment goals found in the Humphrey— Hawkins legislation. Further, 25 representatives of national environmental organizations wrote a letter to Congress in support of the Labor Law Reform Bill of 1978 (Steel Labor, December 1978).

Perhaps one ought to pause at this point and briefly reflect what the motives for these instances of cooperation could have been and how "easy" it might have been for a group to support measures the other side was concerned about. It might be useful to distinguish two types of concerns: (1) concerns of high interest to BOTH labor and environmentalists, and (2) concerns of high interest to only ONE of the two groups. One could argue that it "costs" little to the group with little interest in an issue to express support while this group might hope to derive great "benefits" from this support at other occasions. In other words, tactical considerations would have determined a group's positions. Environmentalist support for labor law reform, Humphrey—Hawkins or OSH (which probably fit the second category), then, should not be taken as too important evidence for labor— environmentalist cooperation. What really counts, this argument suggests, is the LER in regard to high interest areas for both groups such as probably toxic substances control, nuclear power or air pollution control.

While this argument intuitively seems valid, qualifications also come to mind. If an influential organization adopts a formal position, this position likely affects the thinking of its membership and of the broader public —and thus is political—, even if the position was tactically motivated. An organization can not adopt a series of tactically motivated positions without risking the loss of credibility and thus political clout. Assuming that an organization like the Sierra Club is aware of that, and given the interconnectedness of labor— environmentalist cooperative efforts as apparent in Table 2-4, they probably can not be explained as primarily tactical moves. Nor did the demands for Employment Impact Statements forwarded by environmentalists seem to be mostly motivated by tactics.

One may further ask: what does it matter whether support is motivated by tactics or by genuine interests in an issue? I believe it does matter if one seeks to draw conclusions from such instances of cooperation for the LER. If support were primarily guided by tactics, the built-in dichotomy argument would be strengthened since cooperation in that case would be mostly an artifact of political calculation and therefore easily reversible. On the other hand, if support manifests genuine concerns, it would be the political expression of the rejection of the built—in dichotomy view.

The question of what reasons there were for the cooperation of the kinds described, of course, remains still unanswered. Much more in—depth interviewing would have been required than I was able to do. Be it as it may, cooperation in high interest areas to both movements has rather increased than declined at the turn to the 1980s.

Most notably, the LER benefitted from the growing scepticism within labor toward nuclear power. At the same time, the cleavages within labor regarding this issue became substantial. As noted, none of the liberal unions such as UAW, USWA or IAM officially objected to nuclear energy expansion until the Three—Mile—Island nuclear accident occured in 1979. Following that accident, however, the executive board of the UAW called for a moratorium on nuclear power construction until a permanent high—level commission concluded that all the general and specific concerns about nuclear power have been answered (Logan, Nelkin, 1980:8). Similarly, calling for a moratorium, the IAM became the first AFL—CIO member union to break with the official pro—nuclear position of the Federation. By October 1980, nine international labor unions denounced nuclear power in the first 'National Labor Conference for Safe Energy and Full Employment' in Pittsburgh. The conference not only included environmental organizations as participants but, indeed, resolved to build coalitions with the anti— nuclear movement. In March of 1981, numerous union locals joined in the 'March on Harrisburg' as a reminder of the TMI accident. At the same time, however, the building and construction unions and the AFL—CIO continued in their support of nuclear energy. At the first anniversary of the accident, the AFL—CIO Building and Construction Trades Department and 15 construction unions signed the Three Mile Island Recovery Project Agreement with Metropolitan Edison Company, the owner of the infamous nuclear plant (AFL—CIO News, 29 March 1980). At several occasions, it came to direct confrontations between pro— and anti— nuclear unionists.

Besides nuclear power, the labor unions were also divided on other issues pertinent to the LER. In the 1980 Presidential campaign, substantial parts of labor favored Kennedy over Carter, and subsequently supported Carter against Reagan only half— heartedly. While the AFL—CIO endorsed the Carter/ Mondale ticket, the Teamsters union supported Reagan, and a substantial part of the union membership voted for Reagan if it voted at all. The national environmental organizations supported Carter in the elections, but frequently only reluctantly since many of them would have preferred Kennedy. Barry Commoner's ecological Citizens Party was not considered a serious choice by the environmental movement.

2.4.4 The LER in the Reagan Years

The beginning of the Reagan administration could have inflicted great damage to the LER for several reasons. The "supply side" economic policies and schemes for "reindustrializing" America, could be expected to encourage particularly environmentally harmful production. One such example was the plan for large—scale development of oil—shale in Western Colorado —a project also warmly received by the AFL—CIO. The economic recession in the early 80s, moreover, gave rise to fears that the environmental commitments of the unions might by sacrificed for jobs at any price. In addition, the avowed goal of the Reagan government to "deregulate" the country made it likely that existing environmental statutes and regulations would be severely weakened.

While some of the fears about the intended effects of "Reaganomics" for employment and the environment proved accurate, the LER has since rather improved than declined. The Reagan policies and his choice of personnel were soon perceived to be detrimental to both constituencies. Labor unions, consumers, minorities, environmentalists, and the poor soon became the victims of deregulation

33

and the reordering of budgetary priorities. The results were rising membership figures in the environmental movement; a decline of union membership, political and bargaining power; and coalition building including labor and environmentalists.

One major impetus for coalitions was the growing realization that environmental protection and occupational safety and health (OSH) are, politically and physically, strongly intertwined. Labor unions, in the past more concerned with OSH matters than with the environment outside of the plants, have turned to environmental groups for political, and especially public relations, support. Environmentalists, on the other hand, have given more attentio to OSH issues.

The first attempt of coalition building was the OSH— Environmental Network (c.f. Table 2-4) formed shortly after the inauguration of the Reagan administration. However, the network turned—out to be too much of a top—down operation and was not considered an unambiguous political success. More successful was the Clean Air Coalition that protected the Clean Air Act from being dismantled when it was up for re-authorization in 1981. The Act was the only major environmental statute —as opposed to regulations— that the administration tried to change directly under the guise of its deregulation policy. Industrial and service sector unions joined environmental groups protecting the Act while building and construction unions supported the "regulatory relief" sought by opponents. A great success was Solidarity Day in 1981 that brought more than 400,000 labor unionists and members of coalition groups to Washington marching for jobs and social justice. Considered a major victory by environmentalists and a defeat by labor was the abandonement of the Clinch River breeder reactor project in 1983.

The Reagan administration was quite successful in crippling the implementation of environmental and OSH laws and regulations. The EPA, OSHA, and NIOSH budgets were severely cut, staff was greatly reduced, the enforcement activities were drastically curtailed, the promulgation of rules was suspended, the newly instituted Superfund for the clean—up of hazardous waste was barely used, inspections were frequently replaced by "voluntary" industry cooperation, public participation rights were limited, development obtained precedence over conservation and protection of public lands and natural resources, nuclear energy safety rules were weakened, energy conservation and solar energy supports were greatly reduced, urgently needed regulations for controling hazardous chemicals were delayed, established OSHA standards were cut back, and health data collection and dissemination —and the availability of such data— was reduced. This list could be continued almost ad infinitum (c.f. "Indictment — The Case Against the Reagan Environmental Record", March 1982; "Poisons on the Job", Oct. 1982; "The American Environment Under Attack: What Next", March 1983). The underlying philosophy of all this was that economic interests supersede protection, that industry demands were largely heeded, and that "the government ought to get off people's backs" as much as possible.

While the OSHA-Environmental Network was not considered too successful at the federal level, coalition-building has succeeded on the lower level. In numerous states, so—called COSH-groups have been established seeking to achieve on the state level what the federal government would no longer do. These groups focused on preserving the most important functions of the OSHAct on a state by state basis (e.g. "right-to-know" rules) and had the support of the environmental groups. On the electoral level, environmental "Policy Action Committees" (PACs) were formed that cooperated with labor PACs. While I do not have information of the 1984 election track record of these PACs, the better—than—expected performance of Democratic Congressmen might, in part, be attributed to them. Asked about different groups and types of people who contribute money to political campaigns, the public ranked candidates contributing to their own campaigns highest and environmental PACs second highest (Harris Survey, Nov. 1982, in: World Opinion Update, 7(1983):1). Notwithstanding the land—slide victory of

34

Reagan, the environment has continued to rank very high on the polls. While it obviously could not affect the Presidential elections that were largely decided by personality, earlier in 1984 the environment was considered to possess the highest impact on swing votes (Interview Bill Drayton, March 1984).

In retrospect, the first Reagan administration has done more harm to labor than to the environmental movement. Organized labor might well face the question of organizational survival in the long run —of course, not only because of the Reagan administration. Unions have suffered from economic, geographic and demographic shifts, from the recession, from deregulation, from professional union busting, and from "bad press". The Reagan administration, Kuttner (1984) concluded sarcastically, "could not have come at a worse moment". Environmental organizations, on the other hand, definitely profited from the Reagan policies in terms of membership. Their lobbying power has increased and their political involvement generally has grown. At least, environmental mass organizations like the National Wildlife Federation are "beyond birds and flowers" (Chaffin, 1982). For others, they have turned already into a Green Giant (Symonds, 1982).

2.5 Summary

In both countries, the LER has become an issue. In the US, it became politically salient in the mid–60s, in the FRG around 1970. Figure 2–1 gives schematic heuristic curves for the LER as suggested in the preceding discussion. In both countries, the LER declined in the mid–70s but was on the rise again at the beginning of the 1980s. The low levels after 1975 reflect the controversies on nuclear energy. As a whole, the LER was better in the US than in the FRG. The substantial differences in the US among labor unions are also represented.

NOTES

[1] A representative of the German Metal Workers Union once remarked on citizen groups acting on behalf of the interests of workers: "This is as if somebody chewing with a full mouth explains to somebody who is hungry, how he should fast" (Badische Zeitung, 3.10.1978).

[2] There are also good arguments that consideration of the Teamsters would have been warranted. They are the largest union and are certainly affected by auto–related energy price, conservation and pollution control measures. It is probably a safe guess that their positions are not too distinct from those of the building and construction unions. On the other hand, the Teamsters are an outsider in the labor movement.

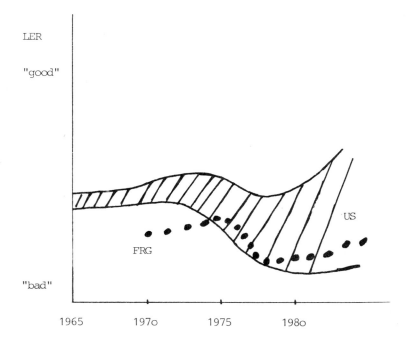

Figure 2-1 : The LER in the US and FRG, 1965 - 1980s

3 Explanation 1: There is an Economic Built-In Conflict of Interest Between Labor and Environmentalism

The reaction one often gets from telling people that one is interested in the relationship between organized labor and environmentalism is the question: "Aren't they in conflict because environmental protection destroys jobs?" Certain jobs would not exist, this thinking goes, if environmentalists had their way. A widely publicized example was the Tellico dam project in the US that almost did not get completed because reportedly a small fish would have become extinct. More generally, the belief in a built-in contradiction between the goals of environmental protection and full employment is based on the assumption that environmental protection measures cost money, increase production costs, and thus threaten employment opportunities. Both existing and new employment are believed to be affected. A firm or a nation which spends money on environmental protection measures, this thinking goes, has less money to spend for investments and thus for jobs. If pollution abatement becomes too expensive but inevitable, the company will be forced to raise prices and, in the extreme, to close down its operations. Internationally, the firm will be at an economic disadvantage with competitors from countries with less stringent environmental requirements. According to this view, conflicts between the employment interests of organized labor and environmental protection interests championed by environmental organizations are natural and unavoidable.

These views suggest the following hypothesis:

1. The perception of a built-in dichotomy between employment and environmental protection has been a central source of conflict between labor and environmentalists in the past.

More specifically, there is the argument that environmental protection can be pursued most successfully at times of economic well-being. Unemployment tends to be low when economic growth rates are high, while, at the same time, there is more money to spend for

37

environmental protection measures on the micro and macro level. Inversely, when the economy is weak, unemployment rises, and anti-pollution investments ordinarily will not only not be made but the pressures to ignore the environment will increase. Energy consumption will also tend to parallel economic activity. I will allude to this reasoning as to the economic dependency argument.

The incompatibility of employment and environmental protection interests due to economic imperatives has also been argued from another angle. The need to raise productivity levels, this argument goes, pits capital spending for wages against spending for pollution abatement. Without rises in productivity, however, industries will become less competitive on domestic and foreign markets. Since labor will not tolerate wage sacrifices, it will abandon demands for stringent environmental controls. This argument has especially been raised in the US where productivity growth recently has been considerably slower than in Japan and Western Europe.

These two arguments suggest two more hypotheses:

2. The goodness of the LER correlates positively with economic well-being.

3. Given the difficult economic situation in the two countries, the perception of a built-in dichotomy between employment and environmental protection interests will persist and thus hinder effective cooperation in the future.

A first test of the saliency of these hypotheses is to look at the perceptions of the general public, labor and environmentalists. How have they viewed the interdependencies of employment and environmental protection? Has, indeed, a perceived incompatibility been a central source of conflicts? To what extent do labor, environmentalists and the public actually believe in this incompatibility? Or have those, who have stressed this incompatibility, done so erroneously or even sought to cultivate this view? To what extent did programmatic statements and actual politics coincide? What are the arguments of those who do not think that employment and environmental protection are incompatible aims? Have the views changed over time? If so, how have the changes affected the LER?

In order to address these questions, this chapter will discuss how the two movements have perceived, in general, the interdependencies of employment and environmental protection, i.e. do they see a dichotomy, a trade-off, or a compatibility. Subsequently, I shall focus on energy related perceptions, particularly nuclear energy. All the views, of course, are embedded in more general economic and political world-views. Issues such as economic growth or the role of industry are closely interwoven with the core themes of employment, environmental protection and energy; and will therefore also be addressed. Third, I will turn to the argument that the LER is dependent on economic well-being. I will examine how labor has reacted to environmental issues at times of economic crises. For the US, finally, I have conducted a simple bivariate statistical analysis of the correlations between a LER indicator and measures of economic performance.

In order to avoid misunderstandings, I should like to stress that this chapter will not attempt to analyze "objectively" what the interrelationships between employment and environmental protection might be. Rather, it will be concerned with the perceptions of these interdependencies.

3.1 The Perceptions of the Interdependencies between Employment and Environmental Protection

How have the perceptions of labor and environmental groups with respect to employment, environmental protection and energy issues affected the LER? If the built-in dichotomy argument were true, then little compatibility of positions could be expected and conflicts would be a likely consequence. But this causal chain does not necessarily go both ways. Conflicts need not imply the existence of a dichotomy. For example, conflicts are likely if two groups attach different weights to different objectives and these objectives are interdependent. Nor will compatible positions necessarily entail a conflict-free relationship. For example, a gap may exist between what is stated in a program and what is pursued in actual politics. In sum, labor-environmentalist conflicts, on the one hand, are conceivable without a built-in dichotomy between employment and environmental protection views. On the other hand, compatible views will not ensure cooperation.

I will address the question, whether the perception of a built-in dichotomy between employment and environmental protection interests might have caused the conflicts in the past and will do so in the future, with respect to five topics: (1) environmental protection as a principal goal; (2) employment policies; (3) "environmental blackmail"; (4) economic growth; and (5) preferences for energy strategies.

3.1.1 Environmental Protection

In both countries, environmental protection as an important social goal was accepted throughout the 1970s and has remained so today. This was reflected in public opinion data, governmental declarations, and by statements of all important political groupings including labor unions. The labor-environmentalist conflicts can neither be attributed to extravagant positions —far removed from those of the general public— of the environmental movement, nor to a principal lack of environmental commitments on the part of labor.

Public opinion surveys show that throughout the 1970s, overwhelming majorities of the West German Public considered environmental protection an "important" or "very important" political goal (Umweltgutachten 1978:447; ZDF-Politbarometer 1980:57). This commitment by the public has rather increased than declined in the 1980s (c.f. Wirtschaftswoche, 28.9.1984: 63ff). Indeed, a high-ranking official of the Federal Department of the Interior in charge of environmental matters observed that "the environmental consciousness in the public has by now charged far ahead of everyday politics. ... The political decision makers have been surpassed by a broad new consensus of basic values among our people" (quoted by Edingshaus, 1980:107f).

In the United States, environmental concerns as apparent in public opinion surveys peaked at around 1970. Ten years later, the issue had lost some of its urgency but the sympathies for national environmental protection efforts remained high (CEQ, 1980) [1]. Public support for the environment remained high in the Reagan years as well (e.g. Bloomgarden, 1983). When the onslaught on the environment by the administration became apparent, the public was appalled but did not blame the President himself for what was happening. The fact that Reagan was reelected in 1984 by an even larger margin than in 1980 means in no way that the public accordingly approved his environmental policies. Even environmentalists gave him the benefit of the doubt:

> Reagan did not see or understand the problems that made regulations necessary.... In his eyes, regulations were not necessary protection but absurd restrictions on the enterprise of reasonable men. Environmental problems were, for the most part, a flimsy pretext for federal control of private activity (Lash,

39

1984:xii).

I now turn to the perception of environmental issues by German labor.
The DGB Environmental Program (Umweltprogramm) of 1974 recognized that
environmental degradation had become a growing threat to human health
and life. While all human beings are affected, workers, and especially
those of lower income, suffer particularly. Their interest in
environmental cleanup is not only vital but also financial and
economic. They —the Program stated— are affected most in terms of bad
health; they pay most compared to their income to mitigate health
damages and to finance measures improving environmental conditions;
they suffer most from a macro— economically wasteful production system
(p.11). Therefore, organized labor must seek to utilize existing
occupational safety rights. These rights, however, are not more than a
first step on the road to effective protection of the work environment,
the Program argued. In addition, labor must obtain co—determination
rights regarding investment planning and decisions, and subsequently
link investments to environmental protection decisions. Moreover,
protecting workers against environmental pollution must become a
collective bargaining issue (pp.23ff). Most environmentalists probably
endorse the 49 theses put down in the program wholeheartedly.

However, the obstacles to the implementation of abstract
environmental goals into effective environmental protection policies
were substantial. On the one hand, the German environmental movement
might be blamed for occasionally seeking environmental protection with
little consideration for the difficulties and cost involved. On the
other hand, economic thinking treating environmental protection as a
costly externality was widespread in labor and elsewhere. Ewringmann
and Zimmermann (1977:16) took the insights expressed in the DGB
Environmental Program as "mostly verbal declarations with only very
limited intentions to make them come true" and concluded that the labor
unions will be "progressive environmental actors" in only a limited
way. In practice, the unions supported environmental protection
legislation often only half—heartedly. Contrary to the DGB
Environmental Program, environmental protection has not become a
collective bargaining issue. Nor have co—determination rights with
respect to environmental matters increased or, at least, become a
central political demand of labor.

Half—heartedness is also an apt characterization for the attitudes
of the bulk of American organized labor. Environmental protection as a
principal goal was undisputed but was often sacrificed to immediate
economic interests. But unlike in the FRG, a politically powerful
group of labor unions belonged to the staunchest advocates of effective
anti—pollution measures and was allied with the environmental movement
at numerous occasions. Nevertheless, these pro—environmental unions
also agreed to extensions of environmental deadlines when their own
industries were affected.

In recent years, gradual but significant changes of environmental
attitudes took place in both countries. In the FRG, in spite of
persistent economic difficulties, the rise of conservatism, and the
ascent of new political concerns, the environment has probably moved
further upward on the political agenda. Budget constraints may in fact
have benefitted the environment because they curtailed possible new
infringements on the environment. Environmental interests became
better organized in terms of organizational longevity, concreteness of
their concerns, and broadness and interconnectedness with other
interest groups. Many environmental activists are also active
trade—unionists and vice—versa.

The labor unions have made a significant turn, recognizing that
environmental protection on balance would rather create than destroy
jobs. They no longer postulated a priority of jobs over the
environment but viewed both goals as complementary. While the unions
usually had agreed to compromises when environmental and job interests

40

in their jurisdictions clashed, they now made deliberate efforts to avoid such clashes in the future. They added environmental experts to their staff; they included environmental matters on their training and education programs, stressing the importance of damage prevention; they sought to sensitize the membership and officials to environmental hazards; etc. They developed own expertise regarding the substitution of hazardous materials and industrial processes, the introduction of time-tables to achieve compliance, the use of the latest technology, or the production of "alternative" products. On the most pressing environmental problem in the country, the decay of trees on a large scale probably due to acid rain, the DGB(1983) issued a position paper that called for

* the use of environmentally benign coal-burning technologies

* the rational usage and conservation of energy in order to reduce emissions

* the tightening of emission standards for carbon-hydrates, heavy metals, SO2, NOx if technically feasible

*the promulgation of ambient standards for further noxious compounds

*stricter emission standards for large power plants and industrial boilers

* the provision of catalytic converters in cars, and for tax incentives for purchasing them

* the implementation of a government program "Securing Employment by Qualitative Growth" amounting to DM 50 billion that should include countermeasures against dying forests

While the DGB proposal has not (yet) yielded legislative results, it might have helped prodding the utility industry in North-Rhine Westfalia, the most populous state in the country, toward concluding an agreement with the state to the effect that most of its old coal-burning power plants would obtain modern pollution-control equipment operating more effectively and ahead of time than required by the law (SZ, 13.11.1984:5). (Even more effective, however, according to the state governor was the "reminder" that a likely success of the Greens in the next state elections would probably mean even stricter requirements.)

At the turn to the 1980s, in the US public support for certain environmental goals had somewhat declined (e.g. for clean air) but new environmental issue areas have gained attention (industrial hazardous wastes, toxic chemicals, drinking water quality) (CEQ, 1980:28). The growing problems with industrial chemicals, toxic substances or hazardous wastes have linked the concerns of occupational safety and health to those around the protection of the natural environment. Neither the public nor labor have responded favorably to the deregulation plans of the Reagan administration. Repeatedly, the swing to the right in the US even fostered labor-environmentalist alliances.

The probably politically most pertinent alliance sought to prevent the dismantling of the Clean Air Act when it was up for reauthorization in 1981. Yet, the labor movement was all but unified over what to do about the Act. The construction unions of the AFL-CIO wanted substantial changes in order to promote new construction. The existing law, these unions argued, puts all of the burden for reducing air pollution on newly constructed facilities, thus discouraging new construction. The UAW favored continuing the strong protection provisions for stationary sources, but supported changes that would somewhat ease the rules for mobile sources. A group of seven industrial unions, finally, some of which belonged to the Clean Air Coalition, wanted to keep the Act basically as it was. They opposed proposed changes, and rather demanded a speed-up in the implementation of a hazardeous pollutants program and specific measures for controlling acid rain. The proposed changes, the industrial unions argued, unduly prolonged the threat to the community and work-place health of Americans:

> Protecting "clean" air areas and cleaning up "dirty" areas are both vitally important. In accomplishing these purposes there is no conflict between economic and environmental interests. A healthy economy cannot exist in a devastasted environment. By forcing "dirty" (nonattainment) areas to clean up -thus reversing the deterioration of the infrastructure in older, industrial areas- the Clean Air Act compels companies to introduce new technologies and modernize facilities which result in more productive, efficient, and competitive operations, thus making jobs more secure in those areas. By controlling the rate at which "clean" areas may be polluted (prevention of significant deterioration), the Clean Air Act slows the wasteful exodus of industries from the "dirty" Northeast and Midwestern regions and California to the "clean" Sunbelt and Western states.
> Claims that weakening the CAA is necessitated by the present economic situation and the need to promote job growth and security are simply false. Pollution abatement and job security go hand in hand -environmental regulations have not been the primary cause of even one plant shutdown. It is a fact that deteriorating and obsolete facilities, which also are polluters, are vulnerable to economic collaps and plant closings. In these cases, job losses are more acurately attributable to the lack of modernization than to environmental protections. Furthermore, the lack of strong clean-up efforts in severely polluted areas makes them less desirable places for investments in new plants and equipment and other types of economic growth. Moreover, the CAA directly creates jobs in abatement industries. A recent EPA study estimates that some 525,000 jobs will be created by 1987 if current environmental enforcement standards continue in effect. (Statement by ACTWU, International Chemical Workers Union, Allied Industrial Workers, IAM, International Molders and Allied Workers Union, OCAW, USWA: In Support of Clean Air, February 24, 1982)

In sum, labor and environmentalists have agreed on environmental protection as a principal goal. Concerns about existing jobs and traditional economic thinking on the part of labor, and lacking patience and empathy by environmentalists often caused conflicts when environmental protection measures were up for implementation. Recent anti- environmental policies have been a cause for labor-environmentalist rapprochement, but have also elucidated the divers interests among the unions. Overall, there was not a built-in dichotomy between labor and environmentalism with respect to environmental protection.

3.1.2 Employment Policies

On paper, the views of German labor and environmentalists on employment always looked fairly similar. Those cases where employment and environmental goals were in conflict were both the exception, and the most publicized and politicized ones. Since 1977, the DGB has been calling for "qualitative growth", a reduction of work-time and the social control of productivity increases in order to sustain a full—employment economy (DGB, 1983). However, also in 1977, the much publicized union demonstrations for jobs in nuclear energy took place (c.f. Section 5.2.3.3). While the labor leadership supported these demonstrations only very reluctantly, for many years they were considered the telling evidence of labor's real interests —proclamations of intent to the contrary notwithstanding.

Most of labor's earlier statements in support of qualitative employment were not taken seriously. The DGB Environmental Program called for accelerated qualitative economic growth as a means of creating jobs. In an employment program, the DGB advocated subsidized housing and urban renewal, investments in education and health services, public transportation and environmental protection (DGB, July 1977). German labor was aware that environmental protection investments in the FRG between 1972 and 1980 resulted in estimated net employment gains of 360,000 jobs (ifo Institut, 1980; cited by Albrecht, 1980). In 1981, the DGB proposed government incentives for investments in energy conservation as a means to create employment on a massive scale[2].

In the last 2—3 years, however, the labor movement was supporting environmental protection for its own sake, but was also well aware of its employment potential. The 1981 DGB Employment Program, modelled after the "Investments for the Future Program" that had created or secured more than 300,000 jobs since 1979 (DGB, 1983), emphasized investments with positive environmental impacts in the areas of waste energy usage; construction of new, environmentally benign coal—fired power plants; the housing environment and urban traffic; noise protection; expansion of public transportation systems; environmentally benign technologies; sewage treatment plants; and investments for cleaning air and water. Notably, the DGB has not included expansion of nuclear power construction in its "wish" list of employment inducing investments.

With growing urgency, the DGB has also demanded a shorter work—time as a means of creating more jobs. In 1984, two unions went on strike for the 35—hour work—week without loss of pay which became the toughest labor conflict in the history of the Federal Republic. The unions have clearly broken with the approaches to employment of the past —notwithstanding the fact, that from case to case environmental concerns were put on a low burner when jobs were at stake.

At first glance, the environmental movement advanced measures to create employment that were quite compatible with those of labor. The BBU demanded an "ecologically oriented economy" (also see 3.1.5), requiring investments for measures improving energy efficiency, solar technology, housing and urban renewal, waste water treatment, clean air, nature protection and conservation, ecological agriculture, active and passive noise protection, and raw materials recycling (BBU, Forderungskatalog..., 1979). The Green Party Election Platform for 1980 stressed that "unemployment is inhuman and uneconomical" (p.6). Its demands included the right to work ("Recht auf Arbeit") [3], the differentiation of work—time, the humanization of the work—place by "democratization instead of polarization", a guaranteed minimum income, and democratically derived rules for negotiating incomes. The Green Party in Hessia advocated traditional labor union demands calling for the introduction of the 35—hour work week; an early retirement option; the reduction of work at night, in shifts, during weekends, in extra—shifts and extra hours to the utmost extent; and, as a long term goal, doing away with work at assembly lines and at piece—rate pay (FR, 8.2.1982:19). Finally, the BUND claimed that environmental investments could create one million new jobs: 400,000 by using energy saving technologies; 300,000 in transportation and housing; and additional ones in agriculture and environmental protection technologies (SZ, 2.2.82:1).

However, similar positions on all these issues so far have not yet meant much active cooperation. Disagreements between labor and environmentalists persisted for various reasons. In the past, labor's verbal commitments to environmental protection and qualitative growth were too often put aside when a project promised a specific number of new jobs. "Employment opportunity costs" were usually not considered, i.e. the jobs which would have been created had the same amount of investment been spent for other uses. For example, environmentalists calculated that nuclear power plant investments yielded considerably fewer jobs than investments of the same magnitude in other sectors. Labor has never refuted this argument but supported nuclear energy explicitly because of the jobs involved in the industry (c.f. 3.1.5.1).

Similarly, highly publicized instances such as Buschhaus have harmed labor's environmental credibility. In that case, the DGB had supported an operating license for a coal—fired power plant which had been newly constructed without scrubbers but would use heavily polluting high—sulfur local coal for several years. In return, two older plants would reduce emissions as an offset. At stake were about 600 mining jobs in this economically depressed area adjacent to the East German border, on the one hand, and the environmental commitment of labor (and that of the federal government) on the other. The DGB and other proponents felt the plant should start operations since the area needed the jobs desperately and overall emissions in the region would be slightly reduced. For the opponents, including individual union bodies such as the IGM and DGB districts, Buschhaus had become a symbol for the environmental mistakes of the past. They considered it a litmus test for the sincereness of the much proclaimed environmental commitment of politicians. While the licensing of Buschhaus was highly controversial within labor, there was also agreement that the issue would, and should, not have arisen had proper environmental foresight been used. Although labor's environmental reputation has certainly suffered, there can be no question that Buschhaus has served as a lesson to labor on the need for preventive environmental approaches.

Another area of disagreement was the approach to employment policies. For environmentalists, promotion of investments in the abovementioned "quality growth" areas, and reducing work—time was the principal approach to employment policies. For the DGB, this approach was only one track. At least equally important for the DGB was the expansion of co— determination rights as a means to improve job security. Socially meaningful environmental and employment policies were cited as important targets for using these rights. Environmentalists have neither opposed nor actively supported this approach.

Moreover, environmentalists have not always insisted on "no loss of pay" in conjunction with the reduced work—time demand. For labor, however, the maintenance of income has been central. It demanded the 35—hour work week without loss of pay. So far, it has rejected job—sharing arrangements, at which environmentalists have looked with sympathies.

Finally, environmentalists rejected the ways in which labor unions actually pursued some of the policies (aside from environmental ones) that were in principle also endorsed by environmentalists. Urban renewal and housing was one notorious example. Referring to practices of the "Neue Heimat", the largest housing conglomerate in the country, which is owned by the unions, environmental groups (and others) have accused unions of condoning or tolerating union—owned enterprises to participate on a large scale the elimination —disguised as "modernization"— of cheap housing on a large scale. An artificial shortage of housing, skyrocketing rents, the destruction of grown neighborhoods and urban environments have resulted, critics say. Labor, in general, has not contradicted these accusations.

The AFL—CIO has acknowledged the positive —although allegedly minimal— employment impact of pollution control. One study estimated

that for the 1970-1986 period, unemployment would be .1% to .4% lower
with pollution control standards than without such standards (AFL-CIO
American Federationist, Oct.1979:4). Like their German counterparts,
the majority of the environmental organizations in the US advocated
various job creating measures but often only with a marginal interest
and in general terms. As a whole, the environmental movement has shown
less concern with employment questions than the labor movement has
shown for the protection of the natural environment. This is also
reflected in the issues selected by labor's Committee on Political
Education (COPE) and the League of Conservation Voters (LCV) for their
Congressional ratings (see Section 3.2 for more details). Of the 304
votes selected by the LCV between 1971 and 1979, only 11 dealt with the
workplace environment. The League included only one other employment
related issue (on environmental blackmail). In the same period, COPE
included 39 votes (out of 298) dealing with energy and the natural
environment. To give another example, the NWF (i.e. the environmental
organization with the largest membership), by 1980 had not passed any
resolution focusing on employment issues. (However, occupational
safety and health concerns have gained increasing attention in the
environmental movement during the Reagan administration.)
    Actively engaged in employment matters for more than a decade
already have been those environmental groups which have had an ongoing
working relationship with labor unions. I will present their proposals
at some length, since they were somewhat counter to conventional wisdom
and since labor has been increasingly responsive (see Section 3.1.5.2).
(In the meantime, these views have consolidated into a broader,
distinctly environmentalist approach to industrial policy.)
    The Friends of the Earth have claimed that the 'soft energy path'
(Lovins, 1976 and 1977) and other measures supported by
environmentalists are also the path to full employment. While the
traditional energy industries belong to the least employment intensive,

        retrofitting old houses with adequate insulation and solar energy
        collectors will create hundreds of thousands more jobs than
        creating the new energy supply needed to make the same houses
        comfortable if they aren't retrofitted. (Not Man Apart, Feb.78,
        in:US Government, 1978:277)

wGoals that nearly all environmentalists are already working toward,
FOE claimed, are fully compatible with full employment. Beneficiaries
would not only be environmentalists and the unemployed but also the
employed poor since they suffered first and worst from a wide range of
environmental insults. But also labor would benefit from the small,
decentralized factories advocated by environmentalists since they would
be able to negotiate on equal terms with a home-town management.
    In a statement submitted to the Subcommittee on Energy of the Joint
Economic Committee of the US Congress, the Sierra Club similarly urged
the development of environmentally benign energy sources as a means of
creating employment at a massive scale.

        The Sierra Club believes that more rapid development and use of
        appropriate, alternative sources of energy would not only reduce
        the pressure on our natural resources, but make good economic
        sense as well. We feel that the problems of unemployment and our
        need for clean energy sources, with prices and supply under our
        control, can be addressed simultaneously. One of the major areas
        where this can be done is through the accelerated development and
        greater utilization of the existing technology in the solar energy
        field. (US Government, 1978:284)

The installation of solar energy equipment, the argument went, is a
labor intensive process. Not only would a $ 2 B investment in solar

45

energy create more than four times as many jobs than if it were invested in the construction of a nuclear power plant, but the ratio of tradespeople to professionals would be also twice as high in the solar case. Another study the Sierra Club referred to claimed that the installation of solar space heating units on only 10% of the new housing units built in California until 1985 would generate approximately 5,000 jobs a year over the next ten years, 4,000 more jobs than an equivalent nuclear alternative. Further, a $ 5 B transfer of funds from highway construction to mass transit would result in a slight increase of total transportation construction jobs. As another area where substantial new employment could be created, the Club pointed to the rehabilitation of existing urban housing. Every $ 1 B invested would refurbish roughly 25,000 units and create approximately 50,000 jobs. An urban rehabilitation program would also offer a chance to introduce energy conservation measures. The Sierra Club's California Legislative Program advocated a 'conservation economy' which would purportedly yield a total net increase in jobs over present policies or projects in California of more than 300,000. The measures included the rehabilitation of low cost housing (120,000 more jobs), maintenance of pollution standards (100,000), public employment rehabilitation (32,000), small farming (16,000) or retrofit insulation (16,000) (perspectives, July 1977:3).

Yet, not only the sheer numbers but also the kind of employment to be created favor the environmentalist employment alternative, the Sierra Club argued. Solar energy jobs would go to people in occupations that are more susceptible to unemployment. In addition, many of the jobs could be filled by training the long-term unemployed. Urban renewal could provide employment for the very people whose neighborhood was effected. Further, the Sierra Club supported numerous local and national employment measures that go far beyond the ordinary scope of concerns of an environmental organization such as the Humphrey– Hawkins bill (as noted already), occupational and safety bills, public work programs, or "plant– closing" legislation [4].

Environmentalists for Full Employment (EFFE) has looked perhaps most systematically of all environmental groups into the relationship between energy and employment. The findings of an analysis of more than 70 such studies are summarized in Table 3–1 and confirm the positions taken by the other environmental groups.

Cleavages on employment issues did not divide labor and the environmental movement in general but rather followed industrial sectors. The Autoworkers, Machinists or Public Employees unions at times cooperated closely with the Sierra Club, FOE, EFFE or local groups. The Steelworkers have been aligned with environmentalists on issues like air and water pollution and employment, but divided on others like 'bottle bills' or nuclear power. Further, while the AFL–CIO Building and Construction Trades Department saw the expansion of energy production as the adequate way to raise employment, the AFL–CIO Industrial Union Department (IUD) stressed the benefits of relying on solar energy, conservation and mass transportation (also see 3.1.5.2). The IUD's "Blueprint for a Working America" (AFL–CIO, 1980:12) predicted that 400,000, 200,000, and 550,000 jobs, respectively, would result from such policies. Groups such as EFFE have used detailed analyses on the employment impacts of environmental and energy policies to push the government to integrated employment and energy planning (see Chapter 6). The overlap of interest between a minority of labor and environmentalism, thus, was substantial on employment related matters. Unlike in the FRG, both sides did not merely share similar views but actually joined forces to put them into effect.

On the other hand, environmentalists and the majority of organized labor have disagreed fundamentally on the wisdom of expanding energy production capabilities as a prerequisite for full employment. Further, the two sides disagreed on the wisdom of supporting large construction projects (such as dams, highways, airports, or oil shale

A. In relating energy requirements to future employment needs, the government has cavalierly accepted the contention of major energy producers that to support employment throughout the economy as well as in the energy industry, continued expansion of fossil fuels and nuclear energy is essential. However, the energy field has not been singled out by federal policy makers as a significant source of new jobs for the 1980's. And the effects of different energy scenarios on employment have largely been ignored.

B. There is growing evidence that emphasizing energy conservation and renewable energy is consistent with high levels of economic vitality in the economy as a whole and would lessen our need for scarce and costly conventional fuels (oil, gas, coal, uranium). Additional research is needed to show in detail how these measures could be introduced, what new industries would be created.

C. Numerous studies show net employment *benefits* from the introduction of conservation and renewable energy measures. Not only are jobs created in the conservation and renewable energy industries, but the reduced consumption of energy also produces a shift in consumer spending that adds jobs throughout the economy. Analyses that fail to take these factors into account perpetuate a bias against conservation and renewables.

D. Studies show that reduced purchases of conventional forms of energy, made possible by energy conservation measures and the use of renewable energy, can have significant employment benefits in many localities. Most regions of the country must import their energy from elsewhere. By curtailing these imports and substituting conservation and renewables, localities can promote their own economic growth and create jobs at home. Again, these jobs will not be limited to the conservation and renewable energy industries, but will appear in the wider economy of the region as well.

E. Most employment impact studies of conservation and solar energy applications have concentrated on the residential sector. But conservation and solar technologies have valuable applications in the commercial, industrial and transportation sectors, where eighty percent of our energy consumption takes place and where significant energy efficiency increases have already been recorded. Failure to examine these areas represents a major gap in the research effort, and future employment impact studies should be expanded to include them.

F. Most studies which have looked at solar energy have dealt with conventional solar water heating systems—rooftop collectors, pumps, and water storage tanks. A few have dealt with wind systems and photovoltaic systems. (Since the ultimate technology that will be used to produce solar cells has yet to be developed or commercialized, these latter estimates are quite unreliable.) None has looked at biomass conversion systems that could collect municipal and/or agricultural wastes and convert them into electricity, alcohol, or methane. Yet biomass is likely to be an important part of our renewable energy future. The construction of biomass conversion facilities, followed by the collection of these materials and the operation of the facilities (as well as by the *production* of agricultural products having high energy yields), are likely to be rich sources of employment, in both urban and rural areas.

G. There is no evidence that the recent studies and analyses of energy-employment interactions have been a factor in Federal energy policy. Furthermore, to the extent that analytical studies are used as an integral part of Federal energy policy making, they do not seem to use frameworks or methodologies suited to illuminating the employment consequences of energy policies. In short, employment has not been a major factor in energy policy decisions.

H. Little attention has been directed to qualitative aspects of jobs in the energy field, to health and safety hazards posed to employees and their communities, and to the broader environmental impacts and social costs.

Source: Richard L. Grossmann, Environmentalists for Full Employment, "The Politics of Energy and Jobs", Remarks delivered to a conference on "Meeting Energy Workforce Needs", sponsored by the Department of Labor, Washington, DC, February 26, 1980

Table 3-1 : EFFE Findings from an Analysis of more than 70 studies regarding energy, economic growth, and employment relationships

exploration and mining) solely because of the new employment these would provide. Some construction unions refused any contacts with environmentalists —who, in turn, no longer sought contacts with these unions. To my knowledge, these unions have not responded to —and certainly not refuted— the employment figures presented by the environmental groups. Here, disagreements on policy may have turned into phobias ("Beruhrungsangst").

In sum, there is a good deal of agreement on employment policies between labor and environmentalists in principle. But when the issue is implementation, disagreements between declaratory and actual policy have been manifest especially in the FRG. In the US, there has been considerable cooperation between influential parts of the two movements although it was also evident that many environmentalists were little interested in employment issues. Particularly on nuclear power, the conflicts between building and construction unions and the environmental movement were irreconcilable. There were also deep cleavages among labor unions. In the 1980s, adverse political conditions in both countries to both labor and environmentalism increased their commonalities regarding employment policies, but led in the US only to a corresponding increase of joint labor—environmentalist activities. Overall, a built—in dichotomy on employment matters was not evident.

3.1.3 "Environmental Blackmail"

"Environmental blackmail" refers to such cases where a company seeks to avoid anti—pollution measures by falsely claiming that these measures would inevitably cost jobs. If such claims are not false, then there is no environmental blackmail. Management might threaten to close or relocate a plant, that is an environmental polluter, for perfectly sincere reasons unrelated to environmental protection. Thus, one needs to discriminate between blackmail and legitimate concerns of management. In reality, such a distinction is often difficult and might require a detailed analysis of each case.

Overall, however, there can be no doubt that environmental blackmail arguments have indeed been used. Kazis and Grossman(1982) have documented numerous instances in the US. Studies have found that a very small number of plant closings ostensibly necessary because of environmental requirements actually occured solely for that reason [5]. Moreover, not only management resorted to what resembled environmental blackmail arguments, but also unions (particularly building and construction unions); in the FRG the work councils of affected companies (c.f. Chapter 5); or local politicians and media in regions highly dependent on one particular industry. Further, labor sometimes faced the difficult choice of either live with existing pollution and employment levels, or accept environmental protection measures that were linked to automation and entailed considerable employment losses.

There are two aspects closely related to environmental blackmail. First, how much information is available to the parties concerned? If a company can back—up the necessity of plant closings, relocations or capacity reductions by plausible data, the environmental blackmail reproach loses credibility. On the other hand, if such information is not forthcoming or, even worse, if a company seems to be interested in impeding information gathering, the case for blackmail will be strong. The second aspect concerns the "goodness" of the LER. Environmental blackmail will be the more difficult, the more labor and environmentalists can cooperate, because "playing—off" one side against the other will work less well.

In both countries, labor unions and (as evidenced by public opinion data) the general public [6] have rejected environmental blackmail threats. The emphasis in the FRG was on the first aspect; in the US, both aspects played a role. The difference in emphasis reflects the different political frameworks in which the two labor movements are embedded.

The DGB Environmental Program put the issue as basically one of economic and political power. It recognized the existence of conflicts of interests. It did not explain them as a "natural" dichotomy between employment and environmental protection but rather as a consequence of the economic dependence of workers. Let me recapitulate the arguments in the Program. Workers are excluded from corporate decisions affecting the environment, their work-place and pay. Such decisions are on automation, changes of production processes, plant openings, relocations and closings. "The employed must constantly fear that they will lose their jobs or suffer pay losses as a consequence of technical- economic measures" (p.20). Management can exploit these fears in order to mobilize against justified environmental interests. This is compounded by the fact that workers and their representatives have only limited access to information in order to verify management claims that environmental protection measures and job security are indeed incompatible. Often, the program argued, management deliberately resorted to environmental blackmail. In fact, the prerogative of firing, the most severe manifestation of the workers' dependence, enables management to blackmail not only workers but all those affected by environmental pollution. Therefore, the DGB stressed, the guarantee of job security would make an important contribution to environmental protection -and the means to achieve job security would be improved co-determination rights.

In the US, co-determination of course was not an issue. Rather, the unions sought to increase the transparency of corporate decisions by including anti- blackmail provisions in environmental legislation such as in the 1977 amendments to the Clean Air Act (AFL-CIO American Federationist, Oct.1978:6) or in the Redwood National Park extension legislation (Wassermann, 1978a and 1978b).

In addition, parts of American labor actively sought cooperation with environmentalism as a means to weaken environmental blackmail threats. Indeed, countering corporate power was perhaps the most important motive for labor and environmentalist cooperation particularly regarding energy matters. Let me exemplify this by the following long quotation from the newspaper of the Steelworkers:

What is becoming more and more evident to labor is that a wedge is being driven between two traditional allies -between labor and the conservationists- in what looks like another round of industrial blackmail. ... When environmental laws were enacted and up to this very day, workers were told that companies are forced to comply with such laws dealing with clean air, water and toxic substances, and must meet the huge expenditures necessary they may be forced to close or reduce operation. Again, a blackmail threat using jobs. Now it is definite that energy is added to the list of scare tactics employed to blackmail working people. Most energy problems are being laid on the environmentalists who are being labeled at times as idle rich eggheads with international loyalties, far-out leftists, no-growth advocates or just plain weirdos. Workers are told that it is this environmental movement that stands in the way of progress; that there is little or no danger in (the) nuclear energy production chain; no danger to the miners exposed to radon daughter gases in uranium mines or in the transportation of radioactive material, the operation of reactors or in the disposal and containment of radioactive waste. Some, in fact, make it sound like low level radiation may even be good for people. Workers and the public are being told that sulphur dioxide is not as harmful as reported; that lead, arsenic, asbestos, and other of the many thousands of poisons connected with industry must be tolerated; that the products we come in contact with, the air we breathe, water we drink and foods we eat

49

cannot be purified or made safe without endangering our economy.
While workers were being told that the environmentalists **and**
consumer advocates are their real enemies, it was the Sierra Club
and not one member of American industry that sided with labor in
recent hearings before the Supreme Court in a case involving
Occupational Safety and Health inspectors' right to enter a
workplace. Most all responsible environmental groups regard the
workplace as a part of the total environment and are supportive of
labor's efforts to make our industrial environment less dangerous
to man. (Steel Labor, Dec.1978:8,9)

3.1.4 Economic Growth

The question of economic growth has been a major conceptual dividing
point between labor and environmentalists. For labor unions, high
economic growth rates often appeared to be a goal per se. Economic
growth traditionally was one cornerstone in the "quadrangle" believed
to govern economic policy besides price stability, full employment and
a balance of payment equilibrium. Lerner and Gorden (1969:295)
observed that "in Western Europe, the modern social process of
self-sustaining growth which supports 'affluence' has become a secular
religion". Many in labor have been deeply committed to this belief
despite the fact that economic growth rates high enough to assure full
employment became less and less attainable.

Environmentalist criticism of the existing growth paradigm was
fundamental. The criticism did not stop at the policy level but
extended to the structures and values prevalent in industrial
societies. The BBU provided a typical account of these views in its
'Catalogue of Demands for an Eco-Concept in the FRG' (BBU,
Forderungskatalog..., 1979), on which the following remarks are all
based. Ecological considerations must guide economic and social
policy. One-sided economic growth which was dominant in the past has
subordinated important goals such as the just distribution of wealth,
human working and living conditions, health protection, education and
leisure activities under the prerogative of frictionless production
processes. The ecological movement would no longer tolerate
uncontrolled quantitative growth where all what counted were
sufficiently high annual percentage changes of GNP. The discussion on
the energy and environmental crisis has led to the recognition that
increases of GNP alone can not be a criterion for quality of life and
can contribute less than ever to the solution of society's problems.
Advantages brought by the technological and economic developments of
the past are increasingly nullified by negative side effects. Wasteful
production has used up raw materials and exceeded the tolerance limits
of eco-systems. Physiological and psychological stresses an strains
have led to 'civilization diseases' eminently costly to society.
Current economic growth patterns have barely lowered the differences
between the rich and the poor within a society and have even increased
cleavages among societies. The continued existence of inequalities
even serves to justify continued growth. Growth is increasingly less
suited to prevent unemployment. The conventional wisdom that more
investment means more production and more jobs no longer holds true
since investments are increasingly made for automation purposes.

The BBU has not advocated zero-growth but reductions of 'damage
growth'. It considered investments, and thus growth, in selected -and
in the past neglected- sectors indeed highly desirable (see Section
3.2.2). But the current profit-maximizing western market economies are
not suited for inducing this kind of growth, nor for solving economic,
employment, energy and environmental problems. Neither are the
production maximizing centrally planned economies of eastern Europe.
The BBU concluded that an ecological economy was needed which, however,
would require structural political and societal changes.

"Qualitative growth" has in fact been a concept which labor had embraced prior to most environmentalists. The IGM had sponsored a major conference on "Quality of Life" in 1972, i.e. at a time when the German environmental movement had barely started. The DGB in the Environmental Program, further, was critical of GNP used as an indicator of economic well-being but has relied on it in support of particular policies. And in the US, the former UAW president Woodcock once remarked in the Sierra Club Bulletin (Dec.71:12):

> Growth given the way it has been and is being achieved can no longer be defined optimistically as a higher standard of living; it must also be defined as a deterioration of the quality of life, urban congestion, suburban sprawl, the poisening of the air we breathe, the water we drink and the soil that nurtures us, the accumulation of garbage, and the steady pressure of a rising population on a finite resource base.

Most in labor, however, did not really appear committed to qualitative growth when hard choices needed to be made. Until recently, they fundamentally disagreed with environmentalists on what the effects of economic growth on environmental protection were. The unions regarded growth as a means of paying for environmental cleanup; environmentalists depicted growth per se as potentially highly damaging for the environment. In the controversy on nuclear energy (see Section 3.1.5), the need for more energy was usually rationalized as a means of assuring economic growth rates which in turn were described as indispensable for high employment levels. Although the DGB and its member unions were aware of both the possible economic and social problems associated with growth, in the face of stern employment problems, they held even a partial renunciation of economic growth unacceptable and as posing a grave risk for political stability (DGB, 5.4.77). American labor, similarly, accepted high growth rates as a principal goal. But as the above quotation indicates, that part of labor that has extensively cooperated with environmentalists defined acceptable growth not only in quantitative but also in qualitative terms. Consistently, these unions distinguished more between what ought to and what ought not to grow than did the rest of labor.
In the FRG, the unions have shown more reserve toward growth inducing policies in recent years (see Section 3.2.1). In part, this may be due to the realization that (practically non-attainable) growth rates of 6% annually for ten years would be needed to cope with unemployment (DGB, 1983). In part, the unions have come to reject growth in areas that they consider socially undesirable or that might cost jobs elsewhere. They opposed the introduction of a communications cable system praised by its sponsors for its growth and employment potential. Labor also opposed increases of military exports against strong lobbies in its own ranks and in industry. Regarding hotly contested projects like new nuclear power plants or the Frankfurt airport extension, the unions have continued to endorse them in principle but have not extensively lobbied for them in public.
In sum, economic growth overall has divided labor unions and environmentalists on the conceptual level even though both groupings were committed to qualitative growth in principle. For labor, growth was a goal; for environmentalists, it was a means. For labor, high rates of growth were primary and what was to grow was secondary; for environmentalists, it was the reverse. Notable exceptions in the US notwithstanding, there was a built-in dichotomy with respect to the growth concept. In recent years in the FRG, the unions have adopted a more critical approach to quantitative growth.

3.1.5 Energy Policies

3.1.5.1 FRG

According to its first statement on nuclear energy issued in April of 1977, the DGB "has always stressed the absolute priority for reaching goal of immediate full employment". The present state of nuclear and other large scale energy production alternatives, the DGB then stated, does not suggest any energy formula which could simultaneously resolve all socio- economic, environmental and health problems. Energy politics, therefore, can only seek to minimize the possible risks stemming from all three types of problems and must necessarily be open to political compromise.

Growth —and thus employment— inducing policies can only succeed, the statement maintained, if energy supplies are sufficient and fairly priced. Estimates of the energy needs for the near and medium future, the DGB believed, must rely on past consumption rates. Past experience shows a close coupling of the growth rates of energy consumption and GNP. Energy savings can reduce future needs but their potential is limited. For the time being, the DGB stated in 1977, increasing energy production capabilities is indispensable. But the ultimate goal of energy politics is the use of no—risk, environmentally benign, resource and cost effective energy sources.

For the short term, the DGB advocated the following strategy:

1. Electricity generating capacity must be adequate to assure growth rates oriented toward full employment.

2. As long as energy savings pose no danger for full employment, all measures apt to support savings must be taken.

3. Usage of domestic coal for electricity generation must expand. That entails replacement of obsolete and construction of new coal fired plants. Expansion of electricity generating capacity based on hydro, wind and lignite coal is not possible. Based on oil and gas, it would mean increased foreign dependency.

4. Increased reliance on nuclear energy is therefore inevitable. However, its use must be limited to the amount necessary for securing energy supplies. All serious objections must be met with before a final and irreversible decision is made. Future reliance on nuclear energy hinges upon a number of conditions concerning the back—end of the nuclear fuel cycle ("Entsorgung"), siting, safety concerns, and information of the public.

Ecological energy policies as sought by the BBU (Forderungskatalog..., 1979) were described as environmentally benign and would be based on renewable energy sources. Energy politics in the FRG —the BBU argued— have in the past almost exclusively aimed at increasing energy supplies and stimulating demand. Energy policies oriented toward the future must use all possibilities to reduce energy needs. The energy consumption rates of the past would in a few decades lead to the exhaustion of fuel reserves, to changes in the earth's climate, to a plutonium economy and hence possibly to repressive totalitarianism, and to struggles for the remaining energy sources. The planned heavy reliance on nuclear energy was soon as the result of wrong energy policies in the past.

The BBU, therefore, opposed construction and operation of nuclear power plants, supports the environmentally sound usage of coal, and proposes a variety of measures geared at more rational energy usage. Its opposition to nuclear energy was based on the standard arguments: the BBU sees nuclear energy as unsafe, not economical, not needed, socially incompatible, and bearing proliferation risks. Second, coal usage is needed for the time being, particularly for electricity generation. The BBU coal policy demands:

(1) A siting policy respecting environmentally overloaded metropolitan areas,
(2) that larger amounts of coal are being used for electricity generation,
(3) the use of imported coal in coastal regions,
(4) the replacement of old coal-fired plants by new ones to reduce emissions and create employment in the construction industry,
(5) the installation of decentralized coal-fired plants in smaller units and the use of waste heat in District Heating Systems, and
(6) the application of the latest technology, in particular fluidized bed combustion and pressurized coal gasification.

Third, a variety of measures enhancing rational energy usage should be taken [7].

Hence, the stated preferences of labor and environmentalists in the FRG regarding the relative merits of various energy sources are more similar than one might expect. A BBU leader, in fact, noted a "total identity in the goals of labor unions and citizen groups" with respect to the three highest ranking energy priorities (Aktionsreport, No.23, April 1981:6): First comes rational energy usage, second usage of renewable energy sources, and third the increased use of domestic coal. He stressed however that "what we will continue to disagree on is the reliance on nuclear energy" which labor had assigned rank 4 but which the BBU totally rejects.

The "total identity of goals" observed above, however, might mean little if one looks at the energy scenarios advanced by the two sides to the Enquete Commission on Nuclear Energy Policy of the German Bundestag in 1980. Table 3-2 summarizes the scenarios for for the year 2030 favored by the DGB and the Oko-Institut (that has become somewhat of a research arm of the environmental movement). As points of reference, actual energy demand and supply figures for the FRG in 1973 and 1978 are presented.

The Oko-Institut expects for 2030 only slightly more than half of the energy needs assumed in the DGB scenario. They will be met exclusively by coal and renewables while the DGB figures reflect its mixed strategy. The underlying economic growth rates are fairly similar.

The figures indicate that the disagreements go beyond the merits of nuclear power as the fourth-ranking energy source. The different demand expectations, for example, differ by a factor of 2. Environmentalists count on much higher savings and use of renewable energy but see no need of oil, gas or nuclear. This suggests that the verbally similar preferences for rational energy usage and renewable forms of energy must mean different things in the scenarios. Moreover, in reality, all this might mean substantial changes of production processes and consumption habits. Many of these changes may be unpopular or threaten vested interests in and outside of labor. Further, while some environmentalists concede a considerable role to coal in their scenarios, others have in fact opposed numerous coal fired power plants.

On the other hand, one must note that the DGB figures have rapidly drawn nearer to the environmental scenarios in the course of a few years. The DGB demand projections for 2030 are little higher than present levels and, indeed, are surprisingly low. They represent a significant reduction of projected demand compared to figures comprising conventional wisdom only a few years ago which then had also been accepted by the DGB and its unions. The lower figures reflect the fact that W.German primary energy consumption in 1981 was not higher than in 1973 (e.g. FR, 17.12.1981:5), and also indicate that the DGB was assuming a higher elasticity between energy and economic growth rates than previously stated. In addition, the German unions have

	DGB[a]	Environmentalists[b]
Annual Economic Growth (in real terms)		
- before 2000	$\geq$ 2%[1]	4% – 2%[2]
- after 2000	1.1%	1.5–.5%[3]
Structural Change in the Economy	trend	
Growth in basic products industry	GNP/2	
Energy Savings	35%[4]	30–70%[5]

	1973[c]	1978[a]	2030	2030
Demand (in M to SKE)				
Primary Energy Needs	379	390	400	216
Energy End Use	248	260	280	150
Electricity Needs		36	49[6]	26
Supplies (in M to SKE)				
Coal	117	105	160	97–125
Oil, Natural Gas	248	265[7]	120	0
Nuclear	4	12	70	0
Renewables		8	50	119– 91

1) as much as necessary for full employment, at least 2%
2) 1981-85: 4%; 1986-90:3.5%; 1991-95:2.5%; 1996-2000:2%
3) 2001-10: 1.5%; 2011-20:1.0%; 2021-30: .5%
4) primary energy consumption by continuing present trends without savings in 2030 = 100%
5) reductions in specific energy end use (base year 1973; median values) for space heating 70%, cars 60%, industrial process heat 30%, electric household appliances 65%, electric motors 30%
6) median values of paths 2 and 3 in a)
7) value corrected, HS

Sources: a) DGB, Wirtschaftspolitische Informationen, Nr.5/1980, Anlage 2 (DGB Statement to Bundestag Enquete Commission on Energy, HS)
b) Öko Institut, Energieversorgung der Bundesrepublik ohne Kernenergie und Erdöl (Kurzfassung), Dr.F.Krause, Dez. 1979
c) Deutscher Bundestag, DS 8/570:6

Table 3 -2 : Comparison of Energy Scenarios for 2030 by Labor and Environmentalists in the FRG

approached environmentalist positions by advocating energy conservation as an area of considerable employment potential.

However, all these disagreements and rapprochements were second to the nuclear power conflict. This conflict was by far the most important single issue for the LER. If the built—in dichotomy hypothesis does not hold on this issue, then it will not be convincing altogether. I will therefore again turn to the nuclear power controversy between labor and environmentalists.

Even on nuclear energy, labor had initially adopted a critical position. The linkage established in the first DGB statement between further nuclear power plant construction and a satisfactory solution to the back—end of the nuclear fuel cycle was seen by many environmentalists as amounting to a nuclear power moratorium if strictly applied. Due to strong political pressures (see Chapter 5), the linkage was subsequently substantially weakened. Even today, many environmentalists believe, the DGB would have to oppose further nuclear power plant construction, would it really adhere to its officially stated conditions. Further, if the DGB took the recent (declining) energy consumption trends and actually applied its criterion of limiting nuclear energy usage "to the amount necessary for securing our energy needs" (DGB, April 5,1977 statement), then nuclear energy expansion would also not be warranted.

The DGB described its mandate in the nuclear energy debate as a three—way responsibility. First, the DGB advocated "active environmental policies": a healthy and livable natural environment is a precondition for humanizing the work environment and for a better quality of life. Second, the DGB represents the interests of all employed people. "This includes the demand for sufficient energy supplies which in turn is a precondition for the realization of the full employment goal and for societal growth". Third, the DGB represents all those engaged in planning, developing, constructing, and operating nuclear plants, including job security concerns (DGB, 5 April 1977).

In the view of environmentalists, the DGB position on nuclear energy is internally inconsistent, its main objective being to keep the nuclear energy option open. Environmentalists believe that the self—declared triple mandate presents a presently irreconcilable conflict pitting the first two interests against the third. A reconciliation of the first and third interests presumes nuclear power being environmentally benign (unless one advocates the conversion of nuclear into non—nuclear industry employment which the DGB does not). As long as the combined long—term effects of the nuclear fuel cycle continue to be highly contested in the scientific community, the toleration of nuclear energy expansion implies a foregone conclusion regarding its environmental feasibility. The second and third interests ostensibly represented by the DGB are also irreconcilable if the contention that nuclear energy investments compete with more labor—intensive investments providing equivalent energy services should turn out to be true. By the time the DGB endorsed the German nuclear power program formally, some of these issues had just begun to be explored somewhat systematically, and thus did not warrant the degree of support the DGB actually provided.

In general, the nuclear energy issue has lost in saliency. German labor has endorsed new nuclear power plants much less determined than 5 years ago —even though it has not formally changed its positions. Some in the IGM believe nuclear power to be pratically dead today because of the high investment costs. The workers at the KWU have "sobered out" about its future potential. In the next couple of years, more than 2.000 jobs, including engineers, will be lost at KWU. The KWU—management reportedly looks intensively at alternative product areas such as alternative energy, solar cells and garbage pyrolysis. Yet, as of this writing (Nov. 1984), nuclear energy once again proved to be the litmus test for the LER. The cooperation between the SPD and the Greens in Hessia, broke apart after five months over a nuclear power related issue. While the Hessian model is certainly not synonymous for the LER, it was carefully watched by labor as a symbol of the political maturity of the Greens.

In sum, the stated positions on energy issues of labor and environmentalism in the FRG show more similarities than differences. However, a comparison of DGB and environmentalist future energy scenarios implies considerably different views on actual politics. The most salient issue was the use of nuclear energy. Important differences exist, moreover, with regard to the actual formulation and implementation of policy. In both cases, environmentalist claims appear valid that German labor has supported policies and projects that contradict its own stated objectives. Moreover, the DGB positions on long-term demand projections, the perceived interdependence between energy and economic growth, the feasibility of energy savings, etc. have approached environmentalist positions. The hypothesis that labor-environmentalist conflicts on energy reflect a built-in dichotomy based on economic imperatives can not be affirmed for the FRG. Conflicts have remained but they appear to be based on political rather than economic factors, as Chapters 5 to 7 will argue.

3.1.5.2 United States

The positions on energy issues taken by American environmental groups were similar to those of their German counterparts. The only differences among the various groups were rather on emphasis and tactics than on substance. In a nutshell, they have come to oppose nuclear power; favored increased reliance on renewable energy sources and conservation; tolerated coal-fired power plants if their need was made plausible and the most advanced technological and pollution abatement designs used; advocated windfall profit taxes; and were ambivalent about the deregulation of oil and natural gas prices. Over time, the most notable shift was the one to a general opposition to nuclear power —as noted, many environmentalists were at one time supporters since they considered it cleaner than conventional sources. Given the relative homogeneity and the detailed description of environmentalist views on the energy- employment relationship in Section 3.1.2.2, I shall devote the remainder of this section exclusively to US labor.

The positions on energy taken by American labor unions were more complex viewed both cross- sectionally and over time. The differences are perhaps most striking, if one looks at the issues as choices on an "energy supply"/ "energy demand" spectrum. Figure 3-1 indicates estimates of the rough positions held by labor and environmentalist groups on such a hypothetical spectrum from 1965 to the 1980s. As a whole, labor has been closer to a "supply- side" definition than environmentalism. The positions of the different unions on this spectrum have been more dispersed than those of environmentalists and of German labor. Over time labor on average has moved in the demand side direction. Differences among individual unions have rather increased than decreased. This increase is attributable to the fact that several influential unions have turned to demand-side positions while others have not changed much. Finally, energy has lost much of its political saliency in the 1980s. Nuclear power has receded as an issue. The international oil market has turned into a byuers's market. Energy efficiency has greatly increased, e.g., energy consumption per GNP dollar fell by 20% between 1973 and 1982. The issue, if there is any, is no longer one of how to provide energy but how to pay for it.

The initial supply-side tilt is apparent if one examines the energy policies advocated by the AFL-CIO in the late 1960s. The AFL-CIO noted that most previous energy demand forecasts underestimated actual requirements. Those for electricity and natural gas, in particular, had "a consistent habit of busting the seams of nearly every forecast" (AFL-CIO, 1969:22). A quadrupling of electric power demand until 2000

56

perception of
energy issue

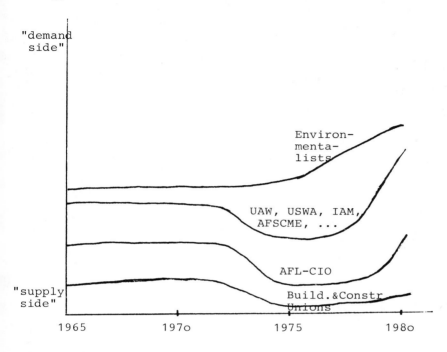

"demand
 side"

Environ-
menta-
lists

UAW, USWA, IAM,
AFSCME, ...

AFL-CIO

"supply
 side"

Build.&Constr.
Unions

1965   197o   1975   198o

Figure 3 - 1 :   Scheme of Labor and Environmentalist Views
                 of Energy Issue in the US, 1965 - 1980s

was thought possible [8]. Therefore, the AFL—CIO called for "swift steps" to supplement existing fossil fuels by new energy fuels; to develop more efficient methods of fuel discovery, extraction, processing, transportation and use; and to develop techniques of electric power generation and transmission. Oil shale and nuclear power were the "two new and enormous sources of energy" expected to play an increasingly significant part (op. cit.:23).

The energy supply—side attitude of American labor prevailing until the mid—70s is mirrored in the following quote from the IBEW Journal:

> The solution to many of our social and economic problems lies in the use of more energy, not less. Employment, transportation, waste disposal, and water supply are directly dependent on the use of energy. Only through the increased use of energy, and great quantities of it, can solutions be achieved. Our quality of life is proportionate to our use of energy. wA rational, rather than an emotional, viewpoint must be taken towards environmental considerations. Our use of energy must increase. (IBEW Journal, July 1972:28)

This view, not surprisingly, was strengthened and put into more concrete terms by the post—1973 oil shortage. The 1975 AFL—CIO convention passed an energy statement labelled "The AFL—CIO Program to Increase Energy Supplies" which saw it as "urgent that the United States launch a massive program" to that end (AFL—CIO, American Federationist, July 1976:3). The recommendations made included

> * a 5—year, $20B government funded crash program with major emphasis on existing energy sources, particularly nuclear energy, domestic oil (including off—shore), coal and coal gasification, liquefaction, and natural gas
> * the establishment of a government corporation for the construction of prototype and new energy facilities which would serve as a cost yardstick
> * special assistance to the electric utility industry such as tax measures and administrative policies to increase electric utility construction and output
> * a major effort toward increasing the domestic use of coal with appropriate applications of technology to minimize pollution
> * government action to promote the public acceptance of nuclear power. The lead time for getting plants into production should be reduced and "vigilant" environmental and safety measures should be continued to minimize risks
> * to stretch out "as necessary present environmental restrictions on energy production and use to reduce energy consumption and facilitate expansion of domestic energy output. This is a matter of timetable, not of objectives. The advance of technology and development of clean energy sources can permit the realization of environmental objectives. The two programs should be viewed as compatible parts of a single problem."
> * the rejection of deregulating the price of oil and natural gas
> * various measures directed against the large oil companies such as the termination of depletion allowances and tax credits; legislation to prohibit horizontal integration and to require the dissolution of vertically integrated companies; and to find ways that would treat giant oil companies as public utilities subject to stringent federal regulations

Regarding incentives to increase energy supplies, this program was close to the positions adopted at the 1975 AFL—CIO Building and Construction Trades Department conference. The conference urged

[...] that a separate National Energy Production Agency be created...; that long term rates which utilities must pay to borrow money be lowered, that the federal government help in all ways necessary to make financing of approved new energy facilities feasible, that the 10% investment tax credit be extended to utilities for an additional 10-year period, that the Nuclear-Indemnity Coverage Law be extended, that federal approval for energy facilities be coordinated, simplified, and improved, that legislation be enacted which will allow the cost of ongoing construction to be reflected in the rates charged by utilities, that the construction of or conversion to nuclear or coal-fired plants be encouraged, and that Congress enact the Coal Slurry Pipeline Act of 1975.

Regarding the AFL-CIO proposals on oil and gas price deregulation and controls of the oil industry, however, the building and construction unions remained conspicuously silent. But overall, the gist of the building trades proposal was well reflected by the AFL-CIO positions.

Yet, this concordance changed considerably within a few years. Not all unions shared the almost unequivocal supply orientation of the AFL-CIO. The views of unions like the UAW, USWA, AFSCME or IAM sometimes indicate deep cleavages to those traditionally shared by labor. While these unions and environmentalists did not agree on all energy issues (one important difference, for example, concerned energy pricing), their views were generally quite similar and converging.

A certain division within labor with respect to energy (and other) issues, of course, is logical regardless of the LER. Conflicts between those who earn a living by producing energy and those who consume it must be expected. The more unions represent workers not only as producers (i.e. at work) but also as consumers, the deeper the conflicts of interest will be between those unions representing energy production workers (including those constructing energy facilities) and the others. Not surprisingly, inter-union cleavages with respect to energy increased particularly when energy prices soared. The differences of views became most pronounced between energy production unions and those unions whose relatively broad (i.e. non-particularistic, c.f. Chapter 7) scope of concern made them most open to the "consumer interests" of their membership. A certain amount of producer/ consumer tension will always underlie the LER, but must not necessarily be a burden on the LER.

The shifts of union positions on energy became manifest in several ways. First, several unions expressed considerable doubt that more energy ought to be equated with more jobs. The treasurer of the USWA, Frank S.McKee, to give one example, warned that energy in abundance does not assure jobs nor the full utilization of human potential. Machines driven by low cost energy have been replacing the human factor in production. Energy costs have been cheaper than labor costs. The machine was often more predictable and efficient. Machines using energy rarely had ailments and never complained about working conditions. Today, McKee argued, the so-called capital intensive industries are also energy intensive and are becoming more so. They are employing less and less manpower while using more and more energy. The present excessive energy usage in the US, he warned, "may result in definite social and economic deterioration of such magnitude that it will overshadow even our gravest depression" (Steel Labor, Dec.78:8). He concluded:

The United Steelworkers of America maintain that unless there is a genuine full employment policy in America that will assure every able-bodied citizen a job —a policy that will require the government plan for full employment— joblessness and recessions will continue to plague the nation regardless of how much power we have. Likewise, energy and the technology it makes possible is turning once—skilled workers into unskilled workers as more and more of their skills are being made obsolete by sophisticated and energy— hungry machines. (ibid.)

Second, all these "deviant" unions were committed to the much stronger reliance on energy conservation and renewable sources in the future. They criticized the lack of sufficient government assistance for these energy sources and cited the danger that the oil companies, which had become "energy companies" already, might be able to control the solar market as well (e.g. IAM, May 6,1979; The Public Employee, Aug.79:3).

Third, while there were no disagreements in labor that oil and gas pricing should not be decontrolled, this issue became increasingly salient. It was argued that particularly in the absence of effective windfall profits taxation and redistribution schemes, deregulation would increase the already soaring oil company profits and would hurt mostly the poor. Further, it would contribute to inflation and thus endanger employment. The unions also gave strong support to end the oil depletion allowance and the foreign tax credit. Several unions went even further calling for an energy price freeze (e.g. IAM, May 6,1979; UAW, Feb.20,1974; USWA 1978 Convention Proceedings:451; The Public Employee, May/July/ Aug./Oct. 1979).

Fourth, these unions urged strongly that the concentrated economic power of the energy industry be broken. They supported legislation requiring horizontal and vertical divestiture of the large oil companies (e.g. IAM, Nov.17, 1978; USWA 1978 Officers Report:89). In addition, the unions advanced various schemes to increase public control over the industry. They picked up the AFL—CIO proposal of founding publicly owned companies that could serve as a yardstick against which oil company data and performance could be compared (e.g. UAW, 1974; The Public Employee, Aug.79:3; USWA 1978 Convention Proceedings:450).

Fifth, those unions increasingly criticized what they saw as a lack of comprehensive national energy planning taking into account the impact on employment. They urged the creation of a Department of Energy in order to coordinate energy and employment policies more effectively. After the DOE had been established, the unions (but also EFFE) continued to be highly critical of the unwillingness or inability of DOE and the Department of Labor to assess the employment impacts of various energy alternatives (e.g. UAW, 1974; The Machinist, April 1978:6; US Government, 1978).

Last not least, opposition to nuclear power within labor was rising. As already outlined in Section 2.4.2, only very few unions rejected nuclear energy outrightly but many began to favor an increasingly cautious approach in the latter part of the 1970s. Besides mounting safety concerns, rising cost'and the Clinch River Breeder program met more and more objections (e.g. IAM, May 6,1979; The Public Employee, Jan.1977:2). By 1981, it was in fact surmised that labor's "honeymoon with nuclear power" may be coming to an end (Askin, 1981).

While not all these developments and demands were at odds with those held by the mainstream AFL—CIO energy supply—side positions, they indicate a propensity to approach the energy problem more politically and closer to the demand—side perspective. Needless to say, the alternative approach to energy issues facilitated the cooperation with environmental groups. But these changing perspectives were also accompanied by —and perhaps even influenced— a reappraisal of the energy policies of the bulk of the AFL—CIO unions.

The shift of emphasis is apparent if one compares the AFL—CIO policy resolutions on nuclear, coal, alternate energy sources and conservation in 1977 and 1979 (EFFE, Labor — Nuclear Power Package, n.d.). In the 1977 resolution, nuclear power and coal received about twice as much space as in 1979. In 1977, it was "clear that coal and nuclear power are the ones this nation must rely upon in the immediate future"; reprocessing, enrichment and fast breeder programs were to be implemented; nuclear power was still expected to grow to cover more than 20% of the nation's energy supply by 2000; and "every effort" was urged to accelerate coal and nuclear power development while protecting the environment, safety and health. Two years later, coal and nuclear power could not be "ignored" since they would play "an important role in reducing US dependence on imported oil"; development of nuclear power was to be "accompanied by expanded research" to reduce safety hazards; and "immediate, careful attention" was to be devoted to nuclear waste disposal.

Alternate energy sources received four times as much space in 1979 than in 1977. In 1977, the US was to "direct its efforts toward developing such other sources" recognizing that they "will be neither cheap nor be developed overnight". In 1979, a "very substantial commitment ... toward advancing solar, gasahol and geothermal technology" was urged; solar energy was ascribed a "tremendous potential" for making a significant commitment.

Energy conservation was considered "indispensable" in both years but the catalogue of conservation measures was almost twice as long in 1979. In 1977, it was still pointed out that conservation does not mean "a diminishment in the quality of life" nor no growth; in 1979, no such introduction was apparently needed.

In its 1979 meeting, finally, the AFL-CIO Executive Council endorsed most of the measures which the large industrial and public employees unions had pushed for several years: the creation of a yardstick government agency; a major conservation effort; a "stiff windfall profits tax —with no loopholes"; a return to government controls on domestic crude oil prices; and the development of alternative energy sources (The Public Employee, Sept.79:8). Similarly, at the beginning of the 80s, AFL-CIO energy policy statements emphasized the need "to break free of oil company influence" in order to control domestic energy prices and finance "major investments in conservation and non-inflationary energy technologies" (AFL-CIO, Industrial Union Department, 1980:6; also AFL-CIO, Feb.16, 1981:4). No mention was made of nuclear energy.

In sum, by 1980 the energy outlook of American labor had definitely moved to positions more compatible to those of environmentalists than ever since energy had become politically controversial. To be sure, nuclear energy and to some extent energy pricing remained a source for labor-environmentalist contention and labor is still closer to energy supply side than to demand side perspectives. Moreover, the statements of the building and construction unions still sound similar to those made in the early 1970s (e.g. AFL-CIO Building and Construction Trades Department President Robert A. Georgine, in: US Government, 1978:217). But, as a general pattern, labor's shift toward the demand orientation and the lower saliency of energy issues seem to parallel improvements of the LER, and certainly weaken perceptions of a built-in dichotomy between employment and environmental protection interests.

3.2 The LER and Economic Well-Being

Various authors have contended that the state of the economy is a major influence on the LER. Watts (1979:173) hypothesized that the size of environmentalism as well as the duration and intensity of environmental conflicts depend on the absolute level of material security and its relative distribution. Lehner (1978:48) saw environmental values become the more important, the more material interests are satisfied. At times of economic hardship, this argument goes, people tend to be preoccupied with making economic ends meet. Similarly, rich countries tend to be more concerned about the environment than poorer ones. When the economy is weak and unemployment is high, environmental requirements will tend to be weakened if they prevent or restrict employment policies or investments. During periods of prosperity, on the other hand, environmental protection is more affordable in terms of both alleged employment losses and financially. Furthermore, one could expect that labor unions pursue more active environmental policies because good economic conditions give them more bargaining power.

But exactly the opposite argument is also plausible. At times of recession, public expenditures might be more carefully scrutinized and thus fewer investments bearing on the environment are made. Moreover, Logan and Nelkin (1980:8) argued that labor- management alliances opposing environmental regulations above all form in periods of economic prosperity. This will be particularly the case with business unionism, i.e. under conditions where union officials sell a service to the membership rather than unions being a cooperative venture of the membership (see Chapter 7 for more details). Logan and Nelkin surmised that business unionism will be more attuned to giving up traditional bargaining rights when employers can afford higher wages, i.e. when the economy is strong. If union leaders can produce less at the bargaining table, then the philosophy of business unionism loses credibility and labor/ management accomodation tends to break down.

The first view implies that during economic crises a built-in dichotomy between labor and environmentalism must surface strongly and conflicts will be particularly pronounced. The absence of such increased conflicts, on the other hand, makes the built-in dichotomy explanation appear questionable. On the other hand, if Logan and Nelkin were right, then under conditions of business unionism, labor-environmentalist conflicts would be minimal when the economy is down. However, their argument also implies that at least as much as economic conditions it is the ideological framework that determines the LER.

What evidence is there with respect to the impact of the state of the economy on the LER?

3.2.1 FRG

Table 3-3 indicates the economic trends in the FRG from 1965 to 1980. In this period, recessions occured in 1967, in 1974/75 and one started in 1980. A toughening of the environmental positions of labor during these periods can not be observed (but rather, as Hagelstange (1979:740), has noted, sudden increases in union membership). In 1967, environmental issues had barely reached the political agenda. In 1974, when the LER was not yet a political issue, the DGB published its rather progressive Environmental Program. As noted, hostile positions and statements toward environmental citizen action groups by labor and political parties had not become frequent before 1977/78 —that is, at a time when the anti-nuclear protests had become widespread, but also when the economic recovery from the recession had well been under way.

The economic depression, which began in 1980, has led to more than 2.2 million unemployed or a 9% rate by the end of 1984. This was the highest level in the country since the early 1950s. Economic growth in 1981 and 1982 declined if adjusted for inflation. However, environmental sentiments have continued strong: Ecological parties have become rooted in the political scene; the Frankfurt airport extension controversy politicized and drew sympathies from the whole country [9]; energy conservation has become a viable option to many people —although, of course, not only as a result of more environmental consciousness [10]; in nuclear power construction, projects under way were completed but no new ones were added; and acid-rain induced large-scale dying of forests found considerable public attention. Budget constraints combined with environmental sentiments have led to increased scrutiny of sulfur oxides emission standards, further highway construction, airport extensions and other construction projects [11]. In 1983 and 1984, the economy grew again but unemployment remained at

Table 3-3 : Economic Trends in the FRG, 1965 - 1983

	1965	66	67	68	69	70	71	72	73	74	75	76	77	78	79	80	81	82	83
unemployment rate in % (1,4)	.7	.7	2.1	1.5	.9	.7	.8	1.1	1.2	2.6	4.7	4.6	4.5	4.3	3.8	3.8	5.5	7.5	9.1
economic growth rate in real terms 2,4,5	5.5	2.5	-0.1	6.5	7.9	5.9	3.3	3.6	4.9	.4	-2.5	5.7	2.6	3.5	4.1	1.8	-.3	-1.2	1.2
cost of living increases in % 2,4	3.4	3.5	1.5	1.3	2.0	3.2	5.1	5.3	6.8	6.9	6.3	4.4	3.9	3.5	4.1	5.5	6.3	5.5	3.6
primary energy consumption increases in % (3)	2.3	1.1	0	7.5	1o.5	7.o	.6	4.4	6.9	-3.3	-5.0	6.5	.6	3.9					
labor productivity 4 (1980=1oo)												86	89	94	99	1oo	1o3	1o6	111

Sources:
1) Bulletin of Labor Statistics, ILO, Geneva, 198o:xviii
2) Ballerstedt, Glatzer   3) own calculations; 1965-1973 only approximate figures
4) Statistisches Jahrbuch, 1984

63

near record figures. The public support for environmental protection clearly has not waned. In addition to dying forests, other environmental issues of national prominence have crept—up such as dioxin effluents from waste—dumps and incinerators, the toxicity of formaldehyde, making catalyctic converters mandatory on automobiles, and —stirring a real sacred cow in the country— whether or not a speed limit on the Autobahnen should be imposed.

Labor's reaction to economic stagnation and decline has clearly not been anti— environmental. While in the 1967 and 1974/75 recessions, relief was sought by Keynesian—style government interventions giving little attention to the (sectoral) targets to be chosen, the aforementioned programs since 1977 targetted specific "qualitative growth" areas (c.f. Sections 3.1.1 and 3.1.2). Between 1977 and 1984, labor changed its rating of environmental protection from something like "to be considered" to "possesses most employment potential". It now considered unemployment and environmental protection complementary: The social cost of unemployment were estimated to amount to 50—60 billion DM per year, i.e. were of about the same magnitude as the estimated environmental damages incurred in the country every year. Thus, the unions concluded, an investment program geared towards environmental improvements would at the same time relieve the unemployment problem.

In the midst of new monthly record figures on unemployment, the DGB called for new SO2 emission standards for new industrial plants allowing less than half as much pollution as existing standards and 25% lower (stricter) ones than those proposed by the federal government (FR, 30.11.82:18). The DGB issued a statement to halt the rapidly dying forests calling for stricter environmental controls (c.f. 3.1.1) and for a governmental investment program slanted toward air improvement measures. The IGBSE representing construction labor has traditionally been critical of environmentalism. Yet, facing a severe recession in the construction industry, the union has called for a program titled "Work and Environment" designed to secure and create 400,000 jobs through environmental measures (SZ, 17.9.1984:24).

Thus within a few years time, labor has come to support environmental policies both on their own merits and because of their employment potential. This was a major turn—around in its overall perception of the interdependence between the economy and ecology. Of course, specific issue areas have remained, were unions have tolerated environmentally dubious projects (Buschhaus, the Rhine—Main— Danube Waterway) or were content with "only" gradually phasing out pollution.

In general, the policies the unions and the SPD have advocated as employment—creating measures, therefore, were quite similar to those endorsed by environmentalists: environmental protection, investments geared at energy savings, extensions of social services, occupational safety and health, humanizing the work—place, public transportation, vocational training, and housing and urban development (FR, 23.1.1982:5).

Contrary to this "progressive" (FR, ibid.) employment catalogue championed by most unions, the SPD and environmentalists, the construction of numerous new nuclear power plants was included in a catalogue labelled "conservative" advocated by the CDU, parts of the FDP, and industry [12]. The IGBE and IGBSE have also demanded the removal of "investment barriers" with respect to power plant construction. Other employment inducing measures listed in the "conservative" catalogue were the introduction of new communications technologies, the privatization of public services, increased automation at the workplace by micro processors, and incentives for private housing construction by granting tax write—offs and reducing tenants' rights. All of the latter "conservative" proposals were opposed by most of labor and environmentalism alike.

Another example of labor's reaction to environmental protection demands at a time of economic crisis is the Industrial Union of Chemical, Paper, and Ceramics Workers (IGCPK). The main industrial

sectors in the union's jurisdiction (chemicals, petroleum) are highly
effected by environmental policies. They ranked first and third in
terms of both total environmental protection investments and the
percentage share environmental protection investments had in total
investments in the 1971 to 1978 period (Albracht, 1980:4).
Nevertheless, the union (which by no means has been an environmentally
"progressive" union) has pursued environmental protection at least as
vigorously in 1980/81 as in the economically fatter preceding years.

In these years, the union's long-declared environmental commitments
were put to a real test with respect to the passage of a Chemicals Law,
the imposition of a fee for waste water effluents, the curtailment of
asbestos, and the dumping of diluted acids (Duennsaeure) into the North
Sea. In all these cases, the union faced the employment versus
environment choice at a period of rapidly growing unemployment. Often,
the choice was not a simple one in the form that environmental
protection requirements forced the entire shut-down of operations.
Rather, companies altered industrial processes or relocated production
to other sites ostensibly in response to environmental demands.
However, while the new production processes or sites were indeed less
harmful for the environment, they also used more modern and labor
saving technologies. Thus, environmental protection was not seen as
eliminating jobs as such. Rather, it perhaps accelerated
modernizations which, however, might have been introduced at a later
time anyhow.

The union has distinguished between environmental protection as a
cause and environmental protection as a pretense for employment losses.
It also pointed out that environmentally benign processes or products
were more competitive than "dirty" ones and, thus, have added to
employment particularly during economically difficult times. No doubt,
the pressure on the IGCPK to relax its pro-environmental positions has
increased during the crisis both from management and the work-councils
in the respective companies (Albracht, IGCPK, personal communications,
13.1.1982). But the union stuck to pro-environmental positions -even
though to watered down versions in the eyes of some critics. It
demanded a long catalogue of measures including increased
co-determination rights in environmental protection matters; more
environmental protection representatives and controls; more information
rights for the public; public control of investments guided by energy
efficiency, environmental benignness and resource consciousness; and
the inclusion of the goal of "ecological balance" into the traditional
quadrangle of national economic goals consisting of economic growth,
full employment, price stability and balanced terms of trade (IGCPK
Resolution on environmental protection submitted to the 1982 DGB
Convention).

At the end of 1984, the union is proud of the progress made. It
concluded a voluntary agreement with the asbestos industry that has led
in most areas to asbestos-free production. The construction sector is
scheduled to be free of asbestos by 1989. By the same year, the
dumping of Duennsaeure will be terminated. Jobs will have been lost
but it is clear to the union that regardless of environmental concerns
productivity effects would have been felt in any case. In areas like
fluidized-bed combustion and recycling, on the other hand, environment-
related employment gains have in fact been made. The unprecedented
shut-down of the Boehringer chemical plant in Hamburg for environmental
reasons, that resulted in 200-300 lay-offs, the union thought was
appropriate. The IG Chemie took it as a -negative- example of how jobs
were jeopardized as a result of management failure to institute
adequate environmental protection measures.

All these convergences of labor and environmentalist viewpoints may
not constitute institutionalized improvements of the LER. But they
clearly indicate the absence of a deteriorating relationship which the
built-in dichotomy hypothesis would suggest. Thus, the evidence from
the FRG —sparse as it may have been— does not support the contention
that economic crisis conditions have affected the LER negatively.

65

3.2.2 United States

3.2.2.1 Two Cases

The responses of the Autoworkers and Steelworkers, respectively, to environmental protection requirements at times of economic crises are two case studies for the validity of the built-in dichotomy hypothesis. They are the UAW's reaction to stiffened automobile emission standards in the mid-1970s and early 1980s, and the USWA's positions toward the crisis of the US steel industry in the 1980s. In both cases, the unions agreed to a modest deferral of environmental requirements in order to secure existing employment, with the expectation of reducing pollution comprehensively in the long term. The question is, to what extent these expectations in fact guided subsequent union policy and resulted in a cleaner environment, or were merely face-saving formulas.

The United Auto Workers have always been a strong advocate of strict environmental standards. Until the mid 1970s, the union did not consider it necessary to reassess its unequivocal environmental commitment in order to alleviate employment concerns. On the contrary, in 1970 the UAW thought unchecked pollution by automobiles a threat to the jobs and job security of autoworkers; and therefore sought to make auto emissions a collective bargaining issue (UAW, 1970). However, to my knowledge, environmental pollution outside of plants has not been entered into union contracts —probably because the National Labor Relations Act constrained collective bargaining to wages, hours and working conditions. Alternatively, but equally unsuccessfully, the union sought legislation that would give workers the right to sue their employers for damages suffered from plant shutdowns or layoffs due to insufficient environmental controls (UAW, 1971).

The UAW's pro-environmental commitment was most tangibly challenged in 1975 and 1981–1983 when changes of auto pollution controls coincided with recessions and job losses in the auto industry. In 1975, a stiffening of auto emission standards and the introduction of fuel efficiency requirements was before Congress at a time when car sales had drastically declined. For the union, tightened requirements bore the threat of higher car prices and continued low levels of car sales. On the other hand, reneging on firm standards would have meant a break with the union's long standing commitment to environmental protection and to the frugal use of resources. The union decided to advocate the enactment of fuel efficiency requirements and of less restrictive emission standards than mandated by existing law. The UAW stressed that its reexamination of emission standards ought not to be viewed as environmental sacrifices in order to support the industry. Rather, it explained both the sales slack and the need for reexamining the standards to be results of the fuel shortage. The less restrictive emission requirements would, in fact, help to achieve cleaner air. Constant and not too stringent standards would allow for production efficiencies and thus yield higher car sales, which in turn would mean the faster replacement of old "dirty" cars and, ultimately, cleaner air. Further, the union argued, given the trade-off between decreased emission levels of new cars and increasing their fuel efficiency, the greater scarcity of fuel made it desirable to increase fuel efficiency while minimizing redundant safety margins in the emission standards (UAW, 1975).

In 1981 to 1983, the UAW faced a similar trade-off when the industry was in its deepest recession since the 1930s and the weakening of national ambient air quality standards (NAAQS), auto emission standards and safety rules was contemplated during the Clean Air Act reauthorization process. The union opposed any changes of the NAAQS, supported the principle and the practice of federal government regulations of emissions from all sources as a means to meet those standards, and supported that health-related impacts be given "the overwhelmingly primary consideration". However, the UAW advocated an easing of CO and NOx standards and revision of the HC standard. Given the fact, the union argued, that auto HC and CO had been reduced by 96% and auto NOx by 76% in the past decade, "secondary" factors such as cost could legitimately be considered. If lower cost show up in lower consumer prices (approx. 300$ per car), then sales volume will be stimulated, thus helping industry to cut unit cost and to allow the capital formation necessary to bring out smaller, cleaner more fuel-efficient domestic cars and trucks.

While the UAW had long been convinced that the less stringent CO standard (7.0 gpm) was sufficient, it supported the extension of the current NOx standard (2.0\gpm rather than 1.0\gpm) more cautiously. It accepted the 2.0\gpm limit based on the conditions that the current compliance system would operate effectively; that uncertainties regarding NOx contributions to acid rain, smog and nitrosomines should be further researched (and, if necessary, corrected by legislative action); that total NOx —from mobile and stationary sources— continues to be in compliance with the NAAQS; that diesel particulate emissions are tightly regulated; and that the government accepts responsibility to monitor and, if necessary, remedy adverse effects stemming from the relaxed standards on firms, workers and communities (UAW, 1981).

In sum, the UAW has agreed to defer some more stringent emission control requirements in order to aid the depressed industry. However, its positions are to be seen in the broader context. The union's sincere commitment to clean air seems undubitable. Where the union nevertheless agreed to possibly significantly reduced standards such as on NOx, the preconditions it felt had to be met were rather elaborate. Indeed, the union had reasons to believe that the bill would not become law at all —which actually has not happened since. As it was explained to me by UAW officials, the union agreed to support some curtailments of the existing CAA mostly for political reasons. It sought to obtain the support of Congressman Dingell (D—Mich.) for its domestic content legislation which the union considered crucial for future autoworker employment. Representative Dingell —being a key committee member both for the Clean Air and Domestic Content legislations— had made its support for domestic content contingent upon UAW concessions on clean air.

The United Steelworkers of America (USWA) union has also been a major supporter of environmental protection, especially regarding air pollution. In 1969, the USWA was the first union organizing a national conference on air pollution with 250 local union officials participating. It was a major backer of the 1970 and 1977 clean air amendments and claims the main responsibility for including provisions in the 1977 amendments that enabled EPA to make inquiries into allegations by companies that pollution control requirements would lead to job losses.

Further, the USWA was the only union represented on the National Commission on Air Quality established in 1977 by Congress. The report of the commission published in early 1981 had a major impact on Clean Air Act reauthorization beginning later that year. The USWA was one of three dissenters to those parts of the commission's recommendations that called for a weakening of the existing law. In particular, those recommendations the union opposed sought to eliminate deadlines for achieving health standards; to eliminate requiring new plants in polluted areas to meet "lowest achievable emission rates"; to allow automatic approval of defective state pollution control implementation plans; and to abandon the air quality management plan designed to limit significant deterioration of clean air outside national parks and wilderness areas (NCAQ, 1981:5—35). Therefore, the USWA was a staunch defender of the existing Act both in the Clean Air Coalition and as one of the seven industrial unions cited earlier (c.f. Section 3.1.1).

However, when employment in the steel industry was affected, the union was willing to accept moderate curtailments of air quality on a case—by—case basis. The shutdown of the steel—making facilities in Youngstown, Ohio, in the fall of 1977 brought to a climax the awareness that the US steel industry was in a deep structural and financial crisis. Cheap imports and reduced demand for steel coincided causing deep sales slumps. The USWA membership declined from 1.4 million in 1976 to about 700,000 in 1982. At the same time, the steel industry in many areas exceeded the primary ambient air quality standards and was approaching the statutory 1982 compliance deadline. The union faced the dilemma of either insisting on the enforcement of the clean air act or endangering the employment of a large part of its membership. A solution was sought in a tripartite committee including the union, industry and the government. Based on the committee's recommendations, the USWA supported legislation (passed in 1981) stretching out to 1985 the 1982 compliance deadline contingent upon a rapid steel industry modernization program.

The rationale for the so—called stretch—out bill was the following. Without modernization, the industry would experience more permanent lay—offs and community dislocations. Yet, the need both to accelerate modernization and to meet environmental obligations would create an investment shortfall. A stretch—out of environmental deadlines, the committee argued, would enable the industry to modernize while complying a few years after the original deadline. The union consented to a modernization program linked to employment and environmental guarantees. The companies had to demonstrate in each case that funds, otherwise available available for abatement, would expended to improve efficiency and productivity. The expenditures could only be made in existing steel communities. The stretch—out would not entail further air quality deterioration nor would it require lower standards than those in existence. In the long run, the union believed, the modernization program induced by the stretch—out would improve air quality while securing employment at present locations (USWA, 1980a, 1980b).

However, the stretch—out has not lead to major investments by the steel industry. The union is convinced, that contrary to industry claims pollution control requirements were at most marginally responsible for steel layoffs. The major layoffs occured before the deadlines went into effect. Particularly the economically marginal plants faced closings. On the other hand, those facilities in which pollution control investments had been made were most likely to stay in operation. Even though the stretch—out legislation was estimated to result in investments of hundreds of millions of dollars, the actual investments were of the magnitude of tens of millions of dollars at most. For example, USSteel had applied for a $156 million stretchout, but spent only six million (Interview Mary—Win O'Brian, USWA, March5, 1984).

The pressure to reduce the stringency of environmental standards has undoubtedly increased under the Reagan administration and the need to revitalize the economy and to "reindustrialize" has served as a justification. Yet, on the whole, labor has not called for weakened environmental requirements (e.g. Chaikin, 1982) nor is it evident that labor—environmentalist conflicts in the US have increased when the economy has declined. In the wake of the 1975 auto depression, the 1980 steel crisis, or President Reagan's public service cuts, the LER got boosts from such events as the Black Lake Conference, the OSHA and Environmental Network, the formation of COSH groups or Solidarity Day.

The traditionally environmentally— minded unions, in general, have not seriously considered reduced pollution control requirements even when their industries were severely depressed. A qualified delay of environmental requirements such as the steel stretch—out was even supported by environmental groups. For the first time in their history, major unions agreed to considerable wage concessions (e.g. Kuttner, 1984; Slaughter, 1983). While environmental concerns had

certainly nothing to do with the concessions, the fact that many unions
reneged from their entrenched goal of improving "wages, hours and
working—conditions" to a much greater extent than from their (much more
recent) environmental commitment suggests that the latter was not just
a passing fad. The support of the building unions for a weakened Clean
Air law does not contradict this proposition, since their environmental
commitment has traditionally been much weaker regardless of the
economic situation.

3.2.2.2 Correlating the LER with Economic Well—Being

All this evidence just cited, of course, is not necessarily
representative and certainly unsystematic. Since some suitable data
are at hand, I will try to examine the impact of economic well—being on
the LER more systematically. I will correlate what can be seen as a
quantitative measure of the "goodness" of the LER (see below) with
economic indicators for the 1970 to 1979 period. If, according to this
measure, the LER was "good" at times of economic well—being and "bad"
during economic recessions, then the economic dependency argument would
be substantiated. On the other hand, if changes of the LER do not
correlate with economic developments, that will not prove economic
impacts to be insignificant but questions the popular notion that
environmental concerns and the LER depend decisively on the state of
the economy.

As part of their lobbying activities, the AFL—CIO Committee on
Political Education (COPE) and the League of Conservation Voters (LCV)
have rated Congressional voting annually for the House and the Senate.
I have derived a measure of the "goodness" of the LER from these
ratings [13].

The correlations between LCV and COPE Congressional ratings between
1970 and 1979 do not show effects of economic trends. Table 3—4 lists
the US annual unemployment rate, economic growth rate, inflation rate
and energy consumption growth rate as economic indicators, and
labor—environmentalist correlations for the House and the Senate. In
the Senate, r is consistently increasing from 1969/70 to 1977/78, while
remaining fairly constant in the House. The recession years of 1974
and 1975 are indicated by high unemployment and inflation rates and
negative economic growth and energy consumption rates. Yet, neither
the House nor the Senate correlations show a drop in these years as one
would expect if the economic influence hypothesis were apparent in the
data. For the House, almost the opposite relationship could be
deduced. Pearson r has low points in 1971 and 1979, when the economy
did fairly well, and peaked in the recession year of 1974. Rho shows
the same trends.

A further breakdown of congressional ratings by party (Table 3—5)
shows distinct differences between Democrats and Republicans.
Democrats are far more in favor of labor and environmental issues than
Republicans. In 9 of the 10 years analyzed, COPE ratings of Democrats
are above 70, while Republicans rate consistently below 30. Deviations
from average LCV ratings are less drastic but ratings of Democrats are
considerably higher than of Republicans. Pearson r is higher for
Democrats but environmental and labor voting correlates positively in
both parties. The slumps in 1971 and 1979 for the total House are also
apparent in Democratic ratings. The lack of an apparent correspondence
between economic trends and congressional labor and environmental
ratings and the much higher support of labor and environmental issues
by House Democrats suggest that less so overall economic trends than
differing ideologies —which are also embodied in the respective
parties— form the background of the LER.

It may be objected to the analysis so far that COPE and LCV in
general have based their ratings on largely distinct samples of votes
and that not even all of the few votes considered by both organizations
were evaluated equally (c.f. Note 13). The high correlations, one

	1967	68	69	70	71	72	73	74	75	76	77	78	79	80	81	82
Unemployment rate % of civilian labor force	3.9%	3.6	3.5	4.9	5.9	5.6	4.9	5.6	8.5	7.7	7.0	6.0	5.8	7.1	7.6	9.7[1]
Economic growth rate in %; based on constant 1972 $		4.6	2.8	-.2	3.4	5.7	5.8	-.6	-1.2	5.4	5.5	5.0	2.8	-.4	-1.9	
Energy consumption growth rate in %				4.8	2.2	4.9	4.2	-2.5	-2.8	5.4	2.4	2.4	.9	-3.9	-2.8	
Annual inflation rate in %	2.9%	4.5	5.0	5.4	5.1	4.1	5.8	9.7	9.6	5.2	5.9	7.6	11.3	13.5	10.4	

Labor-Environmentalist Correlations (Sig. .001)

	70	71	72	73	74	75	76	77	78	79
House Pearson r	.70	.46	.71	.74	.82	.72	.76	.70	.74	.52
House Spearman rho	.82	.56	.68	.65	.86	.71	.77	.69	.63	
Senate Pearson r	.72		.74		.75		.83	.83	.86	
Senate Spearman rho	.73		.74		.73		.73	.83	.84	

Sources:
US Statistical Abstract 1982/83   [1]AFL-CIO, 1983:81

Table 3-4 : Economic Development and Labor-Environmentalist Relationship Trends in the US

Pearson r[1]	1970	1971	1972	1973	1974	1975	1976	1977	1978	1979
all										
Cope mean	49.8 N=373	53.5	52.9	53.9	53.0	59.7	56.5	57.3	51.1	57.3
LCV mean	46.3 N=369	46.0	52.7	45.7	52.3	53.1	54.1	49.4	49.7	46.1
Pearson r S=.001	.70 N=369	.46	.71	.74	.82	.72	.76	.70	.74	.52
Democrats										
N[2]	220	252	254	240	245	291	288	291	289	275
Cope mean	71	73	71	78	77	76	71	72	66	74
LCV mean	56	50	59	58	63	60	64	59	59	57
r	.77	.50	.74	.71	.80	.71	.71	.59	.65	.38
Republicans										
N[2]	149	176	179	191	188	142	141	143	143	156
Cope mean	19	25	27	23	22	25	26	27	21	28
LCV mean	32	41	44	30	39	39	34	30	31	26
r	.42	.48	.72	.64	.75	.65	.61	.62	.73	.50

1) N varies between 430 and 435 if not listed; S ≤ .001
2) lower figure

Table 3-5: LER in House: total and broken down by party 1970-1979

could argue, therefore mean little and the different ratings rather underline the conflicts between labor and environmentalism. The counterargument (c.f. Note 13) is that it would indeed have been surprising, had the two movements had many more votes in common. After all, the LER has tended to be conflictual throughout a good part of the 1970s. Moreover, the different samples reflect the different priorities, one should expect the "labor" and "environmental" movements to have, rather than different positions on most issues. (One must note that a vote was only counted as having been considered by both groups if COPE and LCV meant the very same vote, i.e. votes on the same bill but on different amendments of that bill were not thus counted.) The voting analysis suggests, however, that the labor—environmentalist conflicts were not directly and decisively influenced by economic well—being (see below). It further suggests that the two movements have similar Congressional constituencies. Since, as Chapter 6 elucidates, lobbying Congress and electoral politics have been important activities of both movements, the overlap of their Congressional base offers opportunities for coooperation even though each movement will tend to stress its particular concerns first.

Another objection might be that economic conditions influence the LER without being apparent in the data. The lack of a discernible influence on the LER in the recession year of 1974, for example, may be explained by the fact that Watergate strongly influenced Congressional voting. On the other hand, it is unclear why a general issue even though as severe as Watergate should have decisively affected votes as specific as those used for the ratings.

Whatever may have been the case, in order to minimize the possible influence of overriding political factors on Congressional voting, and to take a more detailed look at the voting behavior under different economic conditions, I have correlated the means of COPE and LCV ratings of the Congressmen in the House state by state with unemployment and unionization rates on a rank—ordered basis. State unemployment rates have been available for each year between 1970 and 1978, unionization rates only for the even years. If the economic influence hypothesis were true, one would expect that states with high unemployment would correlate negatively with LCV and positively with COPE ratings. Further, COPE with LCV, and unionization with LCV would correlate negatively. Table 3—6 shows that the data do not support the hypothesis. Correlations among unemployment and both COPE and LCV are low and positive (rows 2 and 3).

The differences between COPE's and LCV's correlations with unemployment rates are spurious. Unemployment and unionization in row 4 correlate positively between .37 and .55, i.e. states with unemployment problems tend to be higher unionized. Without implying causality, that seems intuitively true. Unionization correlates positively with COPE (.58 to .69, row 5) and with LCV (.50 to .56, row 6). The former appeals to common sense, the latter at least contradicts beliefs in an inherent conflict between labor and environmentalists. Since the ties between organized labor and the Democratic Party are close, one may deduce from these data that the conditions in highly unionized states which tend to be more Democratic, are also conducive to environmental support.

As a further refinement of the analysis, I have ranked the states by COPE ratings, LCV ratings, and unemployment rates, respectively, for each year from 1970 to 1979. Subsequently, the Spearman rho correlations among COPE ratings, LCV ratings, unemployment and unionization rates were computed according to each ordering of the top ten, middle 30, and bottom ten states. Again, the data do not support the economic dependency hypothesis. When the states are ranked according to COPE and LCV ratings, respectively, in descending order, the correlations among the four variables vary widely with unsatisfactory significance levels for the top ten and the bottom ten states. The only exception is a positive correlation (.36 to .52)

72

Spearman rho	1970	1971	1972	1973	1974	1975	1976	1977	1978	row
Cope ratings with LCV ratings	.82	.56	.68	.65	.86	.71	.77	.69	.63	(1)
Unemployment rate with Cope ratings (S)	.16 (.128)	.33 (.009)	.51 (.001)	.45 (.001)	.20 (.082)	.21 (.072)	.25 (.04)	.33 (.01)	.26 (.036)	(2)
Unemployment rate with LCV ratings (S)	.13 (.183)	.24 (.046)	.46 (.001)	.34 (.009)	.18 (.107)	.29 (.021)	.35 (.006)	.31 (.013)	.14 (.158)	(3)
Unemployment rate with unionization	.37 (.004)	n.a.	.55	n.a.	.37 (.005)	n.a.	.45	n.a.	.46	(4)
Unionization with Cope ratings	.65	n.a.	.58	n.a.	.59	n.a.	.65	n.a.	.69	(5)
Unionization with LCV ratings	.50	n.a.	.56	n.a.	.56	n.a.	.56	n.a.	.51	(6)

N=50
S≤.001 if not listed
n.a.=not available

Table 3-6: House correlations Cope ratings, LCV ratings, unemployment and unionization rates of states 1970-1978

between unionization and unemployment of the top ten COPE states. Further, whether ordered by COPE or LCV ratings, the two ratings follow the same order. For the middle 30 states, the COPE and LCV correlations correspond roughly to the national averages, and unionization correlates positively with COPE ratings, LCV ratings, and unemployment rates. Further, ordered by the LCV ratings, the correlations of unemployment with COPE and LCV ratings are positive (unemployment with COPE : .09 to .52, unemployment with LCV : .19 to .45).

When the states are ordered by unemployment in descending order, the correlations involving unemployment rates are spurious and are rather insignificant. Clear positive correlations between COPE and LCV ratings exist regardless of unemployment levels (see Table 3-7). Thus, unemployment does not make a difference for the correlations. There is a difference, however, with respect to the average COPE and LCV ratings in the top 10, middle 30, and bottom ten states. For most of the 10-year period, the high unemployment states have higher COPE and LCV ratings than the states in the middle which in turn have higher ratings than the states where unemployment rates are the lowest. These findings do not only contradict the conventional wisdom that the distance between labor and environmentalists increases when economic security decreases, it may even suggest the opposite: Conditions which are accompanied or manifested by economic insecurity are also favorable to stronger labor- environmentalist ties.

3.3 Summary and Conclusions

The evidence examined supports to some extent the first hypothesis introduced at the beginning of this Chapter, rejects the second, and rather rejects than confirms the third.

Among the German and American public, the perception of a built-in dichotomy between employment and environmental protection was not prevalent. Both issues were well supported even though employment tended to rank higher. The public did not believe that economic imperatives in principle force a choice between employment and environmental protection. To the contrary, the public considered the two goals reconcilable and consistently expressed support for continued government spending on environmental protection even when the economy was depressed. Stated as a forced choice, employment fared better than the environment. However, many have rejected this choice as a valid one.

The perceptions of labor and environmental organizations can be summarized as follows:

1. There is in principal support for environmental protection but labor and environmentalists have disagreed on implementation.

2. The environmental movement has recognized the importance of employment considerations.

3. Labor and environmentalists agree that environmental protection overall does not cause unemployment and —more likely than not— on balance creates employment. Both groups have increasingly recognized that environmental protection might indeed have the greatest short-term job creating potential.

4. Overall, labor unions have rejected environmental blackmail threats. Labor unions have also accepted compromises trading short-term —but politically volatile— anti-pollution policies against expectations of long-term improvements if the latter promised to save jobs. Distinctions between "blackmail" and legitimate arguments of management were not easy. Both sides have recognized that own expertise on the interdependencies among

74

Spearman rho	1970	1971	1972	1973	1974	1975	1976	1977	1978	1979[4]
Cope with LCV										
top 10 states in terms of un-employment a)	.90[1]	.67 (S=.017)	.61 (.03)	.85	.96	.88	.89		.81	.72
middle 30 b)		.37[2] (.024)	.53	.53	.85	.58	.63	.78	.67	.91
bottom 10	.67[3] (.025)	.47 (.087)	.72 (.009)	.70 (.013)	.92	.79 (.003)	.65 (.02)	.73 (.008)		.67 (.017)
Cope ratings										
top 10	51[3]	66	69	72	57	63	63	61	50	53
middle 30	44	49[2]	51	50	49	55	51	51	45	48
bottom 10	51[3]	44	37	37	45	49	50	46	39	38
LCV ratings										
top 10	53[3]	52	59	55	51	60	65	55	43	44
middle 30	41	44[2]	52	43	49	49	47	43	47	43
bottom 10	45[3]	41	34	32	45	50	44	40	39	36

a) at sig. ≤ .1
b) at sig. ≤ .001 if not listed

1) N=27
2) N=29
3) N=9
4) ordered by 1978 unemployment data

Table 3-7: Correlations and ratings of Cope and LCV according to the 10 states with highest and lowest unemployment, and the 30 states in the middle, 1970-1979

energy, employment, environmental protection, inflation and economic growth must be obtained rendering blackmail more difficult.

5. There are labor—environmentalist conflicts on the concept of economic growth although there is principal support for qualitative growth.

6. There are agreements and disagreements on energy both between labor and environmentalists, and among labor unions. Nuclear energy has been the major dividing point but has lost saliency. Both sides are aware of the pertinence of energy issues for employment and the environment. In general, labor advocates increases of energy supplies while environmentalists are "energy demand siders". There is agreement that there should be more control of the energy industry but disagreement on energy pricing. Overall, labor has moved closer to environmentalist positions regarding energy demand projections, the relationship between energy and economic growth rates, and the feasibility of energy conservation and renewables in the future.

Disagreements were strongest where issues were most tangible and immediate. Those employed in nuclear power plant manufacturing, construction and operations saw their jobs directly threatened by the environmental movement. It seems justified to assert a built—in dichotomy between those believing nuclear power to be environmentally destructive and those employed in the nuclear industry. Yet, relatively few jobs actually depended on nuclear power.
Overall, the perceptions of the interdependencies do not warrant the conclusion that employment and environmental protection were believed fundamentally irreconcilable. Most of the conflicts, which undoubtedly existed, were not the result of incompatible basic views but concerned the implementation of particular policies. However, these conflicts on implementation often were substantial. In the US, the cleavages were vertical along industrial sector lines. In some, cooperation was substantial; in others, conflicts were fundamental. Over time, cooperation has increased and —given the pragmatism on both sides— that trend will likely continue. In the FRG, both movements in the abstract shared fairly similar views but very rarely cooperated. The cleavages on implementation were horizontal across the various unions but dividing the leadership from a good part of the membership. These differences between the US and the FRG can not be explained merely by the different perceptions of the issues per se but seem to be based in the different political frameworks such as the unified German labor movement ("Einheitsgewerkschaft") versus the dispersed American movement, or the respective ways the movements were integrated into the political systems.
The evidence examined (which, however, was sometimes inconclusive) does not support the assertion that labor—environmentalist conflicts were most severe when the economy is bad, nor that economic prosperity is a favorable condition for labor—environmentalist cooperation. Further, the lack of an apparent correlation between the LER and economic conditions also speaks against the validity of the built—in dichotomy hypothesis. These conclusions derive from the trends within each of the two countries as well as from a very rough comparison of the two countries: While the FRG overall has been economically better off, the LER has been more cooperative in the US.
Thus, the evidence reviewed in this chapter rejects rather than supports the built—in dichotomy argument. Since this conclusion contradicts conventional wisdom, I will briefly discuss some of the objections which may be raised. One could object that the analysis of labor's and environmentalist perceptions was based too much on statements and programs rather than on actual political behavior. This might indeed have been the case but what follows from that for the LER?

If, especially among labor, the pro—environmental rhetoric was not
borne out by facts, then that must not imply a built—in dichotomy of
views but could have had other reasons such as lack of power, internal
pressure, political considerations, etc. These issues will be
addressed in the next chapters.

Second, one could argue that while the direct effects of economic
difficulties on the LER were not discernible there may well have been
indirect ones. Perhaps, for example, German labor might have pushed
co—determination or collective bargaining demands more strongly, had
the economy been better. In the US, stricter environmental laws might
have been demanded rather than existing ones been defended. Again,
while all this might have happened, not so much the perception of a
built—in dichotomy between environmental protection and employment but
rather the distribution of political strength would explain why it did
not.

Third, some might object that the evidence presented was
insufficient to reject the built—in dichotomy hypothesis. If the
evidence reviewed was too scattered, the COPE/ LCV correlations
unconvincing as an indicator of the LER, and abstract public opinion
statements little meaningful, what evidence would be sufficient? What
follows if there is a lack of evidence for the acceptance of the
hypothesis, and some but perhaps inconclusive evidence for its
rejection? The proper conclusion, if that objection were valid, would
probably be to leave the issue undecided (i.e. the built—in dichotomy
argument ought not be dismissed but neither is it convincing), and turn
to the other explanations for the LER.

NOTES

[1] Annually from 1973 to 1978 and again in 1980, the National Opinion
    Research Center has asked whether "we're spending too much money,
    too little money, or about the right amount" on a variety of
    issues. The environment has ranked high throughout but a gradual
    decline is apparent. In 1980, 48% of the public said that the
    country is spending too little and 31% were satisfied with present
    spending levels. Only 15% believed that the US is spending too
    much, up from 10% in 1978 (CEQ 1980:9) and 5% in 1973 (Mitchell
    1979:17). The CEQ (1980:13) report showed a similar trend from
    1977 to 1980.
        For the FRG, see Note 6.

[2] Most prominently, a member of the DGB Executive Board advised the
    Enquete Commission on Future Nuclear Energy Policy of the German
    Bundestag that 700,000 to 1,000,000 new jobs would be created
    until the year 2000 if investments amounting to DM 500 B would
    also seek to achieve energy savings from improved home insulation,
    heat pumps and district heating systems (FR, 30.4.1980:1).

[3] In the proper meaning of the term, not in the sense of American
    "right to work" initiatives seeking a ban on union shops.

[4] The Sierra Club has actively supported the Humphrey— Hawkins full
    employment legislation. Further, according to Sierra Club
    president• Joe Fontaine, the Club considers the workplace
    environment an "integral part of the environment" (Statement on
    CAA and OSHA Environmental Network,(6.2.81). Moreover, the Club
    sponsored the 'Labor— Intensive Public Works' program as part of
    an urban policy package which, however, failed to pass Congress in
    1978 (Sierra, Jan./Feb.79:11). In Massachusetts, the Sierra Club
    endorsed "plant—closing" legislation, requiring large corporations
    to give one year's advance notice of closings, providing affected

employees with severance pay, and requiring the company to pay a lump sum equal to 15% of the affected annual payroll into a 'Community Jobs Assistance Fund' (Ray Ghelardi, Greater Boston Group, Sierra Club, 25.3.1980). These measures would provide time to work out alternatives to plant closings, give workers time to adjust and find new jobs, and help the community in a transition to other economic support bases.

[5] E.g. League of Women Voters, 1977; Heffernan, 1975; Meissner, Hoedl, 1977; Meissner, 1978; Meissner, 1979; critique of Meissner: Kabelitz, 1980; response to Kabelitz: Meissner, 1980; Feldengut, 1979; Keuter, WdA, 17.5.1979:3

[6] Asking individuals to rank employment and environmental concerns amidst rival alternatives may help to determine how the LER is embedded in public sentiments. Let me cite pertinent public opinion results in some detail for the two countries.

In the US, between 1965 and 1980, environmental concerns —peaking around 1970— were ranked lower than employment most of the time. In 1965, George Gallup asked one of the first questions about environmental issues in a public poll. His interviewers presented a list of 10 national problems and asked which 3 the government should devote most of its attention to in the next year or so. "Reducing pollution of air and water" was chosen by 17% ranking ninth, "reducing unemployment" was mentioned by 35% and ranked fourth (CEQ 1980:7). By 1970, 53% (second rank) mentioned pollution and 25% unemployment (seventh rank). In 1980, unemployment again was believed very urgent (48%, second rank), while air and water pollution had dropped to 24% and rank six. Other concerns have supplanted environmental protection in terms of urgency. Of 12 broad national goals presented for selection as the most desirable, two goals (a strong defense and lowering inflation) each received a quarter of the votes. None of the others which covered a broad spectrum including nature protection was "most important" to more than 11% of the respondents (p.8). Moreover, when presented with the choice between economic growth and protecting the environment, only 1 in 5 respondents chose the statement "we must relax environmental standards in order to achieve economic growth" (CEQ,1980:3).

In the mid seventies, a series of Federal Energy Administration (FEA) sponsored surveys of the American public asked to compare the seriousness of unemployment, inflation and an energy shortage. In December 74 and January 75, 57% thought employment, 31% inflation, and 7% an energy shortage to be the most important problem facing the country. The respective figures for the least important problem were 13%, 17% and 45% (PB 244,985:9). When confronted with questions implying energy-environmental trade-offs, various polls showed a leaning toward more energy production. Substantial majorities in the FEA surveys favored more off-shore drilling by oil companies (78% for, 14% opposed), more nuclear power plants (62% to 27%) and federal government involvement in oil exploration (66% to 26%) (p.11). Yet, the polls also showed clearly that enhanced energy production at any environmental costs were not favored. Only 27% favored (versus 67% opposed) removal of pollution control requirements on oil refineries and 26% favored (48% were opposed) removing strip-mining restrictions (ibid:12). A question which Roper has asked annually since 1973 is: "Are you more on the side of adequate energy or more on the side of protecting the environment?" CEQ(1980:19). In 10 Roper surveys conducted between October 1973 and September 1979, only 1976 was environmental protection chosen by a plurality. Otherwise, the results were similar to those of September 79, when 43% chose "adequate energy", 38% chose "protecting the environment", and 10% said "neither" or "no conflict". In September 79, 47% of those responding to an NBC News poll considered "building a needed refinery or pipeline" more important than "protecting the environment " (chosen by 40%) (p.4).

Questions like the above, of course, are highly hypothetical. As the CEQ (1980:20) report points out, "each trade-off question requires respondents to assume that the choice posed is one that has to be made". Yet, many disagree with the assumption that "adequate energy" supplies are necessarily incompatible with environmental quality. Nor do questions pitting energy against the environment leave respondents the choice between environmentally more benign and environmentally more risky energy sources. As a way of testing public preferences along these lines, RFF in 1980 asked individuals to look ahead to the year 2000 and to select from seven energy sources the two or three that "we should concentrate on the most". They were then asked for the one that should receive "the least effort to development". Subsequently, the percentage points of those holding a source "least" desirable was subtracted from the percentage share of those believing that source to be "most" desirable. On a "most minus least desirable" scale, solar energy ranked first (+55), followed by energy conservation (+32), coal (+27), water power (+21), oil and natural gas (+19), synfuels (+16) and nuclear energy (−10) (CEQ, 1980:22). The high level of popularity for solar energy reportedly is consistent with the results of other polls (p.31).

Opinion surveys further show that the American public in the past 25 years has consistently voted for full employment even if that would require massive governmental involvement. Between 1956 and 1960, the public in 3 surveys agreed by more than 2:1 margins that "the government in Washington ought to see to it that everyone who wants to work can find a job" (in Levison 1980:193ff; also the following results). In 1969, 64% agreed and 26% disagreed with the statement "that the federal government guarantee a job to every American who wants to work even if it means creating a lot of public jobs like during the depression". In 1972, vast majorities agreed that the government is responsible to see that those willing to work can do so, or that it should put those unable to find work on the public payroll. Ninety-three percent agreed in 1975 to the statement that at a time when work is hard to find, "the only human thing to do is to give the unemployed productive jobs so their families can eat".

These results affirm the commitment of the American public to full employment but do barely address the methods to be used to combat unemployment. For example, McGovern's economic program in 1972 called for a guaranteed minimum income. However, polls have clearly rejected such "hand-outs" in favor of an approach emphasizing employment. Would high governmental spending for reducing unemployment also be acceptable given the anti-government mood at the turn to the 1980's? Levison argues that when the issue was employment, the attitudes of the majority of the American people were "hardly conservative in any sense of the term" (p.195). Only when public attitudes toward taxes and the government itself were examined did a widespread opposition become apparent. Thus, popular criticism of government in the late 70s took many forms: 80% felt that government wastes a lot of money, 70% felt income taxes were to high, or 67% felt that there were too many federal employees (Levison 1980:196). But vast majorities also preferred that public spending be increased or kept at present levels for helping the elderly (97%), reducing air poll (90%), making college possible for deserving young people (88%), improving medical health care (87%), helping the unemployed (81%), providing adequate housing (76%), providing better mass-transportation (77%), rebuilding run-down areas of cities

(75%), or for improving the situation of black Americans (72%) (ibid:197; also Warren E. Miller, talk at the Science Center Berlin, 19.11.1981). Levison concludes that there is strong majority support for insuring "genuine full employment", even if it might require to seek an alternative to the conventional conservative and liberal approaches.

For the FRG, a variety of survey results ranking environmental protection relative to other issues are summarized in the Environmental Report (Umweltgutachten 1978:448–452). In 1972, environmental protection was considered the second–most important issue mentioned by 47% only surpassed by the desire for social and economic security (46%) and followed by schooling, education and sience (35%), transportation and road construction (22%), and housing and urban construction (21%).

When people were asked in 1975 to rate the areas where the public sector should and where it should not safe money, environmental protection was named least frequently by those favoring spending cuts in this area (28%) and most frequently by those opposing cuts here (70%). It was followed by expenditures for social benefits (34% in favor of cuts, 63% against cuts) and expenditures for science and research (40%, 58%). A similar question, however without including important areas of concern such as reducing unemployment and internal public safety, was asked in 1977 finding expenditures for environmental protection the least desirable targets for public spending reductions (favored by 7%, opposed by 88%). Of the issue areas offered to the respondents to choose from, subsidies for sports organizations were second (44% for acts, 52% against), followed by national defense (55%, 40%).

A survey in 1977 asked to point out the three areas viewed as most important until 1980 out of a set of 12. Economic policies ranked highest (60%), followed by social security (52%), internal safety (48%) and clearly before environmental protection (28%). A survey in early 1980 yielded the following list of priorities (the items are ranked according to the percentage of people rating them as "very important"): secure employment (81%), price stability (75%), secure retirement payments (72%), law and order (57%), effective environmental protection (51%), good relations to the USA (42%) and to Eastern Europe (34%) (ZDF–Politbarometer 1980:56/57).

In the following, the attitudes of the German public toward trade–off questions involving employment, the environment, energy, growth, etc. are presented. When asked in 1970 whether more money should be made available for housing or environmental protection, 55% chose housing and 32% environmental protection. In 1977, the respective figures were 21% and 64%. When the same questions were asked in regard to road construction and environmental protection, the prefences were in 1970 44% and 44%, and in 1977 13% and 72%. With regard to national defense and environmental protection, the figures were 24% to 63% in 1970, and 23% to 60% in 1977 (Edingshaus, 1980:112). When asked whether it was "above all important, that the economy continues to grow, even though the natural environment will have to suffer", in 1973 14% agreed and 74% disagreed with that statement. In 1977, 24% agreed and 60% disagreed. After the energy price crisis in 1974, the following question was asked: "Scientists believe that environmental protection is only possible if one reduces economic growth and, in addition, energy consumption increases at slower rates than in the past. What do you think: Is environmental protection an urgent problem or should we, because of the energy crisis and difficult economic situation, renounce environmental protection for now?" Eighty percent believed environmental protection was an urgent problem while 5% preferred a renouncement at present.

The same survey also included a trade–off question between

80

employment and environmental protection. Fifty—six percent said
that they would prefer environmental protection even though that
might mean unemployment for the respondent or his family.
Twenty—two percent would opt the other way, and the same number
had no opinion. Three years later, those without an opinion on
that trade—off had risen to 35%, while those preferring
environmental protection had fallen to 45% and those in favor of
employment to 20% (all results summarized in Umweltgutachten,
1978:450f). In two surveys, however, pluralities believed that
environmental protection enhanced rather than endangered the
employment situation. In 1977, 35% of the respondents thought
environmental protection measures would create new jobs, 11%
feared job losses, and 52% could not make a judgement. In 1978,
45% thought more employment, 23% believed as much, and 3% said
less employment would be available (Fietkau, Kessel, 1979:116).

[7] The proposed measures included: (1) incentives for improved
insulation against heat losses,for solar hot water and space
heating, and for energy efficient materials and processes, (2)
elimination of the inverted rate structures, (3) incentives
leading to energy savings, (4) mandatory energy consumption
figures on electric appliances, (5) an integrated program for the
insulation of buildings against heat loss consisting of tax
incentives, subsidies, and regulations; subsidies for urban
renewal must mandate sufficient insulation, (6) more cogeneration
and smaller power plant units, (7) an end to the monopolistic
structure granted to energy utilities and the right to infuse
industry produced electricity into the electric grid, (8) emission
charges for unused power plant heat, (9) expansion of district
heating in densely populated areas, (10) removal of legal and
regulatory obstacles to a decentralized system based on renewable
energy, (11) the introduction of a speed limit on highways and
lower speed limits in residential areas, (12) expansion for R&D
for advanced coal technologies, environmentally protective energy
sources and rational energy usage, (13) public information and
education in schools, the media and at work on environmentally
conscious energy usage, prohibition of advertising for electricity
usage.

[8] Given the widespread assumption at that time that electricity
consumption would increase at a 7% annual rate, the AFL—CIO
expectation of a quadrupling of electricity demand until 2000 was
actually low. An eight—fold increase was in fact to be expected.

[9] One may object that the controversy possibly drew a lot of
sympathy for both positions and thus may not be a meaningful
symbol of strong pro— environmental sentiments. Rather, what
ultimately counts is, that the airport is being extended.
    This objection does not seem valid to me. Even if BOTH
positions had a lot of sympathy (and I have not seen any poll
results while on similar occasions polls supporting a project were
soon published), the amount of opposition has probably been
without precedent. The whole region including SPD and CDU party
districts and locals reportedly opposed the airport extension.
That was not so in the nuclear energy related local protests.
Many middle—aged and old people, i.e. an untypical cohort,
participated in demonstrations as long as they remained peaceful.
I have not heard of demonstrations in support of the extension.
The opponents lost some sympathies because the protests became
violent but not on substantive grounds. Judging about national
environmental sentiments by asking "who won?" seems inappropriate
here. The airport extension was completed but the government has
lost a lot of face. The opponents wanted a state referendum
(which is a highly unusual political instrument) and collected

several hundred thousand signatures to get it on the ballot. However, the Hessian government, and later the highest court in Hessia, ruled it unconstitutional. The belief of many citizens in democratic procedures was badly hurt (which, as Chapter 7 will discuss, has become an issue in the LER). The Greens obtained 8% of the votes in the Sept.82 Hessian elections. This was their best result in any state election up to then. They possibly would have done even better, had the dramatic shift of government in Bonn not have taken place at the same time bringing a sensationally good result for the Hessian SPD.

[10] Energy consumption in 1981 was at the same level as in 1973 but real GNP grew by 17%, and the country's dependency on imported oil has declined from 55% to 45% (FR, 22.10.1981:5). It would be mistaken, of course, to explain the energy savings merely by environmental pressure. The high price levels were certainly a major reason. Another reason was the slackening economy. On the other hand, energy conservation as a desirable and attainable strategy per se is also accepted now. Further, the media are full with environmental arguments for energy savings. A value shift is evident in opinion surveys (Chap.7 will discuss this), seems to be underlying election results (Chap.6), and is suggested by two (perhaps trivial) examples: bicycle sales have reached record levels, and tens of thousands participate in voluntary "car-free" weekends. This was not always so. Only a few years ago, politicians painted pictures of imminent gloom and darkness if no new nuclear power plants were built. Nobody would believe them today. All that boils down to the argument that energy conservation has increased as a credible option for great many people, that it is part of a more general value shift, and that environmental lists profit from these shifts in elections. I am aware that this argument is not "scientific", but short of an attitude survey I don't see how to "prove" it.

[11] It is not easy to separate the importance of budget constraints from environmental reasons regarding the continuation of several large-scale construction projects. There are opinion surveys showing considerable scepticism ("we have enough") toward further highway construction (Note 6). The Minister of Transportation cancelled the extension of the Hamburg airport since it was no longer needed. He also wanted to stop the construction of the Rhine-Danube waterway because cost-benefit analyses no longer support construction. The opposition from environmental groups has led to several court rulings mandating to downsize the planned new airport in Munich. Environmental- political considerations led the Bundestag to postpone a decision on the future of the Kalkar breeder reactor for several years. (The decision to go ahead with the breeder was made but against the votes of the SPD and thus of many unionists.) The Prime Minister of Lower Saxony postponed a decision on reprocessing at Gorleben because it would be politically damaging. The success of the Greens may have helped the government in Hamburg to abandon its commitments in Brokdorf.

[12] One may argue that labor's constituency has been disagreeing with the progressive catalogue. Can the considerable losses of the SPD in several state elections during 1982 perhaps be attributed to its employment policies?
    The answer to this question is not easy and will be touched on in Chapter 6. There is no doubt that especially workers, i.e. traditional SPD voters, switched to the CDU (or not voted at all) at that time in local elections and in the state elections in Lower Saxony and Hamburg. The CDU argued that these switches occured primarily because of the economic development in the FRG

and the respective solutions the parties have to offer (e.g. Zeit, 26.3.82:7).

It is difficult to know to what extent this claim might have been true. One must, of course, consider that the SPD was the major party in power and therefore got most of the blame for high unemployment. This attitude is probably independent of which party is in power and what its policies are. There are many who claim that traditional SPD voters turned to the CDU not so much because of the positions the SPD has taken, but because of the ongoing crisis of the SPD/FDP coalition government in Bonn. The government in Bonn had been repeatedly at the brink of break-up. Both parties had suffered from the public image attached to them of undecisiveness, opportunism, fickleness and being unable to govern. Diverging economic policies advocated by the two parties, to be sure, have been a major cause of their disagreements. The SPIEGEL (29.3.82:22) wrote that the SPD paid the price in the states for staying in power in Bonn. But the price was not only the loss at the polls but also mounting conflicts among the party wings (which in turn has cost votes).

Another reason cited for the switch of traditional SPD voters to the CDU was a widely publicized scandal surrounding the union-owned housing company "Neue Heimat". The Neue Heimat is the largest builder and manager of housing in the nation, most of which was highly subsidized by the government. The company, the unions and politicians, especially from the SPD, had close ties to one another. Analyses of the Hamburg elections —where, incidentally, the headquarter of the Neue Heimat is located— showed that the switches from SPD to CDU votes was particularlyly high in areas of Neue Heimat housing developments. Roughly 10% of the voters in Hamburg live in 40,000 to 50,000 Neue Heimat appartments (FR, 8.6.82:4).

[13] The similarity of congressional voting, of course, is an indirect measure of the LER at best and objections to congressional ratings as an LER index might be raised. One could argue that factors other than environmental or labor pressure influence a Congressman's votes. Another objection might be the fact that COPE and LCV have based their ratings in general on distinct samples of votes. COPE based its ratings for the House on 154 votes and LCV on 184 votes between 1971 and 1979 but only 12 votes were considered by both. The corresponding figures for the Senate are 144 COPE votes, 120 LCV votes, and only 7 joint votes. Not even all the votes considered jointly are evaluated equally by the two organizations: Only 9 of the 12 jointly selected House votes and 3 of the 7 Senate votes were evaluated equally.

Yet, in the absence of a better measure I have relied on the congressional ratings as an indicator of the LER. Several considerations support this decision. First, COPE's selection of votes is a conservative measure of the LER, since large unions with a pro-environmentalists record such as the UAW and UMW were not even members of the AFL-CIO. Unions such as AFSCME and IAM, which are affiliated with the AFL-CIO but have repeatedly disagreed with AFL-CIO policies, are sometimes not represented by COPE's choices of issues or positions adopted on these issues: The IAM, for example, has withheld payments to the AFL-CIO's Industrial Union Department (IUD) since it has disagreed strongly with IUD's energy positions (interview with Mr.Greenwood, IAM Wash., Feb.27,1981). Further, the UAW, IAM and AFSCME also have Political Action Committees on their own. Second, even though COPE and LCV have selected different samples of votes, this probably does not reflect different positions on most votes but more likely shows the different priorities of the two groups. As we have seen, labor has supported environmental protection, and several environmental groups have spoken in favor of job and union

rights.   Yet,   the   votes   on   these   issues   have often not been
selected for the congressional ratings.   Third,   the   ratings   are
used   to   determine   which   candidate   to support in congressional
races.   Section 6.1 shows that COPE and LCV have largely supported
the   same   candidates.Since   lobbying   Congress   and   electoral
campaigns are major activities of both groups,   selection   of   the
candidates   and   thus   a   comparison of congressional records is a
major aspect of the LER.

   The correlations between LCV and COPE Congressional ratings are
taken   as   a   measure   of   the goodness of the LER.   The Pearson r
stands for the goodness-of-fit between the LCV   and   COPE   ratings
for each Congressman assuming a linear relationship.   The closer r
is   to   +1.0,   the   more   equal   are   the   ratings   given   to   the
Congressmen   by   the   two   organizations.   (High   correlations,
however, do not necessarily mean a   high   support   for   labor   and
environmentalist   concerns.   If Congress voted "incorrect" on many
environmental and   labor   issues,   r   would   also   be   high.)   The
Spearman rho is a similar indicator as the Pearson r.   It is based
on rank- ordered data (as opposed to at least interval level   data
for Pearson r).

4 Explanation 2: The Influence of Demographic and Socioeconomic Differences on the LER

Writers and labor leaders alike have pointed to the different socio-economic and demographic base of labor and environmentalism as a potential source of conflicts. Their arguments of how socio— economic differences have become manifest in conflicts have taken various forms. One of the earliest articles on the LER in the FRG, Olaf Radke's (1972) "Thoughts of Trade Unions on Environmental Protection", questioned the abilities of environmental groups to effectively contribute to improvements of the human environment. Radke, himself a labor union official, affirmed the serious stake unions have in environmental protection and that attaining a livable environment required much effort and cooperation. But, he pointed out, environmental degradation had become most severe at the work—place and where workers live. Environmentalists, on the other hand, ordinarily were removed from these environments since they were generally middle—class. Trommer (1976) argued that citizens engaging in environmental groups are privileged since only in some areas of life are they affected by wrong decisions or ignorance. Other people, however, face shortcomings persistently due to structural reasons which can not be corrected by simply forming ad—hoc groups but which require more permanent organizational structures such as labor unions.

With regard to the US, Fiorina (1973) similarly warned that the environmental movement due to its middle—class membership and support base could lose credibility and effectiveness through failure to recognize other legitimate interests of ordinary Americans and thus become perceived as a vested interest. Mitchell (1978:5f) pointed out that voluntary organizations in American society tend to draw their membership from the better educated, more affluent segments of the population; that the environmental groups were no different in this regard; and that this has opened them to charges of "elitism".

The theme that environmentalists lack concern "for the little guy" has also repeatedly been taken up by labor leaders and has been exploited —with little substantiation— to reject environmentalism. One example each from the FRG and the US may illustrate the arguments used.

The former president of the DGB, Heinz—Oskar Vetter, asserted labor's opposition to those groups that claim "highest authority in all vital realms of society". The citizen groups, he argued, have often been a front for affluent citizens "engaged in the defense of their private idyl". He denounced it as unacceptable that workers would have to pay with the loss of their jobs for the shortcomings and shortsightedness of environmentalist energy politicking (SZ, 22.4.77:4). The IBEW painted the effects of socio—economic differences between "them" and "us" perhaps in the most drastic terms:

> Many of the radical environmentalists would deny us what they consider their right. Generally, they are affluent and have had the advantage of formal education. Too often they believe that it is their right to have air conditioning, that it is their right to drive their private autos to environmental hearings, that it is their right to live in the suburbs surrounded by every labor—saving device and gadget. Why must we live in hot, crowded apartments, use public transportation exclusively, and be denied any labor—saving device? If we believe the rubbish that these radicals expound, which they themselves eschew, then we deserve the fate that awaits us. (IBEW Journal, July 72:28)

Occasionally, the arguments also have been reversed. To give an example, Buttel and Flinn (1978:434) reported that those of lower socio— economic status have often been painted as "irresponsible" and "unfortunate laggards in the evolution of 'post— industrial' society". Their only concern, this argument goes, is the improvement of their individual material situation in the short—term. Toward environmental concerns, they are inherently ambivalent if not outrightly hostile.

These arguments can be compressed to the hypothesis that the different social bases of the two movements have accounted for the labor—environmentalist conflicts. In an analysis of membership and public opinion surveys, I will therefore examine the impact on the LER of variables such as age, political affiliation, occupation, income, education, or place of residence. If certain social groups comprise a significant share of the membership of one movement but not of the other, then a necessary condition for attributing the labor—environmentalist conflicts to compositional differences would be fulfilled. The first question raised in this chapter therefore is:

> 1) What are the crucial socio—economic and demographic differences between the memberships of labor unions and environmental groups, and between these groups and national average?

If the membership base of the two movements is considerably different, then the question remains which variables in fact are the crucial ones for the LER. If social class as indicated by the statements above is the main factor, then differences in occupation or income probably matter most. If the conflict is more value—based or ideological not following traditional class lines, then education, political affiliation, or age might be more important. Also, shifts may have occured over time.

On the other hand, the membership base may be different but may not be a sufficient condition for explaining conflictual views on pertinent issues or with respect to other groups. If the different membership compositions do not translate into distinct attitudes and behavior, then Explanation 2 would be hardly relevant for the LER. Two more questions, therefore, must be asked:

> 2) How do labor union members and environmental group members view energy, employment, and environmental issues? Do they

significantly differ from one another and from the general public?

3) If there are important differences (in terms of views, background, or both), how do they affect the LER?

4.1 The Membership of Labor and Environmental Organizations

4.1.1 United States

Buttel and Flinn (1978:434f) summarized the findings of studies concerned with the social base of the American environmental movement, which were conducted until the mid 1970s, as follows: The environmental movement was (upper-) middle class "beyond doubt" and "education, almost without exception, was the class indicator most closely related to environmental concern". In addition, members in American environmental organizations were ordinarily found to be younger, in higher income brackets, leaning to the Democratic rather than Republican party, more liberal, and more urban than the average American citizen and labor union member. But there are also considerable differences among the memberships of the various environmental organizations.

Tables 4-1 and 4-2 indicate the typical composition of US environmentalists. Table 4-2, at the same time, shows important differences among organizations. The data underlying Table 4-2 are from a Resources for the Future (RFF) survey conducted in 1978 of five national environmental organizations including the National Wildlife Federation and the Sierra Club. Environmentalists (leftmost column) differed considerably from the general public (rightmost column). As noted, they are much better educated, have higher occupations, are almost exclusively white, lean strongly toward liberalism while being independent in terms of party affiliation, and have a secular outlook. The data on age of the surveyed environmentalists listed are probably erroneous. The membership composition of the Sierra Club corresponds closely to that of all surveyed environmentalists, while the figures for the NWF deviate markedly with respect to most variables. The General Counsel of NWF told me (interview with Joel Thomas, 23.2.1981), that the NWF membership is more "middle American", less wealthy, less educated than that of other environmental organizations (and probably quite similar to labor union membership). The table confirms Mr. Thomas' view in the particulars of education, occupation, income, political affiliation and religion. NWF members are older than other environmentalists, more conservative, stronger supporters of Republicans, and more religious. Nineteen percent of the NWF members (either themselves or their spouse) are also in a labor union; compared with 13% of the Sierra Club members and 15% of all surveyed environmentalists (interview with Robert Mitchell, RFF, 26.2.1981).

According to union and Bureau of Labor Statistics officials, comprehensive figures on the demographic and socio-economic composition of American labor unions have not been published. While data on individual unions are even scarcer, officials of several unions guessed that the memberships of their unions were similar to national average.

Thus, labor union demographics are piecemeal. Tables 4-3 and 4-4 list characteristics obtained in three unrelated surveys conducted in 1970, 1977, and 1980. Labor union members compared with the average worker are older (1970: 5 years), earn more (1970: $1200 per year), are more likely to be blue collar, and male (80% versus 60%). Compared with the breakdown of environmental membership, union members are considerably older, are mostly in blue collar occupations, earn less, and are more religious. There are similarities also. Unions and environmental organizations alike are disproportionally male, white, leaning to the Democratic party, and have most of their membership in the Northeast and Midwest. With respect to education, occupation, and religion, union and NWF membership were more similar than union

87

	(1) Views of the environmental movement					(2) Members of local or national group 1978	(3) Supporters of envirm. protection at any cost 1978
	Sympathetic No 1980	Yes 1978	Yes 1980	Active 1978	Active 1980		
Male	5%	49%	53%	12%	6%	9%	51%
Female	3	51	57	14	7	7	56
White	4	50	57	13	7	8	54
Black	4	51	39	13	4	6	55
Age							
18-24	2	47	55	15	12	5	70
25-34	4	58	63	14	7	9	65
35-54	4	45	52	15	5	9	49
55-64	5	49	52	14	7	7	46
65-	4	47	50	3	3	6	31
Education							
8 years or less	4	36	43	14	5	2	43
High school grad	4	44	55	15	6	4	54
Some college	6	60	65	}12	8	}13	}59
College grad	5	60	66		7		
Postgraduate	2	56	59	16	4	15	49
Income (1000 $) 1978 (1980)							
Under 6(8)	3	50	45	11	7	4	49
6(8)-14(12)	4	43	56	17	5	4	56
14(12)-20(15)	3	52	56	10	8	8	53
20(15)-30(25)	4	56	60	12	7	7	58
Over 30(25)	4	54	60	14	8	27	52
Party							
Democratic		48		13		5	56
Republican		50		11		7	47
Independent		38		25		10	59
Ideology							
Liberal		52		22		11	64
Middle		51		11		8	54
Conservative		48		13		7	52
Union member[1]							
Yes	4	46	56	16	6	6	63
No		48		15		9	51
Total public	4	50	55	13	7	8	54

[1] 1980:union family

(1) "In recent years, the environmental movement has been very active. Do you think of yourself as: an active partcipant in the environmental movement, sympathetic towards the movement but not active, neutral, or unsympathetic towards the environmental movement?"

(2) "Do you belong to any national environmental organization such as the Sierra Club, Friends of the Earth, the National Audubon Society, or others like these? In addition to the national groups and their local chapters, there are a number of state and local environmental groups of one kind or the other. Do you belong to any of these?"

(3) "Protecting the environment is so important that requirements and standards cannot be too high, and continuing improvements must be made regardless of cost."

Sources: Mitchell, Sept.1978:4; CEQ,1980:44,45

Table 4-1 : Public Views of the Environmental Movement, Environmental Membership, and Support of Environmental Protection in the US, 1978 and 1980

Background Variables

Table 4-2: Demorgaphics of the US Public and five selected environmental organizations in 1978

	All Environ.	Envir. Action	EDF	National Wildlife	Sierra	The Wild. Society	Public (RFF Survey)
AGE							
17-24	13%	15%	2%	6%	18%	7%	19%
25-34	15	24	23	19	21	23	20
35-44	18	17	19	13	21	14	15
45-54	26	12	19	15	17	16	15
55-64	29	16	18	20	10	17	15
65 +	3· / 4·	16	19	27	12	22	16
EDUCATION							
High School	11	6	6	33	7	9	67**
Some College	16	17	11	23	16	14	19
College Grad	24	25	20	21	24	27	8
1-3 years Grad School	29	31	34	16	30	31	6
4 years Grad School	20	22	28	6	22	19	1
OCCUPATION							
Professional, etc.	66	68	78	47	68	63	7*
Managerial, etc.	12	11	10	12	12	13	17
Remainder	22	21	12	41	20	24	76
% upper middle-- upper class	46	50	56	27	47	47	13***
INCOME							
Under $8,000	8	10	6	10	6	9	29**
8,000 -13,999	15	17	9	22	16	15	22
14,000 - 19,999	18	17	17	23	19	16	21
20,000 - 29,999	22	20	21	24	25	21	19
30,000 - 39,999)	15	13	17	12	15	14	)
40,000 - 49,999)	9	8	11	3	6	9	)7
50,000 and over	14	15	20	6	13	17	2
SEX							
Male	60	63	58	54	68	57	48
Female	40	37	42	46	32	43	52
RACE							
White	98	99	99	99	99	99	86
IDEOLOGY							
Strong Conservative	4	2	2	9	4	6	7
Moderate Conservative	19	7	11	38	19	23	38
Middle of the Road	17	9	13	31	16	18	29
Moderate Liberal	14	48	49	18	44	39	13
Strong Liberal	14	24	18	3	12	12	5
Radical	5	10	7	2	4	2	2

	All Environ.	Envir. Action	EDF	National Wildlife	Sierra	The Wild. Society	Public (RFF Surv.)
Political Affiliation							
Democrat	24%	30%·	29%	12%	28%	19%	41%
Ind. leaning to Dem.	16	42	39	16	16	30	11
Independent	16	16	12	19	16	18	10
Ind. leaning to Rep.	4	4	4	21	11	16	10
Republican	13	3	9	27	11	16	10
Other	1	4	3	3	1	1	10
Don't Know	1	1	-	2	1	1	
Assessment of Carter Adm. environ. record - 1st yr.							
Excellent	2	2	2	0	2	3	
Good	19	21	22	9	20	19	
Fair	41	47	43	31	39	41	
Poor	25	21	22	42	22	23	
Don't Know	13	7	13	18	16	14	
City Size							
Large (250,000 +)	25	25	30	12	30	25	24°° / 23°
Suburb	20	10	11	16	20	21	17 / 14
Medium - Small	42	35	25	48	42	43	51 / 47
Country	13	11	8	24	9	11	8 / 16
Present Religion							
Protestant	35	25	30	58	27	41	
Catholic	9	10	11	16	10	9	
Jewish	7	35	25	2	6	4	
Personal ties w/ Nature	28	11	8	16	34	28	
None	7	9	19	4	16	9	
Other	14			5	7	9	
Region							
Northeast	9	12	12	8	5	9	
Mid-Atlantic	18	18	24	19	10	22	
East Northcentral	17	16	13	25	12	20	
West Northcentral	15	4	16	8	10	5	
South	15	17	3	13	17	17	
East Southcentral	2	2	4	3	2	2	
West Southcentral	4	5	2	5	4	5	
Mountain	7	7	4	5	6	10	
Pacific	23	20	22	12	47	10	

* National environmental public opinion survey - Summer 1978. Data are for adults
· NORC All ** NORC 1978 adj *** NORC 1973

Source: Kathryn Utrup, Robert C. Mitchell, Environmental Group Surveys, Resources for the Future, Wash. DC:8f

	in labor unions			not in labor unions		
	all[1]	white collar	blue collar	all[1]	white collar	blue collar
1970[2]						
median age (years)	41	39	41	36	37	43
16 to 17 years	.5%	1.0%	.3%	5.6%	2.4%	5.6%
18 to 24	13.1	16.7	11.9	23.2	21.5	26.1
25 to 44	44.3	42.7	45.6	38.1	42.5	37.6
45 to 64	39.7	37.2	4o.1	29.o	29.9	27.4
65 and older	2.5	2.5	2.1	4.2	3.7	3.3
median earnings (dollars)	86o9	8858	8654	7452	8532	669o
under 3ooo	1.7%	1.8%	1.4%	6.5%	3.7%	5.5%
3ooo to 4999	9.o	7.6	8.4	18.5	13.7	22.8
5ooo to 6999	18.8	17.6	18.1	21.4	19.9	25.7
7ooo to 9999	38.2	37.2	39.9	24.3	24.8	27.3
1oooo- 14999	27.3	27.1	28.4	18.8	22.3	16.2
15ooo or more	4.9	8.8	3.9	1o.5	15.6	2.6
1977[2]						
weekly earnings average (dollars)	262	27o	266	221	255	194
under 1oo	1.4%	1.0%	1.1%	8.9%	5.1%	7.6%
1oo - 149	9.7	7.6	9.o	24.5	19.3	28.5
15o - 199	16.4	15.4	15.2	2o.7	19.4	23.9
2oo - 249	2o.o	2o.9	19.8	14.9	15.4	16.8
25o - 299	2o.1	21.6	2o.6	9.7	11.3	9.6
3oo - 349	21.8	21.o	23.8	11.1	14.o	9.4
35o and over	1o.7	12.5	1o.6	1o.2	15.4	4.2

[1] incl. Service workers here not listed [2] 197o and 1977 figures not directly comparable

Sources: US DOL, Selected Earnings and Demographic Characteristics of US Union Members, 197o, Report 417, 1972:1o,13

_____, Earnings and Other Characteristics of Organized Workers, May 1977, Report 556, 1979:28

Table 4-3 : Age and income distribution of US workers in and not in labor unions, 197o and 1977

	AFL-CIO Membership	All Employed in 1979	
Family income			
under 15,000	23%		
15,000 - 25,000	36%		
over 25,000	34%		
Education			
8 years or less	9%		11% (1)
some high school completed	15		12
high school graduates	45		39
some college or trade school	21		17
college graduates	5		} 21
some postgraduate training	3		
Age			
under 30	13%	16-19	8%
30 - 39	20	20-24	14
40 - 49	22	25-34	27
50 - 59	23	35-44	19
60 - 69	18	45-54	17
70 and older	4	55-64	12
		65-	3
Religion			
Protestant	47%		
Catholic	35		
Jewish	1		
other	11		
no religious affiliation	5		
Sex			
men	80%		
women	20		
Region			
northeast	31%		
south	16		
midwest	34		
west	19		
Party Affiliation			
Democrats	47%		
Republicans	13%		
Independents	30%	(1) civilian labor force 25 years and older	

Source: Opinion Research Survey, National Survey of AFL-CIO Union
Members, Prepared for Committee on Political Education,
Aug. 1980: 51-58; AFL-CIO Department of Research, Union
Membership and Employment 1959-1979, Feb.1980:III-13,III-22

Table 4-4 : Demographic characteristics of AFL-CIO union
members in 1980 and of all employed in 1979

membership and the membership of the other environmental organizations surveyed. The opposite held true for political affiliation.

4.1.2 FRG

The environmental citizen groups in the FRG (which were the politically most active and, thus, crucial part of the German environmental movement) comprise an always changing and highly dispersed movement. Thus, membership statistics are more piecemeal than for the US environmentalists. The picture is somewhat clearer for the electorate of the Greens. The general pattern, however, is fairly similar to that in the US.

The willingness to become engaged in citizen groups and voting for an ecological party correlates positively with education and professional attainment, negatively with age. In 1973, 3% of the West German citizens have at one time been members in a citizen group and 34% could think of situations in which they would become active. Respondents with a complete secondary education (9%), working as employees and civil servants in advanced positions (8%), and who are or might be members of political parties (10%) showed greatest propensity to environmental citizen group membership. In terms of age, those 25 to 49 years old were the most likely to have been active in a group at one time, while the 18–34 years old were the most willing to become active in the future (Infas, April/Mai 1973, in: Kmieciak, 1976: Table X,10). By 1976, acceptance of citizen groups had grown from 34% to 51% while rejection had dropped from 63% to 47% (Emnid Informationen 3/1976, in: Andritzky, 1978:30). A survey conducted in 1977 (Fietkau, Kessel, 1979:110) also revealed a preponderance of the "young" in environmental citizen groups. Twenty–five percent of the members were below 25, 39% between 26 and 35, while the 36 to 60 years old comprise only 16%. On the other hand, beyond retirement age, a considerable increase of environmental interest and activism was notable. While the distribution of preferences by age has by and large remained unchanged and its dependence on education only slightly shifted (Andritzky, 1978:30), acceptance of citizen groups has particularly grown among blue collar workers.

Similarly, the sympathizer or voter of the early Greens was better educated, had a higher professional status and was younger than average. Age seems particularly important, since by several measures the decline of "green" sympathies and growing age coincides consistently (Spiegel, 19.6.78:90, 24.3.80:30). Four years later, after the Greens and their electorate had consolidated the Greens show a "double profile" (FAZ, 3.9.84:11). While the aforementioned upper–middle–class characteristics of most of its voters have remained valid, the Greens have also become attractive to so–called protest voters from the lower classes. Especially unemployed less–educated youth would vote for the Greens –reportedly almost 40% of these youth under 21! In the 1983 federal elections, almost 70% of the green electorate was younger than 35 years.

A breakdown by occupational status of the DGB and ten unions is given in Table 4–5. The top 5 unions have favored nuclear energy, the five unions at the bottom have been more sceptical about it (see Chapter 2). The table shows that —with the exception of the OTV— the pro–nuclear unions and the DGB as a whole represent predominantly blue collar workers while the unions more sceptical about nuclear energy are based to a large extent on white collar workers and civil servants. From 1978 to 1983, blue–collar membership has declined while white–collar and civil servant membership have increased. I have not found breakdowns by age or education of the DGB or most of its unions. The IGM in 1976 had a fairly equal distribution of its membership by age (members in their twenties: 22.5%, in their thirties: 21.5%; forties: 21.3%; fifties: 14.5%) (Ballerstedt, Glatzer, 1979:186).

| | 1978 / 1983 | | | |
	blue collar (Arbeiter)	white collar (Angestellte)	tenured civil servants ("Beamte")	total
DGB (in 1000)	5289/ 5212	1483/ 1711	698/ 823	7471/ 7746
IGBSE (construction)	459/481	41/42	o/o	5oo/523
IGBE (mining)	323/318	45/48	o/o	368/366
IGCPK (chemical,paper,ceramics)	534/515	117/12o	o/o	651/635
IGM (metal)	2238/2148	386/387	o/o	2624/2536
OTV (public service)	534/575	438/511	1oo/87	1o78/1174
IGDP (printing)	134/113	18/31	o/o	152/144
GdED (railroad)	216/189	1o/8	199/182	425/38o
GEW (education, science)	o/o	29/47	124/139	153/185
HBV (trade,banks, insurance)	45/48	247/312	o/o	292/36o
DPG (postal)	116/143	29/45	273/27o	418/458

Source: Statistisches Jahrbuch,1978:552
        Statistisches Jahrbuch,1984:587

Table 4-5 : Breakdown by occupation of the membership
            of the DGB and ten unions, 31.12.1977 and 1983

Also, the Wohlfahrtssurvey conducted in 1978 showed that unionization rates were similar among the ages. It differed considerably among the professions (self-employed: 1.8%, civil servants: 26.6%, white collar: 17.6%, blue collar: 34.3%) and by subjective social affiliation (working class: 31.2%, middle class: 17.7%, upper (middle) class: 9.6%). As one would expect, union members rated the DGB considerably higher than non-members. On a -5 to +5 scale, labor unionists in 1973 gave a mark of +2.9, salary and wage earners rated it +2.1, the population at large +1.6, and non-union members +1.5 (Nickel, 1975:51). Broken down by occupational status and by age as listed in Table 4-6, support for unions corresponded in 1973 and 1975 roughly to the pattern found in the Wohlfahrtssurvey.

In sum, there are substantial demographic and socio-economic differences between the labor and environmental movement in each country. I now turn to the question whether and how these differences have translated into different attitudes toward energy, environmental protection and employment issues.

4.2 Socio-Economic Status and Attitudes on Energy, Employment, and Environmental Protection Issues

4.2.1 United States

Early studies of "public attitudes regarding environmental improvements" in the US indicate -not surprisingly- that those groups most likely to join the environmental movement have also been most concerned about environmental degradation. Table 4-7 illustrates that in 1969 the better educated, those earning high incomes, and suburban residents were the most sensitive to pollution, the most willing to pay for environmental cleanup, and the most dissatisfied with the government's handling of environmental protection. On the other hand, the low income and low education groups most exposed to pollution were among those least concerned. Fiorina explained this paradox as follows:

> The data are consistent in revealing greater concern and greater willingness to do something about the natural environment among the more educated and more affluent segments of the public, among those who live in the suburbs surrounding the large metropolitan centers, and among younger adults. These articulate segments of the public could be characterized as having high expectations and demand for a livable environment, and as having a greater than average intellectual awareness of environmental conditions. People who live in cities, blacks, and persons with and education levels show less concern about environmental conditions. At first glance, this appears paradoxical since it is the lesser privileged segments in our society, especially in the inner cities, that one would suspect have greater contact with at least certain forms of environmental pollution and deterioration. However, it appears that some combination of apathy, low expectation levels as regards the natural environment, lack of awareness of its effects on the quality of their own life, and the perception of other problems as being even more severe and pressing produce an apparent low level of concern. Thus proponents of a greater emphasis on natural resources and environmental cleanup will find their natural allies, at present, among the educated and the affluent.
> [...] Any immediate broadening of the base of support for environmental improvement will require public education to increase awareness of the problem among the lesser educated, lower income portions of our society. (Fiorina, 1973)

94

| | total | blue-collar workers | | white collar | tenured civil servants | self-employed | age | | | |
		unskilled	skilled				18-24	25-34	34-49	5o+
labor unions are very important (1973)[1]	25%	3o%	39%	29%	44%	6%				
ratings of the DGB on a -5,+5 scale (1973)[1]	+1.6	+2.2	+2.3	+1.7	+2.2	-.2	+1.9	+2.o	+2.1	+2.2
labor unions have										
more	44%	4o%		44%	42%	49%				
less	19	17		2o	22	22				
right amount of influence (1975)[2]	28	33		29	22	2o				

Sources: 1)Nickel:51,52
2)Ballerstedt, Glatzer, 1979:187

Table 4-6 : Support for Labor Unions in the FRG by Occupation and Age, 1973 and 1975

Have air and water pollution affected your personal enjoyment of your surroundings and your life in any way?

July 1969: (Harris)

	Yes	No	Not Sure
National	29%	68%	3%
Eighth Grade	15	81	4
High School	30	67	3
College	42	55	3
White	30	68	2
Black	21	69	10
Cities	31	64	5
Suburbs	43	55	2
Towns	25	73	2
Rural	18	79	3
Under $5,000	15	82	3
$5,000-$9,999	29	67	4
$10,000 plus	43	56	1

Would you be willing to accept a $20 per year increase in your family's total expenses for the clean up of the natural environment?

July 1969: (Harris)

	Willing	Not Willing	Not Sure
National	55%	35%	10%
Eighth Grade	32	50	18
High School	58	33	9
College	69	25	6
White	56	34	10
Black	42	38	20
Cities	54	34	12
Suburbs	66	26	8
Towns	47	39	14
Rural	50	41	9
Under $5,000	31	53	16
$5,000-$9,999	58	33	9
$10,000 plus	74	19	7

Thinking about air and water pollution, improvement of land and water, forests, fish and wildlife, recreation and park areas--do you think programs for improvement of the natural environment now receive too little attention and financial support from the Government, now receive too much attention and financial support, or just the right amount?

July 1969: (Harris)

	Too Little	Too Much	Right Amount	Not Sure
National	52%	5%	22%	21%
Eighth Grade	36	6	18	40
High School	55	4	24	17
College	65	4	21	10
White	54	5	22	19
Black	33	6	18	43
Cities	58	4	16	22
Suburbs	66	2	21	11
Towns	42	7	24	27
Rural	42	6	27	25
Under $5,000	36	6	22	36
$5,000-$9,999	56	5	21	18
$10,000 plus	64	4	23	9
East	58	3	18	21
Midwest	53	6	27	14
South	44	4	21	31
West	54	7	21	18

Sources: Fiorina, 1973:31,32
regional breakdown: Erskine, 1973:129

Table 4-7 : Attitudes toward pollution by the US public in 1969 (by education, race, size of community, income, and region)

In the 1970s, a large number of researchers have studied the social base of those concerned with environmental quality. Reviewing these studies, VanLiere and Dunlap (1980:182) found "considerable dissensus with respect both to the evidence itself and its interpretation". Therefore, they examined the bivariate relationships between indicators of environmental concern and age, education, income, occupational prestige, residence, sex, political party, and political ideology reported in several dozen studies which had been conducted between 1968 and 1978. They concluded that

> age, education and political ideology are consistently (albeit moderately) associated with environmental concern, and thus we have confidence in concluding that younger, well-educated, and politically liberal persons tend to be more concerned about environmental quality than their older, less educated, and politically conservative counterparts (p.192).

They found less conclusive evidence for the variables residence, political party identification and occupational prestige which were correlated more weakly and/or less consistently with environmental concern. There were a few exceptions. At the local level, there was consistent evidence for a positive association between urban residence and environmental concerns. Among political elites and the college educated, Democrats were significantly more environmentally concerned than Republicans.

With respect to occupation, nonvertical cleavages were expected to be more important than prestige per se: Business occupations, technology dependent occupations, and nature—exploitative occupations were hypothesized to be negatively correlated with environmental concern. However, VanLiere and Dunlap found the evidence for this suggestion inconclusive because too sparse. Finally, the evidence regarding income and sex suggested that they are not systematically correlated with environmental concern.

By the late 1970s, support for environmental protection had become well established across all demographic and economic subgroups of American society. Surveys have shown consistently (see Note 6, Chapter 3) that a vast majority of the American public did not favor reduced spending for environmental protection —the 1980 elections notwithstanding.

The right—most column in Table 4—1 even has shown that majorities of most societal subgroups were supporters of environmental protection "at any cost". While such an unambiguous declaration of environmentalism seems questionable, it does not support the hypothesis that the different social bases of the two movements have been a direct cause for labor— environmentalist conflicts. In particular, labor union membership even expressed more support for environmental improvement "regardless of cost" than the general public. Mitchell (1978:6) concluded that environmental concerns were not

> the preserve of a small segment of the population... . Belief in the seriousness of environmental problems, support for environmental protection, and sympathy for the environmental movement, all cut across racial, sex, education, and income groups. Among the age groups, support is low only among the elderly.

Similarly in 1980, Mitchell found concerns about six environmental problems fairly evenly distributed across sex, race, age, income, education and rural— urban categories (CEQ, 1980:29). The election of President Reagan must not be mistaken as a vote against environmental protection. A Louis Harris survey in May 1981 showed overwhelming opposition to weakening either the Clean Air Act (favored by 12%) or the Clean Water Act (favored by 4%) (Jackson, Wright, 1981). In September 1981, a Roper survey found that only 21% of Americans thought that environmental protection laws and regulations "have gone too far" while 69% said they were about right or not strong enough (Symonds, 1982). Perhaps even more impressive is the breadth of this support. No more than 30% of any major group —including Republicans, conservatives, poor people, blacks and Westerners— reportedly felt that environmental protection had gone to far. In 1982, similarly, 70% of the US public agreed that "pollution is rising to dangerous levels" while only 18% disagreed (Kessel, 1984:26).

I now turn to the question how different demographic and socio—econom subgroups in the US have viewed energy, employment and environmental protection trade—offs.

In the mid—1970s, the Federal Energy Administration commissioned a series of surveys on these issues. Given a choice between unemployment, inflation and energy shortages, unemployment was cited as the most important problem facing the country by all population subgroups in the US in 1975. While 52% chose umemployment, 25% named inflation and 12% energy shortages. The lower education and income, the higher the concerns with unemployment and the lower the concerns with an energy shortage (PB 244989:3f).

No preferences between cleaning the environment and employment could be made out in June of 1975. Forty—three percent agreed, 44% disagreed with the statement "that the environment is more important, even if it means closing down some old plants and causing some unemployment" (PB 255003:34). Support of environmental protection declined evidently with age and increased with the level of education. White collar occupations favored the environmental option 49% to 41% while the blue collar occupations preferred the employment option 50% to 39%. The environmentally active favored the environment 52% to 35% (ibid.). For several questions pitting employment against environmental protection, the attitudes of the total public, white collar, blue collar, and the environmentally active are listed in Table 4—8. Overall, the percentages in the four columns are quite similar. The views of environmentalists and blue collar workers do not differ much from those of the general public nor from each other. Environmentalists deviate significantly from blue—collar workers only with respect to accepting new industries in one's state which would increase air pollution. But one can infer from the table that the greater the abstraction in the wording of the question, the greater the chance environment would be favored in a trade—off with employment. While an overwhelming majority favored non—degradation of clean air sheds in the first question, one third wanted new air polluting industry to settle in one's own state, and another 21% tolerated such industries after thinking about their positive employment and energy impacts.

A survey conducted among members of AFL—CIO (1980) unions shows strong support for environmental protection among union membership in general. It also indicates some variations among the members. The survey asked union members how much effort they think unions should expend in order to get a set of legislative proposals adopted:

Overall, union members wanted a lot of effort put into these legislative proposals. Ranked on a scale 1 to 3 (no effort equals one, some effort equals 2, a lot of effort equals 3), union members wanted efforts spent on the following proposals in descending order: increase social security benefits (2.39), increase penalties for businesses that disriminate against union members (2.39), strengthen regulations against industrial pollution (2.33), put back controls over oil and gas (2.30), reform tax laws so that corporations pay a greater share (2.30), increase taxes on profits of oil companies (2.25), enact national

	total public	white collar	blue collar	environ-mentalists
clean air areas should be				
kept as clean	94%	93	96	92
allowed to get somewhat				
more polluted	2	3	2	2
Do power plants and oil				
refineries cause air yes	76	78	72	72
pollution? no	10	11	11	12
build power plants and oil				
refineries				
in "dirty" areas	33	25	34	42
in "clean" areas	14	12	15	8
which are clean	8	13	5	6
governmental laws prohibiting				
new industries in clean air areas				
for	41	45	41	36
against	41	42	39	37
new industries in R's state				
causing more air pollution				
for	32	35	34	19
against	52	53	52	56
Do you still feel the same				
if not building these facilities				
would cause unemployment and yes	21	22	20	27
power shortages? no	21	22	24	23

source: PB 249 544:23-26,29,30

Table 4-8 : Perceptions of pollution versus employment
trade-offs in the US by the total public,
white and blue collar workers, and
environmentalists, 1975

health insurance (2.20), limit a corporation's ability to relocate factories overseas (2.15), adopt wage and price controls to fight inflation (2.14), prohibit businesses from asking their employees for political campaign contributions (2.06).... On strengthening regulations against industrial pollution, 53 percent of union members want a lot of effort expended, 32 percent some effort, and 8 percent no effort. Members of government and service unions want somewhat more effort than members of other industries. Younger members are somewhat more interested in having a lot of effort in this area, as are Catholics than Protestants. Finally, straight Democratic voters are more interested in having a lot of effort spent than are Republican union members. eFifty—eight percent of union members want their unions to expend a lot of effort to put controls back on oil and gas prices, while 54 percent want a lot of effort expended to increase the taxes on profits of oil companies. The proportion of those who want a lot of effort expended reimposing controls is slightly greater among union members in the lowest family income and lowest education groups.

<u>4.2.2 FRG</u>

As indicated in Section 3.1, employment and environmental protection have strong public support in the FRG. The same segments as in the US tend to be most environmentally—minded. Fietkau and Kessel (1979:119) reviewing public opinion data from a variety of sources concluded that younger age groups (especially the 20—35 year olds), the better educated and the higher income groups were the most likely to support environmental protection.

The Wohlfahrtssurvey (1978) measured the levels of satisfaction and dissatisfaction with 22 areas of life relative to one another. Satisfaction with the environment ranked second lowest: Only 1.4% were satisfied with environmental conditions. The only area rated even lower concerned the opportunities to become politically active (p.301). Asked about the areas people were most dissatisfied with, the environment was mentioned most frequently (by 34.4%), followed closely by public safety (by 34.2%). Those 18—34 years old were less dissatisfied (30%) than were respondents of age 34—59 (34.4%) —somewhat deviating from trends observed so far. Dissatisfaction clearly declined from higher to lower professions (self—employed: 45.1%, civil servants 43.9%, white collar employees 34.2%, blue—collar workers 29.3%) and social (class) affiliation (upper (middle) class 47.1%, middle class 34.6%, working class 30.7%). It should be noted for all these figures that they are relative to the respondent's (dis)satisfaction with other issue areas. The lesser relative dissatisfaction of the 'young' with the environment might, therefore, be due to the fact that they were more dissatisfied with other areas of concern (housing, income) than the older age groups and consequently mentioned the environment less frequently.

When satisfaction levels were measured for each issue independently on a 0 (least satisfied) to 10 (most satisfied) scale, each the environment and public safety obtained an average rating of 5.0. With respect to the environment, the youngest age group (18—34) was less satisfied (4.5) than the age group 35—59 (5.2) and those above 50 (5.2); the self—employed, civil servants and white collar employees (4.7 and 4.8) less than blue—collar workers (5.2); people describing themselves as working class (5.2) more than upper (middle) classes (4.5). Far below average ranked non—voters (4.3). Interestingly, those most satisfied with the environment tended to be least satisfied with public safety and vice versa. This phenomenon shows clearly among the various age, occupation and class categories, and will be picked up later linking value change to the LER. From 1978 to 1982, the dissatisfaction with environmental pollution relative to other

100

issue—areas had further grown. Ninety—one percent agreed to the statement that "pollution is rising to dangerous levels". If dissatisfaction is measured by one's preferences for tax— financed expenditures for eliminating the cause of one's dissatisfaction, in 1982 environmental protection had reached the top spot, with "development of new energy sources" ranking second and "housing" ranking third (Kessel, 1984:31). Unfortunately, employment—related spending targets were not included.

Three surveys conducted between 1974 and 1977 measured the employment/ environmental protection trade—offs as perceived by different age and occupational groups. One survey asked whether people believed that environmental protection threatened or created jobs (INFAS, in: Umweltgutachten 1978:451). Half of the respondents did not want to express an opinion on this question. Among the other half, three out of four expected that more rather than less employment would result. This ratio was 2 to 1 for those under 35 years of age, 5 to 1 for the 35 to 64 years old, 4 to 1 for labor union members, and 3 to 1 for nonmembers. Thus, labor union members considered the effects on employment slightly more favorably than did non—members and —deviating from other results— the old more so than the young.

Two other surveys in 1974 and 1977 asked the question whether the respondent would support environmental protection even though he or someone in his family might risk the loss of his job as a result of environmental protection measures. Clear majorities (56 to 22% in 1974; 45 to 20% in 1977) expressed support for the environment given that contingency (op.cit.:451f). The groups most likely to become unemployed, i.e. the ages 45 to 59 and the less—skilled, were the least supportive of environmental protection but nevertheless by about a 2 to 1 margin. In 1974, the familiar pattern surfaced again. The young and the higher occupations supported environmental protection by the highest margins. By 1977, the different preferences among the occupations had leveled off almost entirely. The pro— environmental sentiments have decreased among the white—collar and slightly increased among the blue—collar jobs.

Almost ten years later, the beneficial effects of environmental protection for employment seems clearly established. In 1984, only 13% of the public agreed to the proposition that the high cost of environmental measures decreased industrial competitiveness and thus cost jobs. On the other hand, 62% agreed that environmental protection requirements stimulated new technologies and thus new jobs (25% were undecided). Interestingly, union members believed more in the compatibility of environmental and employment than did non—union members. Only 9% of the union members agreed to the first proposition (13% of the non—unionists), 76% to the second (61% of the non—unionists) (Wirtschaftswoche, 28 Sept. 1984:83).

4.2.3 The Environmental Movement and the Anti—Nuclear Movement

Since nuclear power has been such a controversial issue with respect to the LER, I will briefly touch on the membership base of the anti—nuclear opposition. Unfortunately, only very few of the published public opinion results concerning attitudes toward energy options that give demographic and socio— economic breakdowns also distinguish among union and non—union members. Nor do I possess published results from pertinent surveys conducted specifically among union members. The data presented in the following are therefore piecemeal.

In the US it is mistaken to equate environmentalism and opposition to nuclear power for the whole time period considered. Overall, the environmental movement enjoyed considerably higher levels of sympathy than the anti—nuclear movement (Mitchell, Sep.1978:5). Further, those in higher occupations have been higher than average supporters of environmental groups, of environmental protection measures and of nuclear energy! Those environmentally active in the US until the mid

1970s apparently were a different breed than were the more recent anti-nuclear activists. A poll of participants at a large anti-nuclear rally described the latter as predominantly "young, well-educated, liberal and from urban areas" (Science, 31.8.1979). On the other hand, the FEA surveys conducted between 1974 and 1976 found consistently that environmentalists besides suburban dwellers and earners of high incomes belonged to the staunchest supporters of nuclear energy. Those with most unfavorable views were city dwellers, the young, and those who had completed high school but not college. At the end of 1974, all groups favored nuclear energy by at least a 2 to 1 margin (PB 259345: 32).

The support of nuclear power was the smaller the closer a plant was to home. Only 50% to 40% favored a plant within 20 miles of one's home. By far those most in favor were the environmentally active (75%), most opposed were the young (50%) and women (49%) (op.cit.:33). The most serious problem seen associated with nuclear energy was waste disposal (52%). This assessment was fairly equally distributed across socio- economic lines (p.34). By May 1975, 55% of the public felt favorable toward nuclear power, in general, 24% had no opinion, and 21% were opposed. Environmentalists (70%), the better educated (71%) and those with higher incomes (70%) were particularly sympathetic. No subgroup was outstandingly hostile. A 45% to 38% majority supported a nuclear power plant within 20 miles from where they lived. The same subgroups as above tended to be in favor; women (46%), those above age 50 (43%), the least educated (42%), small town residents (42%), Midwesterners and Westerners (each 45%) opposed it most (PB 254592). By 1980, the "not in my backyard syndrome" had permeated the public's attitudes toward nuclear power. Ninety percent would not want to live within five miles of a nuclear plant (Jackson, Wright, 1981).

In the FRG, the politically relevant part of the environmental movement was for many years largely identical with the anti-nuclear movement. Today, nuclear energy has become less politically salient. Yet, the vast majority of the green voters are nuclear opponents at their heart. But, as noted, anti-nuclear sentiments are also to be found within labor. Whole unions as well as "deviant" parts of pro-nuclear unions opposed nuclear energy. The data identifying that segment of union membership are insufficient and confusing. On the one hand, particularly the skilled blue-collar workers have been relatively critical. On the other hand, those unions with a large blue-collar membership have tended to favor nuclear power. Within the general public, anti-nuclear attitudes have grown particularly among segments of the public traditionally distant to environmentalism.

Table 4-9 shows the attitudes of the public toward providing energy from nuclear versus "other" sources expressed in 1976 (Wahlstudie '76) and 1979 (ZDF Politbarometer) controlling for education, profession, age and union membership. The 1976 survey occured at a time when nuclear energy was just becoming an issue; the 1979 poll was conducted after the Three-Mile-Island accident (and thus might somewhat overstate anti- nuclear sentiments). For the total population, the share of nuclear energy supporters has remained the same during the three years -exceeding 37%. However, proponents of "other" energy sources have increased from 30% to 47% while those undecided have decreased by the same amount. Broken down by the four socio-economic variables, several shifts over the three years become apparent. In the 1976 survey, education and nuclear energy support correlated positively, while the preference for "other" ways was apparently independent of a respondent's educational background. Exactly the opposite could be observed in the 1979 survey. In both surveys, higher occupational attainment correlated with nuclear energy support. Blue collar workers were slightly more in favor of the nuclear option in 1976. By 1979, a clear split between skilled and non-skilled blue collar workers had arisen. Among the non-skilled, both options were rated almost equally, while a clear majority of the skilled workers preferred the non-nuclear alternative. In 1976, age was not a decisive factor but a discernible pattern emerged in 1979: the younger the respondents, the higher the

in favor of supplying energy by	1976			1979		
	Nuclear power plant constr.	other ways	do not know	nuclear power plant constr.	other ways	don't know
total	37.7	29.7	32.6	37.5	47.7	14.8
education						
10 grades	25.6	30.2	44.2	34.2	41.0	24.8
10 grades,apprenticeship	38.6	30.3	31.1	40.1	46.5	13.4
secondary schooling	47.9	29.0	24.0	36.4	56.6	7.0
profession(head of hh)						
unskilled blue-collar	29.3	21.4	49.3	37.5	38.6	24.0
skilled blue-collar	35.0	30.9	34.1	32.9	51.8	15.3
civil servants(Tenure),						
white-collar:medium level	40.0	34.0	26.0	39.8	49.8	10.4
same :high level	58.9	22.4	18.7	55.8	41.1	3.0
self-employed:small,med.	32.6	32.0	35.4	41.0	43.5	15.5
same :large	56.3	18.9	24.8	51.1	30.8	18.1
age						
-24	41.1	30.1	28.9	28.4	61.3	10.3
-29	33.5	38.1	28.4	38.5	58.6	2.9
-39	41.6	30.1	28.3	41.8	48.8	9.3
-49	38.3	28.9	32.7	37.1	46.8	16.0
-59	41.3	29.3	29.4	43.8	43.9	12.3
60 and older	32.0	27.4	40.6	34.0	41.1	24.9
trade union member						
yes	42.3	29.8	27.9	39.1	48.6	12.4
no	35.6	29.5	34.8	36.8	47.4	15.8

Source:'Wahlstudie 1976'(2nd wave):215
       ZDF-Politbarometer(July 1979):44

Table 4-9: Public attitudes toward a nuclear versus
       nonnuclear energy option in 1976 and 1979 by
       education, profession, age, and trade union
       membership

preference for "other" ways. A distinction between union and non-union members followed along the lines of the total population. The share of nuclear energy proponents has remained roughly the same, while most of those undecided in 1976 have turned to supporters of "other" ways resulting, surprisingly, in a 49% to 39% majority against the nuclear option among union members.

According to two surveys conducted by the International Institute for Environmental and Society Berlin, in 1980 and 1982, a majority in the FRG still thought that nuclear power was needed (Kessel, 1984:12). But the share of the supporters had somewhat declined in that period —perhaps due to a growing appreciation of the risks of nuclear waste storage.

4.3 Demographic and Socio-Economic Differences, and the LER

Undoubtedly, the average labor union member has a different demographic or socio- economic background than the average environmentalist in the US as well as in the FRG. Further, certain population subgroups have distinct views on the interdependencies of environmental protection, energy and employment. Thus, there is evidence in support of the proposition that environmentalism tends to be a concern of the upper (middle) classes who worry little about how their activities may affect workers and the poor.

On the other hand, the broad consensus among the American and German publics in support of the environmental protection goal indicates that the demographic and socio- economic differences are not paralleled by attitudinal differences. With regard to the issues in question, the compositional differences have not translated into clear-c and distinct attitudes. The distinct socio-economic composition of politically active environmental organizations such as the Sierra Club suggests, however, that the behavior of this stratum, i.e. being, at least, a dues-paying member and perhaps even actively engaged in particular matters, is different from the "silent majority". While, on balance, the compositional membership data support the hypothesis that the different membership base could have been a cause for the labor-environmentalist conflicts, the bulk of the attitudinal data leaves open other interpretations as well.

In the following, I will briefly indicate where this hypothesis lacks explanatory power. Then I will turn to the other ways in which the different memberships have possibly affected the LER.

First, VanLiere and Dunlap found class indicators such as occupational prestige and income to be, at most, weakly related to environmental concerns. Consistently, even though moderately important were age, education and political ideology. If the compositional differences were an important reason for the labor-environmentalist conflicts, then material well-being would not be the crucial factor but cleavages of values and world-views found in groups of people significantly different with respect to variables such as education, age and political ideology.

Second, the relationships of the Sierra Club and the NWF, respectively, toward labor unions do not support the socio- economic factor hypothesis. The demographic and socio- economic composition of the NWF resembles much more that of labor unions than that of the Sierra Club. Yet, the Sierra Club has cooperated closely with parts of the labor movement while the NWF has not. This may be explained by the possibility that more educated, higher socio-economic status people may tend to be less parochial in their perspectives and have a longer time horizon. They may therefore be more inclined to cooperate with other interest groups. There is a paradox in the respective LERs of NWF and the Sierra Club only if one assumes that a better LER requires respective memberships to be more similar.

Third, some unions have alluded to the different membership bases of the two movements but have made a point that these differences must not preclude cooperation. The UAW, for example, known to be on good terms with environmentalists, has stressed that workers benefit from environmentalist activities —and be it only from spillovers. UAW's vice— president Odessa Komer gave a sarcastic example: It has been known since the 1930s, that exposure to PCBs at the workplace was found to cause severe skin problems. But as long as its toxicity was related only to occupational exposure, it received little attention. Political attention was given, however, as soon as it appeared to be a threat to the natural environment and its wildlife. Komer concluded:

> Put simply, there wasn't much scientific interest in studying PCB's as long as they were destroying the health of workers. When they showed up in fish and eagles, though, then suddenly it becomes worthy of intensive scientific investigation. It is exactly this kind of double standard that angers those of us in the labor movement so much. (Black Lake Conference, Sunday:4)

Socio—economic cleavage along an amalgam of non—prestige occupational differences and generational/ world—view lines seems more plausible than the class—based hypothesis. VanLiere and Dunlap noted the possible importance of negative associations between environmental concerns, on the one hand, and business occupations, technology dependent occupations, and nature—exploitative occupations on the other. Buttel and Flinn (1978:446) concluded that mass environmental attitudes "may be more accurately characterized as expressions of generational —rather than class— interests". Generational conflicts may be manifest in terms of valuing present versus future costs and benefits differently. Educational differences conceivably could have resulted in looking at different levels of complexity of the issues — both in substantive and political terms.

The importance of occupational cleavages surfaces in the aforementioned survey of AFL—CIO members conducted in 1980. Union members were presented with the possiblity of various groups who might support a candidate's campaign for political office, and asked how the support of that group would influence their inclination to vote for or against that candidate. Among the groups were a labor group, the oil industry, a civil rights group, women's rights groups, and an environmental organization (Opinion Research Survey, 1980:36). The only groups eliciting strong responses were labor groups, which produced a strong positive response, and oil companies, which produced a strong negative response. When support comes from an environmental group, equal numbers of union members would be inclined to vote for (31%) and against (32%) that candidate. Members of construction unions and members living in the West would be less inclined to support that candidate while members of government and service unions as well as younger members would feel more inclined to do so (p.38). Almost the same pattern of negative and positive attitudes (higher education, in addition, correlated positively with support) prevailed with respect to civil rights and women's rights groups, and toward Ralph Nader.

Although I will discuss the ideology— influence hypothesis along the lines of Inglehart's "Silent Revolution" in great detail in a later chapter, I will now briefly present data pertaining to the socio—economic basis of this revolution. As a reminder, Inglehart (1977) and several other authors have suggested that in Western societies a value shift from what he calls "materialist" to "post—materialist" goals is occuring. Higher emphasis on quality of life issues, his argument goes, is a central element of this shift. Such a shift might improve the LER in the long run.

The same groups, which tend to be members or supporters of the environmental movement, also tend toward post-materialism. Inglehart found in a 1972-73 survey that 31% of the US population shared materialist and 12% post-materialist values (the rest being of the mixed type) while the respective figures for the FRG were 42% and 8% (p.38). The fact, that environmental concerns started several years earlier in the US than in the FRG is concordant with these figures. An analysis of the electorate of the Greens found that the "new left" upper middle-class green voter had a distinct post-materialist value-system (FAZ, 3.9.84:11). In a seven nation analysis, the most important predictor of the value type was education, followed by age, party affiliation, church attendance, and occupation (of the head of household), nationality, union membership and sex (p.93). Most post-materialist are university educated 16-24 years of age (39%, materialist 13%). The respective figures of those with only a primary education at the same age were 13% and 31%. Post-materialist values clearly decrease with age and increase with education (p.82). Furthermore, middle-class households were found to be more post-materialist than working-class ones (p.74). Similarly, people who support conservative political parties were less so than those who support parties on the left. Labor union members were somewhat more likely to be post-materialist than non-members. Affiliation with a party to the left was linked with a tendency to support post-materialist values (p.92).

Thus, socio- economic groups congenial to environmentalism were found to be more post-materialist than labor union members which in turn were more so than the average population. But working class households which make up most of labor union membership, were more materialist than average. This suggests that the value-based splits extend into the labor movement. It might explain the differences between construction and services oriented unions surfacing in the above cited AFL-CIO membership survey [1]. It might further explain the gradual incline and subsequent stabilization of pro-environmental sentiments within the labor movement as the composition of the organized labor force has been changing.

Demographic and socio-economic trends of the membership of labor unions and environmental organizations, as well as of those subgroups particularly congenial to them, on balance appear favorable to decreased labor-environmentalist conflicts, if one attributes some validity to occupational and world-view explanations. Tables 4-10 and 4-11 show that in the US and in the FRG, those groups with relatively pro- environmental attitudes also make up increasing shares of the labor force (or, as with respect to educational attainment, of the total population). As noted, US union membership in 1970 in comparison with environmental membership was older, more blue-collar, less educated, more religious and earned less. Table 4-10 shows that the US labor force between 1960 and 1979 has become younger (e.g. in 1960, 39% of the labor force were less than 35 years old; in 1978, 51%), less blue-collar, more female, and has changed from work in goods-related industries to service sector employment. The population as a whole and, by inference, the work force as well, has become better educated. Thus, the overall long-term demographic shifts of the population and the labor force indicate greater labor-environmentalist affinity.

These shifts in the population are also reflected by shifts of relative union strength within the house of labor. Service workers and government unions have had rapid membership increases while union membership as a whole has been stagnant. As listed in Table 4-12, AFSCME membership has increased from 235,000 in 1964 to more than a million now. Similarly, SEIU membership has almost doubled since 1968. Much of those high increases, of course, have been due to low past unionization rates in these sectors. But the new service-sector unions (the United Food and Commercial Workers, the Service Employees, the Communication Workers, the Hospital Workers), including government unions, have given a high priority to organizing. This aspect of the shifts should benefit the LER, since these unions have also

	1960[a]	1970[a]	1979[a]	1981[b]
age				
16 - 19	7.3%	8.9%	9.6%[1]	8.4%
20 - 24	10.6	14.3	15.3	15.3
25 - 34	20.9 38.8	20.6 43.8	25.8	28.0
35 - 44	23.1	19.5	18.4	19.4
45 - 54	20.7	19.8	16.5	15.3
55 - 64	13.0	13.1	11.3	10.8
65 and older	4.4	3.7	3.0	2.7
education[2]				
less than high school grad.	58.9%	44.8%	34.1%	
four years of high school or more	41.1	55.2	65.9	
four years of college or more	7.7	11.0	15.7	
occupation				
white collar	43%	48%	51%	53%
blue collar	37	35	33	31
service	12	12	13	13
employment by economic sector				
goods-related industries (mining, manufact construction)	38%	33%	29.5%	
- manufact	31	27	24	
- construction	5.4	5.1	4.8	
service-related industries	62	67	70.5	
- services	13.6	16.3	18.8	
- government	15.4	17.7	18.0	

1) in 1978   2) in % of total population over age 25

Source: a) US Statistical Abstract, 1979 : 395,144,415,408
        b) US Statistical Abstract, 1982/83

Table 4-10 :   Demographic Characteristics of the US
               Labor Force, 1960, 1970, 1979 and 1981

	1961[1]	1970[1]	1978[2]	1983[3]
age				
15 - 20		8.3%	8.8%	8.3%
20 - 30		20.3	22.9	23.2
30 - 40		24.5	24.1	21.8
40 - 50		21.4	23.2	25.8
50 - 60		15.1	16.8	17.0
60 - 65		6.5	2.4	2.6
65 and older		3.8	1.8	1.3
education				
number of students in 1000 in				
elementary and primary schools	5343	6347[2]	5718	4247
secondary schools	848	1379	2013	1961
colleges, universities	343	528	946	1273
(population in M	56.9	60.6	61.3	61.4)
occupation				
self-employed	12.1%	10.7%	8.8%	9.3%
white collar §	29.9	36.2	44.7	47.0
blue collar	48.1	47.4	42.4	39.5
(§: incl.tenured civil servants)				
employment by economic sector				
production	48%	49%[2]	45%	41.5
trade and transportation	17	17	18	18
services	22	25	31	34
--------------------				
energy,water,mining		2.0%	2.0%	2.0%
manufacturing (w/out constr.)		39.3	35.8	32.7
construction		7.8	6.8	7.8
commerce		12.0	11.9	11.9
transportation,communication		5.6	5.8	5.5
banks,insurance		2.5	3.1	3.4
other services		13.4	16.0	18.6
public service,social insurance		6.5	10.1	10.9

Sources: 1) Statistisches Jahrbuch, 1971:121,72,15,125
2) Statistisches Jahrbuch, 1979:93,29,338/9
3) Statistisches Jahrbuch, 1984:97,98,357

Table 4-11: Demographic Characteristics of the West German Labor Force, 1961, 1970, 1978 and 1983

	1964[a]	1968[a]	1972[a]	1976[a]	1980[b]
United Auto Workers (UAW)	1168	1473	1394	1358	1357
Electrical Workers (IBEW)	806	879	957	924	1041
Machinists (IAM)	808	903	758	917	784
United Mine Workers (UMW)	450[1,2]	1	213	277	245
Oil, Chemical, Atomic Workers (OCAW)	162	173	172	177	154
Operating Engineers (IUOE)	311	350	402	420	423
Sheet Metal Workers	117	140	153	153	161
State, County, Municipal Employees (AFSCME)	235	364	529	750	1098
Service Employees (SEIU)[b]		389	484	575	650
United Steel Workers (USWA)	965	1120	1400	1300	1238

[1] Membership not reported to BLS

[2] 1962 figure -included for comparison

Sources: a) 1979 Union Directory, DOL (Sept.1980):91
         b) US Statistical Abstract, 1982/83: 409

Table 4-12 : Membership Trends for Selected US Labor Unions,
1964 - 1980 (in 1000)

109

increasingly supported environmental and OSH causes. In addition, the membership of the service sector unions consists of cohorts that tend to be supportive of environmental goals. Government union membership is highly educated, government and service unions have a high proportion of women members, tend to put more trust in endorsements given by environmentalists and other liberal causes, and want more efforts than members of other unions put into strengthening regulations against industrial pollution.

On the other hand, traditionally pro–environmental unions such as the UAW and USWA have suffered tremendous losses by the decline of their industries. While one might argue that the building and construction unions or mining unions, which have tended to be in conflict with environmentalists, have also experienced an erosion of membership, and that the relative influence within the AFL–CIO between these two camps, therefore, has remained fairly stable, the decline of key industrial unions must certainly hurt the LER. It affects the LER directly, since their resources (financial, staff support, research, logistics, campaigning) that had been put to good use for environmental causes now allow for much less. But in addition, as Kuttner (1984) points out, these unions will tend to become the "representatives of a few high–paid workers rather than a broad force for social justice". "Deindustrialization", this thinking goes (c.f. Section 6.4), turns America into a two–tier society largely devoid of the traditional middle–class, including skilled unionists. What remains of these industrial unions, Kuttner argued, might confirm the image of unions as a "selfish and shrinking elite", defending nobody and little else than those already well–off.

In general, the same trends of a "post–industrial" society are evident in Table 4–11 with respect to the FRG. They too suggest a gradual increase of importance of social strata with relatively positive attitudes toward environmentalism. Within the labor movement, however, more continuity than the US has experienced can be expected. Although service sector union membership is also slowly growing, the relative shifts are much less profound than in the US (see Table 4–5). In the DGB, the share of blue–collar members has decreased from 73% in 1974 (Weber, 1976:108) to 67% in 1983. Yet those effects on the union structure come less to bear. The same union losing blue–collar members will benefit from white–collar gains. Moreover, due to industry–wide bargaining in the FRG, the evolution of a two–tier wage structure seems much less likely. What troubles the German unions a good deal more is their slackening attractiveness to the young. In large unions, such as the IGM, OTV or HBV, the membership under the age of 25 has declined by 4% to 6% (Buente, 1984:9). But, on balance, the prospects for the LER as a result of demographic and structural–economic changes look better in the FRG than in the US.

4.4 Summary

The demographic and socio–economic bases of labor and environmentalism in the US and in the FRG have been different. Some differences of perceptions have certainly grown out of the distinct membership bases. However, on a variety of energy, employment, and environmental protection related issues, the respective memberships have shared similar views to a considerable extent. Over time, their similarities have rather increased than decreased. As far as one can make a distinction, the dissensus between the population subgroups with respect to positions supported by unions and environmental organizations, respectively, has been less along traditional class lines and more along occupational, educational and value–based lines crossing class differentials. The labor–environmentalists conflicts in the past are not sufficiently explained by the different membership of the two groups.

[1] The surveys cited in Tables 4–3 and 4–4 revealed important differences among occupations, and thus among unions. The 1970 and 1977 surveys noted that in the building trades earning differentials between union and non–union workers were as high as 40% to 50% while they were smallest (about 5%) in the white collar sector. In 1977, construction and transportation were the highest paying–industries for workers represented by labor organizations (p.3). In 1980, a slightly higher proportion of communication and government union members reported incomes in excess of $25,000 (p.55). Nearly all union members with postgraduate education were members of government unions, as were more than one–third of those with college degrees. Those with less than high school education were primarily clustered in construction and manufacturing unions (p.56). There were more Jewish union members working in government than in any other industry (p.57). Relatively high proportions of women were found in sales (41%), communications (39%), service (32%) and government unions (27%) while only 6% of the construction and 8% of the transportation union members were women (pp.57f).

5 Explanation 3: The LER and Internal Decision-Making

Statements by union leaders have repeatedly labelled the decision making within unions as democratic and that of environmental organizations as lacking transparency. Public opinion surveys report high approval rates of unionism and environmentalism in the two countries but also much distrust in union leadership in the US. Further, opinion surveys and grass-root activities within labor show that labor's official political stand on issues like nuclear energy development is not shared by, at least, large minorities of the union membership. Opponents of the pro- nuclear policies of German labor, in fact, charged that an "Atomfilz" (Mez, Wilke, 1978), i.e. vested interests of union officials, the energy industry, and government agencies, have decisively determined the energy policies of the German unions. The question therefore arises how open has union policy making been to controversial views.

This section will examine the internal decision-making processes of labor unions. It will ask whether the institutional and constitutional arrangements within the organizations allow for democratic interest formulation, articulation and implementation, or whether leadership and apparatus can shape policies largely independent of rank-and-file attitudes. For the FRG , I will particularly be concerned with the relationship between works councils and unions. For the US, I will focus on the question of whether or not those industrial and public employees unions that have frequently cooperated with environmentalists tend to be more democratic than the building and construction unions.

How does internal decision-making conceivably affect the LER? The more internal union decision making is a factor, the less plausible is the built-in dichotomy explanation for labor- environmentalist conflicts. As long as environmentalism is decisively carried by non-institutionalized grass-roots support and the more open a labor organization is to bottom-up interest articulation, the easier could environmentally conscious union policies evolve. In this case, environmental groups should find it easier to cooperate with democratic unions at all levels of organization, while conflicts would have to be expected in particular with undemocratic unions. On the other hand, if environmental concerns are already institutionalized or even well rooted in union leadership but not in union membership, then the situation is possibly reversed. If the union is democratic, close cooperation between labor and environmental leadership may not be tolerated by the union members. If the environmentally conscious union is undemocratic, pro environmental union policies would more or less be imposed on the membership.

5.1 External and Internal Constraints for Union Democracy

The degree of union democracy, or lack thereof, is not only determined by the internal tensions between —in the extreme— a whimsical leadership and a militant membership. Nor does the assumption suffice upon which (in Lipset's terms) Michel's iron law of oligarchy rests, i.e. that "all leaders of mass organizations [are] inherently self—interested conservative oligarchs" (in:Cook, 1963:217). Highly important also are the constraints imposed by the conditions of industrial relations, interest group politics and economic policy making. For the US and the FRG it is safe to say, that the labor movements in both countries have a basic interest in the preservation and long—term utilization of the production, employment and wage potential of the existing capitalist economic order. "Cooperative labor unions...are mediators (Vermittlungsorgane) between the needs of high capital turnover (Kapitalverwertung) and the interests of the wage earners" (Bergmann 1973:242). They are interested in "optimal wage levels" which assure the international competitiveness of the industry, necessary investments and long—term liquidity of a company while obtaining wages as high as possible given these constraints (Scharpf, 1978:19).

How does that affect union democracy? To obtain the optimally high levels, the unions depend decisively on their membership in two ways. First, they must attract and keep as many members as possible since size gives the union political and bargaining weight. Second, the membership must be sufficiently "conflict—oriented" as it is the conflict orientation which enables the union to do tough bargaining. However, the dual interests in maintaining the existing order as well as membership attractiveness and conflict—orientation —Scharpf argues— pose a dilemma for union democracy. A strong leadership at the cost of democracy will help to curtail excessive wage demands of the membership but will also tend to attract fewer members and dampen the members' readiness to strike. A union, on the other hand, granting too many rights to members may prevent sufficient controls by the leadership to obtain agreements that lie in the general interest. Democratic unions at the cost of leadership efficiency may also reduce the union's bargaining strength if the lack of leadership strength enhances intra—union factionalism.

Bergmann (1973:245) similarly, called the process of will formation circular and contradictory.

It is circular because the results of the discussions in the union bodies are pre—determined by the technical rules of macro—economic wage setting. It is contradictory because it needs to legitimate by consensus what can not be legitimated: demands which are determined by the (at the time) prevailing constellation of macro—economic relations and defined by "technical rules" can only be accepted but not be legitimated by norms of just distribution. Nonetheless, the will formation process must create the impression that the discussion is on norms of just distribution on which a consensus will be reached.(...) The circular and contradictory nature of the will fomation process in a cooperative union results in a double bind. On the one hand, the will formation process must put up a screen against the open and unregulated articulation of membership interests and against the discussion of the underlying norms of social equity: the articulation of membership interests must be quantitatively and qualitatively limited. On the other hand, the screening—off and limitation must be accomplished without disciplinary and repressive methods. Otherwise, the process of will formation could not appear free of compulsion and democratic and would therefore lose its fundamental legitimizing function.

The unions solve this quandary, Bergmann argued, by subjecting the internal will formation process to "restrictive mechanisms". They allow the unions to avoid putting their legitimacy to test by the unconstrained articulation and discussion of membership interests. If necessary the organizations can prove their legitimacy by the fact that members do not revolt or exit from the organization.

5.2 Union Will Formation and Decision Making in the FRG

The foregoing theoretical discussion of the constraints for union democracy suggests two questions: (1) What are the constraints and (2) how do they apply to union decision making and will formation with respect to energy and environmental policy in the FRG? In response to these questions, following a brief introduction into the formal organizational structure of German labor, I will give a summary description of the institutional barriers to effective participation of union membership. Subsequently, I will examine several of these barriers with respect to energy policy making in the unions. These barriers are: Convention procedures, reporting in the union press, and the role of the works councils in internal union politics. Finally, I will briefly address the distribution of influence among the various unions regarding energy policy making.

5.2.1 Formal Internal Organizational Structure

The levels of authority as specified by the constitutions in the DGB unions comprise the local administrative units ("Verwaltungsstellenbereiche"), the regional units (in some unions state units), and the national convention. In addition, the union is present at the company level. Here, union representation stands on two legs. The official union body consists of the "Vertrauensleute" elected by the union members in the company. The second leg, albeit formally independent of the union, consists of the works councils which are elected by the workers regardless of whether they belong to the union or not. Will formation in the union occurs from level to level by delegates who vote on union policy and hold elections for leadership, commissions, and committees at the various levels of organization. The highest authority is vested in the national convention. Its decisions are binding for all union bodies. The convention elects the executive ("Hauptvorstand"), an executive board ("Beirat") as the highest authority between two conventions, and two control organs. According to the constitutions, all union bodies are linked to the delegate system and, therefore, are formally responsible to represent the interests of the membership and its delegates.

5.2.2 Shortcomings of the Organizational Arrangements

In principle, Bergmann (1979:211) states, the membership could utilize the delegate system to bring personnel and policy matters to the convention and change existing leadership and positions. However, all existing studies of organizational structure and organizational reality of labor unions in the Federal Republic agree that the members have in fact only few opportunities to exert influence on the will formation process and control on the union apparatus. (ibid.)

The major shortcomings are not the delegate system as such but, according to Bergmann (1979), three institutional characteristics. First, leadership and membership rights are out of balance in favor of the former; second, union leadership has much leeway in making collective bargaining decisions; and third, the works councils have an undue influence on union policy. I will summarize Bergmann's arguments now especially with respect to his first and third point. His second point is less relevant for the LER.

1. There is an imbalance between decision making and control powers of the union leadership and apparatus, on the one hand, and the rights granted to the membership and the union bodies close to membership influence, on the other. First, the central control organs can not effectively control union leadership. The authority is held vague by the union constitutions and is not binding for the executive. Although mandated to control the constitutionality of leadership policy and its accordance with decisions passed by the convention, not the control organs but the executive has the right to interpret the constitution and convention mandate.

Second, members of the executive are often ex-officio members of organs that are meant to control the executive. In the IGBSE, IGCPK, OTV, IGDP, and others, they are convention delegates; in the IGM, HBV, and IGBSE, they are Beirat members. At the 1982 DGB Convention, for example, the great majority of the delegates were full-time union officials, i.e. employees of the union executives (SZ, 21.5.1982:2,3). Regional executive officers, moreover, are frequently in the national executive either as full time (IGBSE, DPG, OTV, NGG) or advisory (IGM, HBV, GBT) members. They are elected but must usually be confirmed by the national executive. This oligarchical tendency is strongest in the IGBSE (Bergmann,1979:212).

Third, the national executive has often the right to nominate for election and/or confirm the elected non-salaried members of the local administrative units and their salaried officials (in IGBE, IGBSE, IGM, IGCPK, GED). For IGBSE, IGBE, IGCPK, and IGM, the same applies at the regional level. The criteria for such interventions are held vague and wide open to interpretations.

Fourth, most union constitutions do not exclude staff members from becoming delegates. For those unions where figures are available (IGM, IGCPK, OTV, GTB), their share lies at 20% to 30%. A similarly privileged position, compared to the ordinary member, is held by full-time works council members ("freigestellte Betriebsrate") who are usually another important group at the conventions. Union staff and works council members probably add up at most conventions to absolute majorities.

Fifth, most conventions proceed in a pre-planned fashion and have become "acclamation bodies for the union leadership" (op.cit.:213). The elections to the executive occur usually without opposition candidates. Further, resolution committees play a particularly crucial role with respect to the policies adopted at the conventions. Since hundreds and sometimes thousands of resolutions are proposed, the committees sort, select, and formulate resolutions and compromises and suggest their adoption or rejection. Usually, the convention follows the proposals made by the resolution committees. Because the union executive influences the composition of the committees and controls their work, the resolutions are often tailored to the executive's policies. "They are flexible and open to interpretation" and do not restrict the executive more than condoning it (op.cit.:214). In addition, the incumbent leadership also chairs the convention which means additional controls against unwanted surprises.

Sixth, the national executive of all union controls the union publications and has, therefore, monopoly over communications with the membership and its will formation. With rare exceptions, only opinions in agreement with that of the executive are being published. The relative autonomy of union journalists after WWII was soon abolished. At least temporarily, a formal "pre-censorship" even existed in the IGM and DPG (ibid.).

Seventh, the DGB has sought to curtail the opportunities for union members to influence will formation within the labor movement from the outside. This restriction becomes important if internal channels are not sufficiently open or accessible. Union members are not allowed to identify their union affiliation when they sign non-union statements and petitions, since it "creates the impression in the public that the unions have internal disagreements" (FR, 7.5.81:4 and 27.7.81:1,4).

2. Union constitutions contain few —compared to their importance—regulations on collective bargaining. The final decision—making rights lie with the national executive. Its only major limitation is the membership referendum vote ("Urabstimmung") on strikes. However, it is also up to the executive to decide whether such a vote should be held or not. Thus, membership rights with respect to this still most central union activity are rather restricted.

3. Although the union constitutions give only marginal attention to the works councils and although these are formally independent of the unions, the works councils are the "second pillar" of the organizational structure next to the delegate system. They serve as a substitute for the union at the work place where they act as 'honorary' union organs particularly recruiting and informing members. As specified by the Works Constitution Act, they represent work—place related interests. The works councils have a relatively strong position vis—a—vis unions. They can largely determine the amount of union influence at the work place; their political base is relatively autonomous of the union; and they have an overwhelming influence at the local and a considerable influence at higher union levels. Works councillors usually comprise a relative, often even an absolute majority among convention delegates.

The substantial influence of the works councils on union politics tends to reduce rather than increase the conflicts between labor and business. More conflictual politics would narrow the leeway for independent company wage and social policies. The cooperative wage politics of the past have essentially been based on an alliance of the works councils in the major companies and the national union leadership. In internal union politics, the works councils have become an effective instrument for "membership mediation" (Bergmann, 1979:216).

5.2.3 Internal Organizational Arrangements and Energy Policy Making

5.2.3.1 Conventions

The imbalance of power between leadership and membership has decisively influenced the positions on energy policies, and thus the LER, adopted at union conventions during the 1970s. An examination of the proceedings at 20 conventions of the IGCPK, OTV, IGDP, IGM and DGB between 1968 and 1980 shows that with one exception, the position of the national executive on energy policy always came through. A total of 79 resolutions related to energy were submitted to the delegates, seventy—two of which at 7 conventions held in the critical years between 1977 and 1980.

The pattern is always the same. Resolutions submitted prior to the convention are reviewed by the resolution committee ("Antragsberatungs—Kommission"), grouped and then a recommendation is formulated. In the

OTV, the executive elects the resolution committee members, while they are elected by regional delegates in the IGM. Usually, the recommendation is held vague looking like the least common denominator of as many resolutions as could be covered and official union policy. It was rare that any single one of the resolutions submitted included all the essential features of the recommendation finally made. Since as many as 22 resolutions on energy have been submitted to a single convention, the committee has often reformulated the union position into a single "Entschliessung".

Most of the work of the resolution committee is done prior to the convention. The convention itself lasts several days and follows a tight and well maintained schedule. Experienced union officials loyal to the leadership chair the convention. The convention rules are usually proposed by the executive at the beginning of the convention and subsequently adopted. Several unions —among them the OTV, the IGM until 1977, but not the IGDP— required that the recommendations of the resolution committee be voted on first even if amendments had been proposed. This rule gives an additional advantage to a leadership seeking approval of its policies. For example a delegate, who would support the general direction of the recommendation but who wants to have a particular item changed, would have to obtain a majority in order to vote down the recommendation, propose his amendment, and then have a vote on the amended recommendation again. (The IGM had followed this rule until the 1977 convention when it was proposed again but rejected by the delegates in favor of allowing votes on amendments with at least 50 delegate signatures prior to voting on recommendations (IGM 12. Ordentlicher Gewerkschaftstag (1977), Protokoll:61ff). Convention votes on issues are voice votes. Voting strengths are only approximate and are written into the protocol as estimated by the chair.

The debates on the convention floor on energy policy in the years since 1977 were controversial but, with one exception, the recommended resolutions have always found a majority. Nuclear energy was always at the center of the debate on energy policy. The resolutions of the "opposition" came usually from the union youth. At the 1980 IGDP convention (which was the one exception), two resolutions, both including the demand for a stop of nuclear power plant construction and operation, were brought to a vote. The resolution committee recommended adoption of the more moderate one after eliminating the demand for a halt of nuclear power plant operations. After an extensive debate on amendments in which no nuclear energy supporter spoke, the recommendation was not only overridden but two additional demands for better alternative energy incentives and nationalization of the energy industry were included.

Of those examined, the most controversial conventions on energy issues were the OTV convention in 1980, the IGM conventions in 1977 and 1980, and the IGDP convention in 1977 (22, 13, 13, and 8 resolutions, respectively, were submitted). At the IGDP 1977 convention, a pro—nuclear position based on highly stringent conditions and the nationalization of the energy industry was adopted. Resolutions calling for different forms of nuclear energy moratoria and those for a support of the DGB position were rejected. The 1977 IGM convention had to decide on 13 resolutions ranging across a wide spectrum of conditional and unconditional acceptance and rejection of nuclear energy. The debate was extensive but the recommended Entschliessung had clearly more supporters among the delegates although the nuclear opponents outnumbered the supporters among those who spoke by 8 to 5. Notably, the most outspoken proponents were works council members of the Kraftwerk Union, the largest German nuclear manufacturer. A motion to terminate the debate was finally carried. The Entschliessung was adopted by a wide margin after the IGM token commitment to the goal of nationalizing the energy industry had been reaffirmed. The choice at the 1980 convention came down to the recommended Entschliessung and a resolution submitted by the IGM youth caucus. The debate was again controversial albeit less lengthy than three years previously. A motion to limit a speaker's time from ten to five minutes was rejected. Nuclear opponents and supporters were equally divided among the speakers but the Entschliessung carried "with relatively few opposition votes" (Convention chair; Protokoll:424).

The OTV convention in 1980 makes a case in point for how much power the union leadership can wield. Already the previous two OTV conventions without debate had supported the leadership views: at the 1972 convention, the main speakers on energy had even then declared the discussion within the OTV on national energy policy closed (Protokoll:327). Klaus and Stiller (1979:79) described the 1972 OTV sentiments toward the utility industry and its plans to rely on nuclear energy as "extraordinarily positive and hardly clouded by second thoughts". Since then, however, union statements had become more critical. The 1980 convention began with a motion to amend the convention rules in a way that would allow to vote on each resolution separately instead of voting on the resolution committee recommendation first. The supporters of the motion argued that often vague and open-ended resolutions were recommended by the committee which would replace without any voting the more precise and binding resolutions originally submitted. They pointed out that OTV conventions take place only once every four years and that the number of resolutions could, therefore, not be an argument against the motion (Protokoll:40–44). Nevertheless, the motion was rejected. When the debate also touched on the question of how the resolution committee operated, another feature of leadership power became apparent. During the committee meetings, the staff member in the executive responsible for the subject matter discussed is usually present. The staff, indeed, advises the committee what action to recommend to the convention (p.43). Thus, the circle of leadership control is closed. Since, aided by the convention rules, the convention will almost certainly adopt the recommendations made by the committee, and since the committee's recommendations have been influenced by the executive, one must conclude that the convention no more than rubberstamps executive policies.

The debate on energy policy at the 1980 OTV convention was based on 22 resolutions, five of which tended to favor and 15 to oppose nuclear energy, while 2 dealt with other matters. Several of the resolutions asked that a broader discussion within the union must be possible. The debate was extensive with 5 speakers on each side but was cut-off by a motion to terminate the debate although 15 speakers still wanted to speak. Following the cut-off but still prior to the vote, however, OTV president Kluncker took the floor invoking his Executive privilege to provide "factual information". He gave a passionate speech in favor of the recommended resolution which, immediately following his speech, was also carried.

5.2.3.2 Union Press

I will now turn to the reporting on energy issues in the union press. The newspaper of the IGBE, "Die Einheit", is a loyal organ of official union policy with respect to energy. Its basic position warns that a stop of nuclear and coal power plant construction would cost employment. In order to stress the importance of coal and nuclear energy, the paper has repeatedly published editorials and columns from leading politicians and businessmen. Klaus and Stiller (1979:54) who reviewed the nuclear energy debate in the labor union press commented on the Einheit:

> Astounding ... is the hurry by which the union paper adopts the positions of the employers' side. It reports again and again the immensely high figures of threatened jobs cited by the supporters and owners of atomic power plants, but consistently 'forgets' to include more detailed break-downs and reasoning. (...) Articles

providing substantive information on the benefits, necessity and problems of nuclear energy production are very rare. Questions concerning safety and the back—end of the fuel cycle are pushed aside, alternative energy sources are rejected as unrealistic and uneconomical. A solution to the environmental problems are expected from A.Schmidt's (the IGBE president,HS) formula: 'As much nuclear energy as necessary, as much coal as possible.' It is hardly possible to describe the coming problems in a more non—committal way.

Klaus and Stiller's description is illustrated by the following listing of newspaper headlines. In the first seven months of 1979 —a period chosen at random—, 12 out of 13 issues of the Einheit examined referred in their leading headline on the front page to an energy crisis: "The Risk Grows" (1.1.79); "Crisis Follows the Price Poker" (15.1.79); "Minister Stresses:Coal Is Important" (15.2.79); "Oil Poker Continues. Higher Prices Already in March" (1.3.79); "Pressure on Oil Consumers" (15.3.79); "Have Nots in Raw Materials" (1.4.79); "Crisis Roundabout Lubricated by Oil. Arafat: The War Will Come" (15.4.79); "Let's Go For Coal Now " (1.5.79); "The US Lacks Gas. China Goes for It. The British Take Coal" (15.5.79); "Chancellor: Away from Oil. Gorleben Blocked" (1.6.79); "Does the Crisis Threaten Conflicts?" (1.7.79); "Does OPEC Hit Again in Six Months?" (15.7.79).

The IGBSE union paper "Der Grundstein" reported with greater differentiation but did not carry a controversial debate on union energy policies. It repeatedly advocated increased reliance on energy conservation and renewable energy sources, and pointed out that solar technology might create 50—100,000 jobs. But articles on the possible risks of nuclear energy, Klaus and Stiller (p.60) argued, have been lacking. The paper began to print a series of extremely one—sided advertisements advocating full employment through economic growth and more nuclear energy. The ads were sponsored by prominent works council members of the nuclear industry who had joined under the label of an "Aktionskreis Energie". However, the readers responded with a barrage of protest letters and the series was terminated after the second of twelve planned advertisements.

The "Gewerkschaftspost" of the IGCPK has also supported the union leadership's energy policies but has pointed to possible, even though unlikely dangers to the work and natural environments in the nuclear industry for chemical workers. The official union position on energy corresponds to the one of the DGB. However, the letters to the editor opposed the official position. In the 1975 to 1977 period, only one letter supported the civilian usage of nuclear energy. The spectrum of opponents was broad. Some called for coal power plants instead; others accused their union of having supported with almost no qualifications the positions of the government and the 'atom lobby' (Klaus, Stiller:65).

The newspaper for the IGM membership, "Metall", contained comparatively detailed and balanced reporting on the energy controversy before the union adopted an official position. In the winter of 1976/77 following the demonstrations in Brokdorf, it published a series of six articles titled "blessing or curse" of nuclear energy written by scientists from the University of Bremen known as nuclear energy sceptics. The series included two articles on nuclear energy and employment. The articles came to the conclusion that a decision for or against nuclear energy must be separated from strategies to achieve full employment (Metall 4/77:14, 5/77:14). The articles were followed by a flood of letters. I counted 69 letters published in 14 issues of the Metall during 1977 on nuclear energy (politics), 15 of which were pro—nuclear, 46 were opposed, and 8 neutral. Arguing the pro— position were particularly members of the works councils in the nuclear industry. Klaus and Stiller (p.75) noted that for the first time "bodies of the industry affected, particularly works councils, have spoken up independently of the union and acted as a 'pressure group'

119

for nuclear energy within and outside of the union". However, among the critics of German nuclear power politics were also the labor union representatives of the KWU in Offenbach. They implicitly criticized the politics of the works councils for "trying to force through their group interests" (Metall, 25—26/76:12).

After the IGM adopted its first official position on nuclear energy in March 1977, however, the Metall coverage of energy politics conspicuously quieted down. In the December issue, nuclear power was picked up once more because the articles by the Bremen scientists "had not been non—controversial" and a more "factual debate" on nuclear energy was wanted by supporters and opponents alike (Metall 25—26/77:7—10). This time, several scientists from the nuclear energy research facility in Julich were the authors and they gave their presentation more of a scientific touch than the Bremen group. They came to the conclusion that nuclear energy in the FRG was both feasible and desirable. Subsequently, only four letters were published all of them criticizing what they saw as one—sided pro—nuclear positions. A factor in favor of the relatively balanced view taken by the Metall might have been the editor—in—chief who later became known as an outspoken nuclear critic.

The "otv—magazin" focused on the technology of various reactor types and their state of development. The debate raged most heavily in the first six months of 1977. In that period the magazine published 22 letters to the editor taking positions on nuclear energy —8 in support and 14 opposed. Almost all of the letters in support came from employees and works councils of nuclear facilities. Subsequently, controversial discussions in the magazine on energy issues almost disappeared.

5.2.3.3 Role of Work Councils

The strong influence on nuclear energy policy of works councils representing members in energy related industries at the conventions and on will formation in the union press has already been indicated. Indeed, the activities of the works councils might have been the decisive influence on union energy policies.

As noted, the DGB made the first official public statement on energy policy on April 5,1977. The statement had been preceded by discussions among staff working on environmental issues and the Economic Policy Council of the DGB. The discussions led to a draft statement which was discussed by the DGB executive and which was subsequently circulated among the unions and the DGB regional units ("Kreise"). Based on the internal debates, the "energy unions" (IGBSE, IGBE, IGCPK, IGM and OTV) and the DGB departments for economic and social policies composed the final April 5 statement.

Klaus and Stiller (1979:47f) called the differences between the draft and final statements striking.

> The former differentiates among the various interest positions with respect to nuclear energy, reviews the history of the nuclear industry critically and describes unemployment as immanent to the economic system; in the latter, all insights disappear behind 'full employment oriented growth policies'.

Central to —and provoking opposition from the works councils— the April 5 statement was "the hard linkage between the licensing of new power plants and precisely defined progress in the nuclear Entsorgung", i.e. the back—end of the fuel cycle (op.cit.:162).

> Nuclear power plant construction work in progress must continue speedily. However, operating licenses for these plants may only

be granted if the Entsorgung strategy has been solved satisfactorily —or, respectively, if it is ascertained that such a solution will be at hand in the near term. In the latter case, the operating license may only be granted up to a specified date and under the unequivocable condition that an extension will be impossible if the [Entsorgung, HS] requirement is not met in time. Construction licenses for nuclear power plants presently in the planning stage may only be granted if the Entsorgung problem has been solved. (DGB, 5 April 1977)

Botho Riegert (1980:162), the responsible staff member on energy in the DGB Department for Economic Policies, gave the following account of what happened subsequently. The political opposition (mainly from citizen groups and parts of the political parties against the Entsorgung site in Gorleben) grew. At the same time, it became doubtful whether the energy industry really wanted the Entsorgung center constructed speedily, Riegert contended. Decreasing energy consumption growth rates had resulted in considerable excess capacities of electricity generation —that, and merely for economic reasons, required an extended delay of new power plant construction. Thus, had the Entsorgung center been constructed at the capacity planned, it would have been far from being sufficiently utilized. To be economically viable, more power plants needed to be constructed first.
The DGB linkage, which had sought to accelerate a solution to the Entsorgung issue, was now about to accomplish the contrary. It blocked further power plant construction due to the non—resolved Entsorgung issue which, in turn, remained unresolved since power plant construction had been blocked. A typical chicken—and—egg situation had arisen. The energy industry responded by blaming the DGB linkage for endangering power plant construction jobs. As noted, the workers in the affected companies also grew restless. The respective works councils formed action groups (among them the aforementioned Aktionskreis Energie) and harshly criticized the DGB Entsorgung linkage. Ten thousand workers demonstrated in Bonn and 2,000 in Hanau for securing their jobs by continuing nuclear energy construction. Similarly, the employees of the NWK, the utility constructing the plant in Brokdorf, protested in the streets. The IGBE went on a signature drive that was also supported by works councils of the metal and chemical industries. The works councils of KWU and BBC wrote letters to the Chancellor protesting the plant construction stops. All activities were organized and actively supported by works council members (Klaus, Stiller, 1979:49,50,74,81). Most discomforting for the unions, the works councils organized the mass rally in the Dortmund soccer stadium for November 10,1977. From the union perspective, they planned the rally "with the best intentions but probably without fully understanding the economic background outlined above ..." (Riegert:162).
The DGB reacted in two ways. Two days prior to the mass rally, the DGB executive "supplemented" its April 5 position. The political debates as well as a new study make it necessary, the new DGB position stated, that "the interests of the workers and population directly affected" be given closer consideration. The safety report of the Radiation Protection and Reactor Safety Commissions had concluded, the DGB now argued, that the "Entsorgung center is principally feasible from a technical and safety perspective". The infamous linkage was virtually abandoned. Those politically responsible should therefore

grant the construction permit for the planned Entsorgung center as rapidly as possible. In addition, they should make sure that the reprocessing and waste disposal center can be completed and take up operations as fast as possible. (...) ..it can not be in the workers' interests that a long—term, general construction stop for nuclear power plants is maintained. The DGB Executive therefore believes that construction permits for new nuclear power plants currently in the planning stage can be granted in justifiable cases. Energy as well as the employment needs and preservation of the technological capabilities of the nuclear industry must be taken into account (in: WSI Mitteilungen 3/1980:166).

Second, the DGB unions decided to mobilize for and themselves lead the mass rally. The presidents of each of the five energy unions spoke at the rally attended by 40,000 to 50,000 workers. Incentives granted by the employers like counting the day as a paid vacation, chartered buses and pocket money reportedly helped to achieve the high turnout. Riegert(p.161) wrote that the unions wanted to counter the danger "that the public is suddenly confronted with another large workers' organization besides the DGB unions in the energy sector which may offer a different organizational structure and policies".

A newspaper commented that the union leadership was afraid that the rally might turn into an "anti-union event" and therefore decided to conduct the mass rally itself. By "channelizing" the rally, they hoped to save "environmental and other balanced arguments used in the energy and growth debate" from disappearing entirely (FR, 11.11.77:2; in Klaus,Stiller:50). The CDU, usually at odds with the DGB, here even expressed its agreement with the DGB and the works councils (SZ, 12.11.77:2).

Clearly, the works councils of the utility and nuclear industry had become a factor that indeed threatened the established union structure and positions. The IGM appeared to take the threat particularly seriously. In the opening speech to a conference titled 'Energy Politics and Labor Unions', IGM president Loderer stressed:

> In the face of growing political and social tensions, there must be no common front of works councils and management in metal industries, and particularly the energy industry. In the energy sector ... but also elsewhere, works councils and the union must stand shoulder to shoulder. That will only be possible, brothers, if we discuss the disagreements among us frankly but also stand united to the results of our internal discussions. (IGM, 9.2.78:5)

Subsequently, a discussion circle for IGM works council members and Vertrauensleute from the nuclear industry was established (IGM Metallpressedienst, 17.10.79).

5.2.3.4. Energy Policy Making among the DGB Unions

The "energy unions", and among them the IGM, have had the largest influence on the energy policies adopted by the DGB. As mentioned in the last section, a draft of what became the first official DGB statement on energy on April 5, 1977, circulated among all unions while the final draft was written by the DGB and the "energy unions".

The position finally adopted was almost identical to the one the IGM had at that time. IGM president Loderer declared in late March that his union an the DGB took the same view on nuclear energy (Metall 7/77:3). He defined the IGM mandate for being engaged in nuclear energy in the same three ways as later stated by the DGB. The first DGB position also put forth the same conditions for continuing nuclear energy construction and production which the IGM had adopted. It is thus plausible to assume that the April 5 DGB position was indeed developed by the IGM. At a later occasion, Loderer (IGM, 9.2.78) in fact explained that the IGM was o.k. earlier than most other organizations concerned about nuclear energy and that following the adoption of the position of the IGM council, "I myself have worked extraordinarily hard on the DGB Executive Board to have the same position agreed to" (p.14). The DGB has relied on the "Arbeitsgemeinschaft Kerntechnik" (AKG) as an advisory board for nuclear energy matters. The AKG is administered and staffed by the IGM and OTV, and, ostensibly, is independent of the energy industry (Riegert, 1980:163). However, mostly union members employed in the nuclear industry are members in the AKG (interview Mr. Hecht, OTV, 10.7.81). Other permanent inter—union energy fora do not exist (ibid).

Formally, each individual union can adopt "sovereign" positions. Commonly, these positions are respected by the DGB or other unions even if they do not share these views. However, the printers union's resolution adopted at its 1980 convention calling for a nuclear power moratorium was harshly criticized by vice— president Karl—Heinz Hoffmann of the OTV (FR, 21.10.80:2). Opponents of nuclear energy within the labor union movement, subsequently, criticized "this in the history of West—German labor unions unprecedented event". Large unions ought "not to put a muzzle on small unions" if their internal discussions lead to anti—nuclear positions (AKL Info, No.19, Jan.1981:3).

5.2.4 Will Formation and Decision Making on Energy in West German Unions, and the LER

The "restrictive mechanisms" (so plausibly summarized by Bergmann), to which union will formation is subjected to have obviously applied to the energy debate within the unions. Controversies have existed and have been expressed on the convention floors and in the union press but the decisions have been leadership controlled. The debate in the press was particularly vivid in the IGM and OTV during the first months of 1977, and particularly one—sided in the IGBE. By letter counts, the union membership did not approve of union energy policies. At the conventions, the "Kongressregie" by the leadership was also effective. The leadership has particularly relied on its prerogatives to chair the convention and to influence the composition of the resolution committees. The influence of works councils to select delegates has probably also been a factor to explain the convention positions but was not examined here. But the works councils in the energy industry have definitely been a major influence in support of the pro— nuclear positions taken by the DGB and the major unions. They have exerted their influence in part directly through mass activities, but also because they have much weight within the IGM. Among the DGB unions, the "energy unions" —and primarily the IGM— have decisively influenced the DGB energy position and have also criticized at least one union for adopting anti—nuclear positions.

The implications of the internal will formation and decision making processes of German labor on the LER are possibly vast. First, they support contentions that positions might have become official union policy even though a substantial minority (and perhaps even a majority) of the union membership has not agreed on these positions. Second, declarations of intent such as stated in the 1974 DGB Environmental Program (see Section 3.2.1) might have been put into effect if membership pressure could have been exerted. Thus, the perceptions and the political behavior might have been more congenial to labor—environmentalist cooperation if the "minority views" within individual unions and of individual unions and the DGB could have come to bear. In that case, of course, the built—in dichotomy explanation further loses plausibility. However, in the absence of more extensive membership opinion data than those presented in Chapter 4, the precise impact of the restrictive mechanisms on the LER is difficult to assess.

What was the membership response to the shortcomings of union democracy? Of the three principal options of exit, voice and loyalty

(Hirschmann, 1970), the first has apparently not been chosen by many. As noted, the unions in the FRG have gained members throughout the 1970s. Therefore, it would be plausible to conclude that either union democracy can not be all that bad or that the membership does not care much about it. Opinion surveys, indeed, have shown that unions as such are highly valued by the general public and, even more so, by their membership. Thus, a base of loyalty certainly exists. But studies have also shown that loyalty based on a "proletarian" consciousness previously common among workers has become replaced by more "voice" that was expressed by growing membership figures, readiness to go on strike and more activities and debate within the unions (Herkommer, 11'79:717).

More "voice" also surfaced with respect to energy and environmental issues before the unions shifted emphasis toward increasingly environmentally compatible positions. Chapter 4 made evident that labor union members adopted views increasingly at odds with official union positions. Also, labor unionists reportedly belonged to the most active members in the environmental and other citizen groups. Furthermore, activist union members joined to opposition caucuses in numerous companies running against the official union candidates in works council elections (and, subsequently, were often expelled from the unions). Indeed, labor union members in opposition to official union policies on energy, the environment or housing issues formed a network of at one time more than forty local groups throughout the FRG. Thus, the restrictive mechanisms aided to increase conflicts within labor and to the opening of new channels beyond leadership control. On the other hand, organizational cost could have been even greater if, for example, the energy industry works councils had actually broken with the DGB unions in late 1977. Without speculating on that trade-off any further, the important consequence to note for the LER is that shortcomings of union democracy hindered official labor-environmentalists cooperation but fostered inofficial ties involving activist parts of labor.

On a more abstract level, the role of the works councils and the dominating influence of a few large unions on decisions ostensibly reflecting the interests of the whole labor movement both point to the importance of institutional and ideological factors on labor's positions, its politics and the LER. The institution of works councils (being formally external to the unions but at the same time a pillar within the unions) is a product of the West German political system in general and of its labor- management relations in particular. Another German characteristic is the "Einheitsgewerkschaft" concept which enhances labor's image of unity. Both issues will be taken up in the next two chapters.

5.3 Internal Union Politics in the US

The previous discussion of the internal structures and processes of the West German unions has focused on constraints on will formation and effective sharing in decision making of the membership. It has not asked the question of what makes a union a democratic one. In the German case, this question was not so pertinent since the undemocratic features appeared to be rooted in the basic system of interest intermediation (with the Einheitsgewerkschaft concept and the principle of social partnership as important determinants). In the US, on the other hand, the union movement is less homogeneous and the corporatist integration less pronounced. The labor movement is far more diversified not only by sheer number but also by age, heritage, jurisdictions, ideology, and —of course— with respect to the LER. Thus, the freedom of action of each individual union in the US in principle seems considerably greater than in the FRG.

A look at US union democracy, therefore, as a possible distinguishing feature for inter-union differences is warranted. Are those unions that have cooperated with environmental groups more democratic than those that have not? To start out with, one needs to clarify what constitutes a democratic union. This question has no easy answer. For H.W.Benson (1979:1), the requirements of a healthy union democracy must resemble the standards of democracy written into the US constitution like free speech, free press, free assembly, the right to elect or change officers through the peaceful process of fair elections, or fair trials before impartial tribunals. Edgar James (1978:250) came across three distinct theories of what is the central institutional purpose of unions. The first theory emphasizes bargaining militancy, the second responsible behavior compatible with the prevailing economic order, and the third responsiveness to membership desires and interests. James decided "that any theory of union governance attentive to the general goals and purposes of unions should allow for the possibility of viable non-elite challenges to leadership" (p.249). Similarly, John Edelmann (1974:175) noted the importance of adequate mechanisms for giving effective recognition to the views of the opposition.

In a review of the literature on union democracy, Alice Cook (1963:28) reported the findings of several researchers that union democracy may be more the product of a union's goals and the breadth of controls it can exercise from within than of its internal mechanisms. Membership control and union ideology seem related and, significantly, the business union (c.f. Chapter 7) tends to succumb to bureaucracy. "Union democracy may thrive best when oriented toward broad issues and attempts to contribute to the community and not just to collective bargaining" (Tannenbaum and Kahn, 1958:237, in:Cook:28). Cook(p.219) came to distinguish three alternative standards to apply in making a judgment about union democracy:

> The first would set aside any possibility that the internal government and administration of a union can be democratic and would content itself with measuring union democracy in terms of its contribution to general industrial and social democracy. The second would look upon the union as a public government in miniature, asking that it separate and check and balance governmental powers, operate with a two- or multi-party system, enunciate and defend the rights of individuals and minorities, and create an independent judiciary, even, if necessary, going outside its own ranks to fill its judicial bench. The third, while accepting the union as a political and governmental institution, would emphasize its limited goals and special problems. Hence the applicable standards of democratic practice would vary somewhat from those of public government, providing, for example, representation of special interests short of erecting a full-fledged party system, and including an evaluation of the democratic essentials in leadership, bureaucracy, administration, membership participation, and communications.

5.3.1 A Model of Union Democracy

After a detailed empirical study, Cook concluded that the third alternative was most preferable. Her "model democracy" is based on the principles of separation of power and membership rights, and includes the following features:

First, the leadership or executive has the major responsibility for proposing policy as well as exercising it. "The democratic requirement is that they submit their proposals for full and free debate, acceptance, rejection or amendment by the legislative branch" (p.222). A cabinet (e.g. executive board) aiding and controlling the officers must provide a clear separation of functions between the two branches. The cabinet should include rank and file members. The distribution of power among the officers at the various union levels should be well defined and sufficient autonomy for subordinate bodies must exist. While various checks and balances are needed, the union government's superiority over the collective bargaining apparatus must be clear. A strong leadership must not be equated with an undemocratic one.

Second, the legislature must have the power to draw up its own agenda. In order to work effectively, the legislature should have its own executive board (that is distinct from the cabinet) and a rationally elaborated committee structure. While the executive has the main policy initiation responsibilty, the legislature must equally have the possibility of initiating policy. Hearings should be instituted as a legitimate way to express opinion, even critical opinion. Channels for initiating proposals by individuals and groups must exist. If the convention is to control the executive branch, it must have access to full information, e.g. through permanent legislative committees with hearing powers, including the power to hear officers. The legislative branch must have authority over officers conducting collective bargaining. The constituents must have fair and easy access to the convention delegates.

Third, judicial independence must exist both at the local level where most disputes or charges originate, and for the bodies to which appeals can be made. The creation of either public review boards of outsiders or of a board of distinguished unionists comparable to union trustees seems feasible.

Fourth, procedural requirements to assure fair elections such as secret ballots, voting machines, independent election committees or outside supervision, and free access to the ballot box by all members must be guaranteed and are partly required by law. However, the significance of elections goes far beyond procedures. They must offer members the opportunity to approve or disapprove the results achieved by the officers in the expiring term. "The problem is how to provide not just choice but genuine alternatives ... in each election and for all officers" (p.232). Opportunities for nomination and free flow of information independent of the incumbents' influence must exist. A multitude of subsidiary organizations can provide opportunities for non-incumbents to gain political experience and show their competence.

Fifth, the assignment of some measurable degree of self-government to the intermediate union bodies "is intimately related to union democracy" (p.235). These bodies must be seen as the "training grounds for men and ideas". Absolute autonomy is not desirable since the union locals would break-off as independent units. But the locals should have a wide range of rights and responsibilities.

> The initial power to discipline members; to decide within limits on such matters as dues rates, participation in benefit programs, political activities, and public demonstrations; the nomination and election of delegates, business agents, and representatives to local-wide committees; the organization and administration of education programs —all these powers and undertakings provide the subordinate body with a reason for being, an opportunity to achieve identity and a sense of having some responsibility for its own destiny.
> (Cook:234)

Sixth, the members must have the rights of open admission to the union, of free speech and free assembly within the union, and opportunities for participation in union activities. The issue of free speech and free assembly is not so much the ability to tolerate individual dissidents but is rather called when it involves the activities of independent factions within unions. The answer is not necessarily the institution of party systems but the full political development of the existing intermediate bodies. Unions which have a variety of activity programs, even if they are non-political in nature, afford their members the opportunity of getting training in political skills —speaking, administration, building an organization, making up an agenda, chairing meetings, making reports or joining with others in making decisions. Having or not having these skills makes the difference between membership ability to exercise effective political controls over their organization and leaders, or merely registering "yes" or "no" votes on their proposal and performance. Approaches to fulfillment of democratic goals, Cook(:239) concluded, must begin with a strengthened legislature, other elements will then follow.

5.3.2 Democratic Features in Environmentally Relevant Unions

It would exceed the focus of this work to apply the features of Cook's model of union democracy diligently to the unions examined here and then rank them according to how democratic they are. Rather, Cook's model will serve as a general guide in the following discussion of union democracy of the environmentally relevant unions in the US. For the UAW, USWA, IAM, OCAW, AFSCME and IUOE, I will examine to what extent the six features of union democracy have been realized.

For Edelman, the UAW "is probably the most democratic of the major unions" (p.179). While Edelman arrived at this opinion after a long and active life in the labor movement, Jack Stieber (1962:167) came to the conclusion that the UAW "must be considered a democratic union" following a detailed analysis of the union's inner life. The most serious shortcoming, according to Stieber, was the lack of an institutionalized opposition which the UAW shares with all other unions but one. All International officers and members at large of the International Executive Board (IEB) are elected by a roll—call vote on one slate. The president presides at conventions and IEB meetings, thus an effective separation between executive and legislative functions does not exist. The IEB is the highest authority between conventions. The president appoints and removes all International representatives, hires staff, convenes the IEB but must also report to the IEB. The IEB may reverse any action of International officers, has the power to authorize strikes, issue charters, punish subordinate bodies, establish administratorships over locals, and it is the appeal board. The IEB has put administratorships on locals a few times but interference by the International has been rare. Officers and delegates are elected by secret ballot according to detailed election procedures. While the Reuther elections since 1949 have not been contested, vice—presidents and regional directors faced frequent opposition, and only a small number of convention delegates is elected without opposition. Members to convention committees are appointed by the IEB from accredited delegates. Officers and staff can not be members unless they are truly accredited delegates. Discussions on the convention floor are extensive and opposition views are being expressed. However, procedural requirements have made it difficult for opposition views to become policy. Roberts' rules of order apply, including the ban on amendments and substitutions from the floor until a committee recommendation has been voted down. "Taken together with the absence of any voice by the convention in the selection of the convention members, this prohibition tends to make the delegates' function one of approving or disapproving administration policies, rather than determining policy ..." (Stieber, 1962:24). The union leadership has always tried to avoid time consuming roll—call votes on policy issues, and has at a few occasions rather withdrawn a proposal than risked a rollcall decision. Taken as a whole, Stieber concluded, the rules governing UAW conventions are certainly as democratic as those of most other unions.

A feature unique to the UAW and applauded by all observers of union democracy is the Public Review Board (PRB). It serves as an impartial highest court with jurisdiction over appeals, except for those relating to collective bargaining policy. Established under Reuther in the

1950s, and composed of respected persons from outside the labor movement and independent of the union power structure, the PRB can even overturn IEB decisions. The PRB has not weakened UAW leadership while it strengthened union democracy. Nevertheless, the PRB has not been emulated by any other major union (H.W. Benson, 1979:202).

Besides constitutional determinants, the variety of intermediate bodies operating on a broad range of issues, the weight given to community activities, and the large and qualified staff probably altogether helped to create the opportunities for junior members to develop the skills believed so essential for a democratic union according to Cook's sixth feature.

The USWA has a less democratic reputation than the UAW. The power of the executive is at least as vast as the UAW's with respect to the convention as well as to subordinate bodies. Unfair election practices were repeatedly alleged when strong opposition movements challenged the incumbent leadership. The following discussion of institutional features is drawn from Ulman (1962).

The powers of the International president include (1) the interpretation of the constitution, (2) directing the affairs of the union between sessions of the IEB, (3) authority to inspect any local or district, (4) the authority to appoint, direct, suspend, or remove organizers, representatives, agents and employees, (5) fixing their compensation, (6) the appointment of convention committees, and (7) being convention chairman. The first, second, and fifth of the powers listed are subject to IEB approval. The IEB consists of the International officers elected by referendum vote and the district directors who are elected by the district membership. Since the president can direct, appoint and pay all staff, he has considerable leverage over the district directors. The IEB can remove International officers and district directors after a trial. The IEB may have rollcall votes giving increased voting strength to the International officers. The International executive has also been the locus of power on economic matters. It, and not the local, is the contracting party in all collective bargaining agreements, and strikes must be authorized by the IEB. The International can suspend local charters, remove local officers and appoint administrators. The IEB is also an appeals board.

USWA conventions are held every two years. Staff members may be delegates if so designated (i.e. not necessarily elected) by the locals. The committees are appointed by the International president (who has usually placed one half of the committee assignments at the disposal of the district directors in order to yield a wide representation), and are routinely approved by the convention. The influence of the staff has been considerable. Headquarters staff is assigned to the committees two to three months prior to the convention. Staff specialists analyze and classify the resolutions submitted by the locals and then draft resolutions for the approval of the committee. At the same time, the staff has always constituted a sizeable bloc of convention delegates and has affected voting —and non—voting— decisively. On the floor, committee reports must be considered first and can not be amended before voting. The constitution allows rollcall votes but, as of 1962, none has ever been held. Thirty percent of the votes is required to demand a rollcall. Since many elected delegates carry several votes but the non—elected staff delegates usually only one, and since the 30% limit is determined by counting heads, not votes, the substantial staff presence (estimated in excess of 20%) can effectively prevent rollcalls from being held.

The referendum election of district directors and the International officers by the respective membership—at—large poses, in principle, the best opportunity to express discontent and, indeed, has been utilized in practice. In 1957, the first contested election for International president was won by the incumbent by a far narrower margin than expected. In 1959, the LRMDA required a local by local breakdown of votes of union elections and made it possible to get some idea of who voted for whom. Since then, not one incumbent Steelworker administration won a majority of the votes in basic steel. (H.W. Benson, 1979:228). Complaints about fraudulent elections on the district (particularly District 31, i.e. Chicago) and national levels have frequently been made. In the 1973 District 31 race, the insurgent Ed Sadlowski was first defeated by the "official family candidate" but in the rerun (after charges of fraud and a suit in federal court) under Department of Labor supervision, Sadlowski won by almost 2 to 1 (H.W. Benson:232; also James, 1978:344ff).

The IAM shares with most other unions the substantial powers vested in the executive which make effective membership participation in union policy formulation difficult. The following remarks are based on Perlman (1962).
The International Executive Council (IEC) members are elected by referendum vote on one slate. The IEC recommends the slate but the locals ultimately make the nominations. All officers may retire from age 60 on and must retire at age 65. The IEC and the convention have the same authority to initiate legislation. Somewhat unique, the referendum has been the major policy making instrument. Decisions made by the convention only become binding when affirmed by a referendum. The resolutions committee is appointed by the International president from among the elected delegates. Elected officers and representatives can be recalled through a referendum vote, and several attempts doing that have succeeded in the union's history. Yet, the referendum device is not necessarily a sign of democracy. It tended to favor the incumbents since they can afford to travel the country. More important, participation in the votes has been low, up to 1959 never exceeding a 50% turnout.
The International executive may revoke the charters of union locals if a trial has been held. In general, however, the International president has acted against locals only with great caution. The union has a complex network of due process and the standard trial procedures. If necessary, the International has been ready to intervene against subordinate bodies on behalf of individual members. The union has done political lobbying for years, has established state councils to influence state legislation, and has conducted grass-root campaigns earlier than most other unions.
Perlman concluded that altogether, the IAM should be rated as a democratic union. IAM president Albert Hayes was selected to head the AFL-CIO Ethical Practices Committee in 1956-57 presiding over the trials of the Teamsters and other unions. Galenson (in Perlman:v) took it as evidence for the IAM's "enviable record as one of the cleanest of the large American trade unions". However, Hayes has also been accused of having "used the authoritarian powers available under the union's pre-LRMDA constitution to expel reformers" and that he certainly "could not recognize legitimate democracy" (Benson, 1979:196).

There are very few unions that are as democratic in structure (if the term is defined as the existence of institutional means by which the members can achieve policy) as the OCAW, Rothbaum (1962:vii) argued. It is the only American union with a predominantly lay, i.e. non professional, executive board. The delegates to the conventions as well are usually non-professionals. International officers and staff members are prohibited from being convention delegates. The administration can not dominate the subject matter of the convention. The four most important committees have their membership selected by the district councils rather than by the executive as it is common in other unions. Nor have conventions been dominated through leadership control of debate but rather it allows free and fair discussion. "Unlike the disciplined conventions of many other unions in which the delegates must ratify the administrative program, the OCAW conventions range over many issues and the leadership program is often rejected or extensively modified" (p.51). Where democratization has not inhibited

129

administrative efficiency, it has as a whole gone unchallenged. The OCAW has created a system of democratic participation that goes far beyond the opportunity to remove the incumbent officeholders without fear of intimidation, retaliation, or corruption of the election process. The union has had probably more contested elections than the average union. The judicial procedures are in general good. Appeal procedures are freely available and utilized. Temporary administratorships over locals have been used sparingly (no more than ten cases between 1945 and 1960). Executive officers and IEB members can be recalled by referendum votes initiated by locals but no recall proceedings have been utilized between 1945 and 1960.

While AFSCME has the usual structural features granting the essential policy making powers to the executive, it has been uniquely threatened by secessions. Virtually everywhere in the US, an AFSCME member, group or local can drop out of the union, or effectively dissolve a local, in a single day. Since the union represents public employees, it does not fall under the various national labor laws which protect bargaining relationships for a limited period and which forbid groups or individuals to split-off from a bargaining unit. Thus, union democracy has been almost a condition sine qua non for union growth and progress (Kramer, 1962).

The power of the executive in the IUOE is more extensive than in the other unions discussed so far (Mangum, 1964). The relationship of the general executive board to the general president is, in practice, more analogous to that of a board of directors to a chairman who is at the same time chief executive officer. The executive board is not much able to control the president as mandated by the constitution. The board is advisory rather than directive.

The general convention and the entire membership acting through the referendum are the two legislative bodies of the union. Under the referendum system, the local unions have the power to initiate proposals affecting the constitution, policy and recalls of any general officer. However, relatively high limits are set until a local initiative can become effective. The convention is also strongly influenced by the executive. The basic work of the convention is performed by seven committees which are appointed by the general president. Until 1960, when the LRMDA applied for the first time, the constitution had been silent on the method of choosing the convention delegates. Some locals elected their delegates; in others, the business manager or the local executive board appointed them. But regardless

> of election or appointment, it is the business representative and local officer who have the interest and time to attend and are in position to get themselves elected. To be effective in log-rolling for desired convention action, a local delegation must go united under its business manager. The result is a convention strongly influenced by sophisticated full-time union leaders rather than first-convention rank-and-file members (Mangum:213).

Formally, the freedom of the delegates to discuss issues on the convention floor is restrained only by customary parliamentary procedures. Yet, on each individual issue, the majority of the delegates is likely uninterested or uninformed, and tends to accept the recommendations of the committees. "Through the committee process, most of the work of the convention has been accomplished before the first gavel sounds" (p.212).

While the instruments of revolt are always available to a well organized opposition, opposition candidates have rarely been nominated against an incumbent administration at a convention. The odds are on the side of perpetuation in office. General office vacancies occuring between the conventions (which are held every four years) are filled through appointment by the general executive board. "Since general officers are, in fact, ordinarily reelected term after term for life or until retirement, neither of which are likely to coincide with convention timing, the board is self—perpetuating for all practical purposes" (p.218).

The McClellan Senate Committee investigation led to devastating conclusions on union democracyy and integrity: "Democracy in this vital union is virtually nonexistent"; "trusteeships have been imposed —for no apparent reason— as a means of continuing domination over the affairs of a number of locals..."; "extensive collusion between union officials and management" were some of the conclusions of the committee (in Mangum:198). However, Mangum argued, most of the accusations were based on individual cases and should not be generalized. At times, the imposition of trusteeships on recalcitrant locals has been widespread but the need to resort to International supervision has decreased. IUOE locals have remained highly autonomous on many matters. The internal judicial procedure is typical of those of most unions. Appeals to the general executive board have offered effective protection against unjust local decisions. IUOE leadership has proven itself to be remarkably effective and, hence, has protected members' interests despite falling short on democracy. Mangum concludes that most International unions could not survive as mass democracies. In his view, the IUOE at the International level meets the test of a constitutional democracy, while no such blanket generalizations can be made for local union governments.

5.3.3 Union Democracy and the LER

There is no clear pattern relating union democracy and union proximity to environmentalism. For one thing, the discussion of IUOE internal procedures does not suffice to describe those unions that have tended to be in conflict with environmental groups. Unfortunately, an account of internal policy making of the IBEW and other building and construction unions has not been available to me. Nor did I analyze in detail environmental and energy policy making based on convention proceedings. But also, if one compares the IUOE with the other five unions presented, the differences of internal democracy are more of degree than of substance.

None of the unions examined can live up to Cook's model. In particular, the separation of power between the executive, legislative and judicial branches is inadequate. The union convention has the highest authority but the incumbent leadership can substantially influence the proceedings and policy decisions. Except for the International Typographical Union, no American union has an institutionalized two party system. As a rule, only a rudimentary independent judiciary exists. The major exception here is the United Auto Workers's Public Review Board. As noted, procedures to ensure fair elections are required by law but widespread fraud seems to have occurred especially in the USWA. The locals have considerable autonomy, definitely more than the local units in the German unions. Strong reform movements from within have surfaced, sometimes successfully, in the USWA and UMW. Only four unions with less than 700,000 members provided for the election of convention committee members, despite the important role occupied by committees at conventions (Stieber, 1962:21). Usually, the committees were appointed by the body with the function of a cabinet which makes it extremely difficult for the delegates to control the convention and, thus, official policies.

Based on the six unions just examined, the hypothesis that democratic unions were more pro— environmental than undemocratic ones can neither be confirmed, nor rejected. Given the constraints for a "model democracy", the reviews (which, it must be noted, were completed in the early 1960s) rated the UAW, IAM, OCAW and AFSCME as democratic. All these unions had good relations with environmentalists. Interestingly, all these unions had consciously encouraged local and community activities which mark Cook's sixth feature of democracy and have been a forum of labor- environmentalist interaction. This feature, in fact, might be the major difference regarding union democracy between business and industrial unionism.

The USWA's democratic reputation has mostly suffered from election frauds which were perhaps a consequence of lacking democratic opportunities at the conventions. Conceivably, the large industrial unions adopted official positions on social, including environmental policies that were more liberal than those of the membership at large. On the other hand, it was the same USWA region (District 31 – Chicago) that both challenged the incumbent national leadership and filed a suit against a nuclear plant. Moreover, a "dissident" union local protested the environmental stretch—out bill supported by the International union.

The IUOE received a bad mark by the McClellan hearings in the late 1950s although, according to Mangum, unjustly so in regard to union democracy at the International level. Local practices, of course, are determined by the smaller scale and greater mobility of the building industry. This is different in industries operating at a larger scale. The business manager of building Locals has to seek local jobs for the members which increases the likelihood that above all parochial interests are advanced and that currruption may occur. In business unions, Cook's local democratic "training ground" may especially be absent. Regarding energy policies, it will be interesting to see to what extent the postulated shift to a greater demand orientation (see Section 3.1.5.2) will foster ties between environmentalists and building unions on the local level.

6 Explanation 4: The Political Frameworks and the LER

Political and institutional factors have likely affected the LER in the two countries: Both movements have been important political actors; the issues they are concerned with involve crucial national decisions; their constituencies —and those they perhaps antagonize— are large or vocal or both; the tactics they employ are conceivably influenced by the national political frameworks, etc. Furthermore, differences in political influence of the movements in both countries can be expected to be a consequence of the structural differences between the two political systems. The differences of influence, in turn, possibly are a central explanation for the LER.

This chapter and the next will discuss the following propositions:

1. In the FRG, labor has been more integrated in the political system than the environmental movement. The stronger integration has contributed to the fact that labor has become a factor of order with respect to environmental and energy policies. Environmentalism, on the other hand, has been a countervailing power. The labor—environmentalist conflicts in the FRG, in part, have been a conflict between a factor of order and a countervailing power.

2. Labor in the US has been less integrated in the political system and environmentalism more so than in Germany. Therefore, the LER in the US was less determined by factor of order/ countervailing power discrepancies and, as a whole, was more cooperative.

3. Political/institutional and ideological factors account also for the that the labor movement in the US was less homogeneous than in the FRG. The considerable diversity within US labor allowed for cooperation especially with large industrial, public employees' and service unions although profound conflicts existed

133

with building and construction unions. In the FRG, the relative homogeneity of labor has discouraged cooperation with environmentalism.

4. While parts of labor have been a factor of order with respect to environmental and energy politics in both countries, the reasons differed in the two countries. In the FRG, mostly political or institutional reasons accounted for labor's factor of order role while ideological reasons were crucial in the US.

The key terms used in this chapter and the next such as "integration into the political system", "factor of order" and "countervailing power" warrant some elaboration. They must be viewed both from the vantage points of labor or environmentalists, on the one hand, and with the eyes of an outside observer on the other. In the former case, we are interested in how the movements themselves have seen their role in the political system, i.e. their traditions and ideologies. Chapter 7 will discuss the influence of ideological factors on the LER. In the latter case taken up in this chapter, the issue is political. Characteristic features of the political structure and of institutions must be examined: How could the labor and environmental movements, respectively, influence national policy making on the issues in question? How much access did each movement have to government agencies, the legislature, the courts and the political parties? Were there substantial differences in terms of access opportunities and political affiliations between the US and the FRG, on the one hand, and between labor and environmentalism on the other? More generally, were there major differences of the state– economy relationships in the two countries? Underlying all these issues, of course, is the question how these possible differences translated into the alleged factor of order/ countervailing power cleavages and thus the LER.

The labels "factor of order" and "countervailing power" have been particularly salient for the German situation. While there is agreement that environmentalism in the FRG essentially has been a countervailing power, both labels have been attached to labor's political role. Since the factor of order– countervailing power distinction is possibly a central explanation for the LER, I will briefly elaborate where on that continuum German labor has been placed. According to Grebing (7'1973:393f), conservative critics saw labor as a countervailing power while liberals criticized it as a factor of order. In the conservative view, the unions aim at ruling the state via eradicating private business by a planned economy; they bear the danger of a syndicalist and collectivist economy and society; at the least, their strive for power disturbs –if not destroys– the pluralistic balance in society and the state. Liberal labor union critics, on the other hand, argue that the unions have turned into an instrument to incorporate the workers into the status quo of the given political and economic power structure; they are acquiring the status of a quasi–public institution fulfilling public functions. From this perspective, the unions have become a "blind power", "guardians of the existing", a system–immanent factor of order that distributes system–stabilizing gratifications to its members and that disciplines them to keep capitalism functioning; they have fallen from the heights of a proletarian organization, oriented toward achieving mankind's emancipation by class struggle, to become a service enterprise, to a sales agency of human labor, to an insurance company specialized in insurance against the risks of strikes and lock–outs.

Grebing herself took a medium position asserting labor to be both. Its role is essentially determined by the "existential conditions" within which they operate: Labor unions have been formed and have operated as the representatives of the immediate interests of those who have to sell their labor in order to make a living. They are "immanent to capitalism and, therefore, do not call into question the existence of the capitalist economy and society which is based on division of labor and privately— owned means of production"(p.395). This fact draws them toward the factor of order end of the spectrum. On the other hand, organized labor continuously controls the state to work for social justice ("Sozialstaat") and to assure democratic public will formation ("Rechtsstaat"). In that regard, it acts as a countervailing power.

In a first part, this chapter will examine the basic nature of the state— economy relationship in the two countries and the role organized labor was able to play in it. Subsequently, I will turn to the different access opportunities available to labor and environmentalism by the Presidential system in the US and the West German Parliamentary system. In particular, I will discuss the different opportunities to affect decision making in the national legislatures and to participate in electoral politics. In the third section, I will discuss the consequences of the political and institutional factors for labor and environmentalism in energy politics.

6.1 Political Integration of Labor in the FRG and the US

While both German and American politicians like to label the mode of interest intermediation in their polity as "pluralistic", political scientists in both countries asserted that "corporatism" might be a more apt description (Lowi, 1969; Schmitter, 1974 and 1977; Alemann, 9'1979; Berger, 1981). This distinction seems also relevant for the LER. In a pluralist system, the state and the various organized interests act fairly independently from each other; in a corporatist system, the constituent units are

> recognized or licensed (if not created) by the state and granted a deliberate representational monopoly within their respective categories in exchange for observing certain controls on their selection of leaders and articulation of demands and supports. (Schmitter, 1977)

According to Schmitter (1974:107), corporatist forms of interest intermediation are gradually displacing pluralist ones. This displacement as it affects the LER, my argument goes, has progressed further in the FRG than in the US. The US has remained more pluralistic than the FRG or, in other words, the degree of interlock between the state and organized interests is higher in the FRG than in the US.

The way industrial relations manifest themselves is a crucial characteristic of a system of interest intermediation. In order to focus the notion of "corporatism" on the system of industrial relations and subsequently distinguish the role of American labor from that of German labor, let me present Alemann's (9'1979) conditions for the existence of what he called "societal corporatism":

> (1) the increasing concentration of the economy has the result that individual economic decisions have direct effects on the whole society

> (2) consequently the labor unions are forced to extend the degree of national and international organization and interest articulation

> (3) the state intervenes deliberately and actively into the "private" economy using global steering mechanisms, directed investment incentives, and subsidies

> (4) the state and the organized interests of capital and labor cooperate in these economic policies

135

(5) particularly as a result of social–democratic or socialist party governments, large reform–oriented labor union organizations are included in the cooperation

(6) formal and informal channels are created allowing for the incorporation of the main economic actors (wage–price–commissions, concerted action, social contract)   (p.561)

For Alemann, most of these conditions are met in the FRG and other West European states. In my view, they are met more fully in the FRG than in the US. State interventions in the economy in both countries have constantly risen but were higher in the FRG —as the growth of government consumption and welfare benefits as a fraction of GNP for example indicates (FRG in 1965: 28%, 1978: 36%;US 1965: 22%; 1978: 29%). At the same time, the instruments of governmental economic steering have multiplied, become refined and were conscientiously applied. Baring (1982:136), for example, reported that since the late 1960s, the federal government basked in the belief that the FRG was "second to none" in having put John Maynard Keynes into effect. Quite contrary sentiments have permeated the American political culture. Andrew Shonfield (1965) argued that

> Among the Americans there is a general sentiment, shared by both political parties, of the natural predominance of private enterprise in the economic sphere and of the subordinate role of public initiative in any situation other than a manifest national emergency. The West Europeans, who have no such assumption ... have in consequence been spared the awful doctrinal wrestling, in which Americans tend to engage whenever any bit of the economic field has to be divided afresh between the public and private sector. (cited by I.C.Bupp, 1977)

The German unions have been among the staunchest supporters of state intervention in the economy and have been represented in numerous public and private bodies. The "representational monopoly" postulated by Schmitter perhaps is most apparent in the fact that the German Constitution guarantees labor unions the right to (autonomous) collective bargaining ("Tarifautonomie"). In return —Schmitter's next condition seems also true— the unions implicitly observed controls over their articulation of demands. The German unions were repeatedly applauded for the "Augenmass", the restraint, they showed in their wage demands. In addition, the labor movement itself owns and controls large enterprises in the banking, housing, and insurance sectors. American labor, in general, both has had less political clout than the German unions and also has been more reserved toward state intervention. In part, this can be attributed to the business union tradition discussed in Chapter 7, in part to the different American political culture and heritage.

The different conditions in the two countries are particularly pronounced regarding the rights labor possesses to affect pertinent decisions in government and industry. Summers (1979:258) distinguished four political levels at which workers and unions may have opportunities to affect political decisions: at the governmental level through the political process or membership in government bodies, at the industry level through collective bargaining, at the enterprise level through membership on supervisory or governing boards, and at the plant or shop level through works councils or union representatives.

At the governmental level in both countries, workers have opportunities to participate in the political process directly and through their unions. But the differences between the two countries are large. For about ten years and until its withdrawal (in protest against employers' actions against co–determination), the DGB had been a party (together with business and government) in the "Konzertierte

Aktion". Conceived of by the first Social-Democratic Minister of Economics, Karl Schiller, this was a top level forum concerned with national wage policy and policies relating to employment, economic growth, social insurance and social expenditures. No equivalent forum has existed in the United States. Only in a few industrial states, says Summers, "do American unions have the political effectiveness approximating that of German unions, and in many states they have almost no political weight at all". Moreover, the German unions have nomination and representation rights on many public bodies. To name just some of the politically and economically relevant bodies, the unions possess the right to nominate candidates for the boards of the federal employment agency (Bundesanstalt fur Arbeit); for judges in the labor courts and social courts (Sozialrichter); for members of the administrative councils of the federal postal service and the federal railroad; the right to send representatives to most of the councils governing the radio and television stations (Rundfunk und Fernsehrate); and to send representatives to the governing boards of public health insurance and old age insurance plans (Giessen, 1976:21ff). In the United States, union representatives sit only on few boards and commissions of consequence; and most of the advisory councils on which they sit "serve little more than perfunctory purposes" (Summers:258).

At the enterprise level, "the contrast between the two countries is even more complete and its implications more significant" (Summers:258). In the FRG, labor is involved in the management of the enterprise through representatives on the supervisory board (Aufsichtsrat). Under the Co-determination Acts and the Works Constitution Act, workers and unions have a voice in naming the managing directors, deciding on dividends, and affecting company policies including investment decisions (Summers:258; Der Gewerkschafter 4/81:34f). Workers representatives (in part employees of the enterprise and in part union representatives) have ordinarily almost parity with the shareholders on the board. However, certain rules give the shareholders a majority in case of tie votes. Actual parity exists for enterprises with more than 1000 workers in the mining, iron and steel industries ("Montanmitbestimmung"). Expanding co-determination rights or, as with the Montanmitbestimmung, defending it against a gradual erosion, (e.g. FR 30.7.80:4, 9.8.80:5) has been a major policy goal of German labor since its existence. In the US, there has been no worker participation at this level and, indeed, the unions have tended to reject such a role. Only recently have several unions obtained co-determination rights in exchange for significant wage concessions (Kuttner, 1984).

Workers participation at the industry and shop level combined in the FRG corresponds roughly to the opportunities offered by the system of collective bargaining in the US. However, the levels at which negotiations are conducted are significantly different. In the FRG, usually industry-wide agreements between unions and employers associations are reached. In the US, collective agreements are typically negotiated between a union and a single employer.

Another difference testifying to the stronger political integration and influence of German labor is the fact that unionization and collective bargaining rights in the FRG are guaranteed by the Constitution. This has helped to consolidate union strength while organizing in the US has become an uphill battle. In the US, the labor law dating back to the 1930s (the Wagner Act) has been frequently amended in Congress and many of its provisions circumvented by management. After the Labor Reform Act sought by the unions was defeated by a filibuster in 1978, the Wagner Act had to be considered "a dead letter" (Kuttner, 1984:20). Non-union companies had developed sophisticated, often illegal tactics designed to prevent unionizing in their facilities. Anti-labor consulting firms proliferated. "Illegal union-busting is risk-free", Kuttner observed, "since there are no real penalties for breaking the law" (ibid.). It has increasingly become the norm that an organizing drive is broken by firing pro-union workers. According to one estimate, about one worker out of twenty who signs a union card in an organizing drive is fired —enough to send a definite signal to other workers on the verge of joining the union. Moreover, unions must first circulate cards, then win an election, and then negotiate a first contract. These delays allow management to interfere —often illegally, albeit effectively. As Kuttner points out, even when a majority of workers have signed cards, in only one of three cases will the union eventually win a contract (ibid.).

Thus, at two of the four levels discussed, the political influence and the degree of integration of German labor was clearly considerably greater than of its American counterpart. At the other two levels, although differently implemented, German labor had no less influence than the American unions. German labor's influence has certainly been used —in Grebing's terms— to defend and expand social justice and democratic rights. But the other characteristic of German labor is that it acted as a 'factor of order' with respect to issues like energy or environmental protection. The effects of this factor of order role will be described in the third section of this chapter.

6.2 Electoral and Party Politics

The presidential political system in the US has for a variety of reasons been more open to the influence of interest groups than the parliamentary system in the Federal Republic. The differences in the two systems in part explain why environmentalism gained access to the US Congress but only very late to the German Bundestag, and thus developed substantially differently. Moreover, they contributed to the fact that German labor is more powerful than American labor.

In the parliamentary system of the FRG, and contrary to the American system, the government is responsible to the legislature and can even be recalled if only a parliamentary majority can be found. This difference is of crucial consequence for interest politics in the two countries. The federal government in the FRG can stay in office only as long as it is supported by a parliamentary majority. If the majority is lost, the government is replaced by another one. "The stabilty and cohesion of a parliamentary majority are thus identical with the stability, acting capacity and resistance to crisis within the governmental system " (Steffani, 1969:294). The system can work only if the parties employ discipline. The most important decisions in the Bundestag, therefore, are pre—determined by the party caucuses, the leadership of the coalition parties and the parliamentary committees. On the floor, the results of the committee and caucus work are usually accepted by almost unanimous votes of the parties in power.

In a presidential system, the executive ordinarily cannot be recalled by the legislature. The government, therefore, depends less on party discipline. In the US the written constitution is older than the modern parties, and, indeed, the founding fathers did not think highly of parties. Unlike in the FRG, the political parties do not even have a Constitutional mandate. Tenure of office and stability of the executive are not dependent on stable parliamentary majorities. Voting along party lines is much less pronounced in Congress than in the Bundestag. The individual member of Congress is far less dependent on support from his party than his Bundestag colleague with respect to both his voting record and his reelection.

6.2.1 Access to Congress and the Bundestag

The differences of the two systems have important ramifications for interest group politics, and thus for the LER.

Pressure groups try to further their interests at all levels of decision making by influencing public opinion, and by influencing

138

other interest groups, parties, single members of parliament, administration and government. This is their legitimate claim in the US as well as in Germany and other countries. But while pressure groups in the US try to influence less the parties, as such, and instead work more on single members, this approach appears to be far less successful in Germany since every member is subjected to party discipline. Party discipline protects the single member in case of overwhelming pressure by interest groups. This leads pressure groups to try to bring their representatives as salesmen and sources of information into the parties themselves. The result is that many members of the Bundestag are at the very same time members of pressure groups. They certainly are in final analysis subject to discipline but they also try to take care of the fact that an inner—party consensus will not be reached too easily at their expense. (Steffani, 1969:304f)

How do the access opportunities for labor and environmentalists to the German Bundestag and US Congress compare? In the FRG, labor's access to the legislature and the political parties was far better than that of environmentalism. The German unions have been well represented on the political scene, particularly since the SPD has become the major governmental party. To give an illustration, in the 1969–1972 Bundestag, 218 of 518 Bundestag members were also members of one of the DGB unions (an additional 68 members belonged to other union—like organizations outside the DGB). Of the 218 Bundestag union members, 198 alone were SPD representatives. Most of the Bundestag unionists were organized in the OTV (86), in the IGM (31), or in the GEW (21) (Marchal, 1972:90). In 1979, more than 90% of the full time union officials were members of the SPD (Der Gewerkschafter 7/79: last page). All heads of the DGB unions are SPD members or officials. Further, several former union leaders joined the cabinet of the federal government. Vice—versa, high—ranking SPD party officials have also assumed union leadership positions. In an elite—survey, 83.5% of the 87 union leaders questioned named the SPD as the party they preferred most (Hoffmann— Lange, 1982). All full—time members of the executives (hauptberufliche geschaftsfuhrende Vorstandsmitglieder) of the IGBE, IGM and HBV have been members of political parties (Schmollinger, 1977:144). In sum, in terms of interlocks of personnel, German labor's presence as a pressure group as suggested by Steffani was certainly assured —especially under a SPD—led government.

Labor's close political contacts had come under criticism from its own ranks but reportedly were "vehemently justified" at the latest DGB convention by IGM President Loderer. Neither in other European countries nor in the US or Japan, he argued, do there exist as many contacts between the government and the DGB unions as in the FRG. Indeed, he thought it necessary to stress that "we are into politics in order to represent, and not to betray, the interests of the membership" (SZ, 19.5.1982:2). The fact that this issue has arisen at all in the convention debate shows that the purpose of labor's political activities have become controversial within its own ranks.

Up to the formation of "green" electoral lists in the late 1970s, environmentalism did not have a party base even remotely comparable to the role the SPD played for German organized labor. Indeed, had environmental interests been effectively represented by a political party, environmentalism would unlikely have developed as a citizen—group—based, extra— parliamentary movement and probably would have been less politically salient. There were certainly members of the Bundestag, who were also active in an environmental organization and raised environmental issues on the Bundestag floor, but as a whole the Bundestag and the parties were felt to be unresponsive to environmental pressures. Typically of many similar statements, the Council of Environmental Experts noted that with respect to the natural environment, the political parties "have created the impression of shying away from fundamental discussions while broad segments of the

139

population feel visibly insecure and active minorities have begun to debate new perspectives and changes of value" (Umweltgutachten 1978:464). While many "environmental" laws have been passed, environmental groups usually have criticized them for lacking teeth. Many environmentalists, in fact, did not believe that those laws were primarily meant to correct environmental deficiencies but saw them first of all as attempts to appease the strong environmental protection sentiments.

Particularly in energy policy–making, the active environmentalists faced what they saw as a "great coalition" of all three parliamentary parties in the federal and state governments, i.e. regarding energy demand projections, power plant siting policies, nuclear energy policies, energy research and development, etc. Within the SPD (in particular), a strong environmental faction formed but was never strong enough to force through policies that were opposed by the Schmidt government wing. Thus, environmentalism as a forceful interest group was not only non–existent in the Bundestag but for many years deliberately refrained from relying on parliamentary lobbying as a major course of action.

Unlike in the FRG, lobbying in Congress has been an important activity of both labor and environmentalism in the US, since the individual Congressman is far freer to decide on how to vote than his German counterpart and is thus a more meaningful target for interest groups. It is therefore not surprising that environmentalism in the US has formed large national, Washington–based organizations. It is worth noting that exactly those labor and environmental groups that tended to cooperate most extensively with one another also emphasized political lobbying. The Sierra Club under David Brower's leadership in the 1960s changed from predominantly an outing club to an active political lobby. Indeed, the intensity of the Club's political activities cost it its tax–exempt status that in turn led to Brower's ouster from the Club and the Formation of Friends of the Earth by Brower. Further, the UEC was formed in 1970 with Congressional lobbying as an explicit central objective. The NWF, on the other hand, has done little Congressional lobbying and also had few contacts with labor.

On the part of labor, those unions that first embraced political lobbying have also tended to cooperate more with environmental organizations. The distinction follows roughly old AFL versus CIO lines. Examples of environmentally cooperative, former CIO unions are UAW, USWA, OCAW and UMW while IUOE, IBEW and other building and construction unions were affiliated with the old AFL. Special cases are the IAM and AFSCME. While both were formerly affiliated with the AFL, the IAM underwent a rapid transformation from a traditional craft to a modern industrial union and was one of the first major unions to take up political lobbying in the 1950s (Perlman, 1962). AFSCME as a public employees union by its nature was distinct from traditional craft unionism and was permanently engaged in political activities virtually from its very beginnings.

The ratings of Congressional voting by the AFL–CIO's COPE and the LCV representing environmentalist views introduced in Section 3.2 can be used as an indicator for the political clout of each movement in Congress and how much their interests overlap. Table 6–1 summarizes the voting records from 1971 to 1979 for the Senate and the House on which the ratings were based. In both houses, labor was more successful than the environmentalists winning about 60% of the votes compared to roughly 50% of LCV. But this figure also indicates that –unlike in the FRG– environmentalists must also be considered established in Congress. However, only a few votes have been considered by both groups which points to the two distinct foci of interest [1]. The voting records nevertheless show that the two movements have similar Congressional constituencies. In Section 3.2, positive correlations at the .7 levels were reported, i.e. the same Congressmen tended to vote with, or against, labor and

	sum 1971-79	71	72	73	74	75	76	77	78	79
Senate										
LCV: No.of votes considered	120	8	11	13	8	13	18	26	8	15
No.of votes "correct"	61	2	5	8	4	3	12	14	7	7
% of votes "correct"	51%	25%	45%	62%	50%	23%	67%	54%	87%	47%
COPE: No.of votes considered	144	12	1o	11	11	22	2o	2o	19	19
No.of votes "correct"	9o	5	5	8	9	14	11	15	9	14
% of votes "correct"	62%	42%	5o%	73%	82%	64%	55%	75%	47%	74%
COPE and LCV: No.of votes considered by both[3]	7	2	1				1	2		1
and evaluated equally	3	1[a]	1[b]					1[c]		
and voted "correctly"	2	0[a]	1[b]					1[c]		
votes considered by both but evaluated differently were won by		LCV[d]					COPE[e]	COPE[f]		COPE[g]
House										
LCV: No.of votes considered[2]	184	14	13	19	17	21	23	2o	3o	27[1]
No. of votes "correct"[2]	86	3	6	8	9	12	12	8	17	1o
% of votes "correct"	47%	22%	46%	42%	53%	57%	52%	4o%	58%	37%
COPE: No.of votes considered[2]	154	12	11	11	11	23	23	23	2o	2o
No.of votes "correct"[2]	91	7	6	6	7	17	17	2o	11	12
% of votes "correct"	59%	58%	55%	55%	63%	74%	74%	87%	55%	6o%
COPE and LCV: No. of votes considered by both[3]	12	1	2		2	1		1	1	4
and evaluated equally[2]	9		2[h]		1[i]	1[j]			1[b]	4[b]
and voted "correctly"[2]	3		1[b] 0[b]		0[i]	0[j]			1[b]	1[k] 0[k]
votes considered by both but evaluated differently were won by		LCV[d]			COPE[g]			COPE[l]		

[1] votes counted only once even if they were given double score by LCV
[2] votes falling short of a 2/3 majority are considered "incorrect" even if a simple majority was reached
[3] counted are only same votes, i.e. votes on the same bill but on different amendments are not counted

[a] Butz nomination [b] Occupational Safety and Health [c] strip mining [d] SST
[e] bottle bill [f] Clinch River breeder development [g] Dickey-Lincoln dam
[h] water pollution -curb of environmental blackmail [i] land-use planning
[j] strip-mining failure to override veto [k] windfall profits tax (2x); synfuel monopolies [l] 17 water projects

Table 6-1 : Senate and House Voting Records on which LCV and COPE Ratings were Based

environmentalists. As noted, all these findings are conservative regarding labor—environmentalist Congressional concordance since COPE's ratings did not include the views of environmentally cooperative unions such as UAW, AFSCME or IAM that rated Congressional performance on their own.

6.2.2 Electoral Politics

The differences between the US Presidential system and the German Parliamentary system are also manifest in electoral contests. In the FRG, the political parties nominate the candidates, finance and organize the campaign, draft the positions and slogans —in short, are the main carriers of the campaign. The voter decides how many seats each party will obtain but the party ultimately decides who will fill the seats. Further, federal law provides for re—embursements of electoral campaign expenses to the political parties corresponding to the share of votes received. In the US, the election is much more centered on the individual candidates. In order to win, first, the party nomination and, second, the election, the candidate has to appeal primarily to sponsors and the voter at large, and not to the party organs. The candidate —and not the party— organizes the campaign, designs the campaign strategy and has to seek financing. Unlike in the FRG, financing will have to come mostly from private sources. In sum, the American electoral system is considerably more open to influences from special interests and the public than is the German system.

This difference has affected the LER in the two countries in important ways. In the FRG, the interlocked relationship between labor and the SPD gives influence to the unions with respect to candidate selection and political positions. Environmentalists, on the other hand, have lacked a power base in a political party until recently and could not compete in elections with any reasonable chance of success. This was one reason why the German environmental movement became so decentralized and tended to embark in extra— parliamentary activities.

Since the late 1970s, however, German environmental groups began to participate in elections as well. Because that was not considered to be promising within existing parties, separate ecological electoral lists and parties began to form. German electoral law stipulates that a party has to win at least 5% of the votes cast in order to obtain parliamentary seats. This hurdle was first surpassed in a state election in 1979 and in many more state elections since. But it proved insuperable in several states, the 1980 federal election and the 1979 election to the European Parliament. On the federal level, the diverse ecological electoral lists have consolidated into the "Greens" that entered the Bundedtag in 1983. Thus, ecological parties now are a fact and must be expected to stay. However, they should not be mistaken as fully replacing the citizen groups. Rather, the Greens form an additional leg of the environmental movement while the citizen groups continue at the grass roots level —and, in fact, are encouraged to do just that by the Greens.

The ramifications of the new party for the LER are complex and, in part, speculative. In the short and medium term, they are likely to increase the labor—environmentalist conflict since they extend competition to the electoral level. Electoral analyses indicate that the Greens compete above all with the SPD for votes. In 1980, 36% of the Green voters had formerly voted for the SPD and another 36% were new voters that in the past had also tended to vote for the SPD. In 1984, 52% of the Green electorate had voted for the Greens before, 20% had been SPD voters and 13% were new voters (FAZ, 3.9.84:11). Given the narrow majorities in several states and the closeness of the FDP to the 5% limit, even a few percent of Green votes can make a difference. In the Berlin (1981) state elections, where the Greens received about 8% of the votes, their success has contributed to the downfall of the SPD/FDP coalition that was replaced by a CDU/FDP coalition government.

In Schleswig-Holstein in 1979, 4% ecological votes prevented a SPD/FDP government since the SPD and FDP would have surpassed the CDU without the candidacy of the Greens. In the elections in Hamburg and Hessia, the SPD and the Greens combined received a majority of the votes and entered into negotiations for the "toleration" of a SPD government [2]. In Hamburg, the talks were never concluded because the SPD won a land-slide victory in newly held elections (in the wake of the change of power in Bonn) that rendered support by the Greens obsolete. But the negotiations were successfully concluded in Hessia: a government was elected, one budget passed and another budget with succint green coloring agreed upon. However, the toleration was abrogated by the Greens after five months due to disagreements over the licensing of nuclear fuel-cycle fabrication facilities located in the state.

In addition to still considerable substantive differences, both sides in a conceivable SPD/Green partnership face severe conflicts from within. One major problem for the SPD is the heterogeneity of its electorate. On the one hand, there are substantial sympathies for the Greens. Prior to the 1983 federal elections, reportedly 46% of the SPD voters favored the Greens being elected into the Bundestag (Spiegel, No. 28 1982:22). Another –SPD sponsored– study showed that in 1984, 29% of SPD voters considered the Greens to be the party closest to the SPD (Perger, 1984). On the other hand, the CDU also has been attractive to great many SPD voters: "Being the better CDU offers the best chances to the SPD" (Perger): 43% of the SPD voters perceive the CDU as their second choice, 51% of the SPD voters consider the Greens as their last choice.

No wonder, in several elections since 1981, the SPD has not only lost votes to the Greens but also to the CDU. Especially workers who tended to be traditional SPD voters in the past switched to the CDU. In order to stem these losses, the party must decide whether it should try to integrate those voters tending to the Greens and thus risk even more losses to the CDU, or whether it should draw a clear line to the Green constituency and seek to hold on to the workers. This choice was summarized most succintly in the so-called "Lowenthal Thesen" on "The Identity and Future of the SPD" causing considerable political upheaval in the party (FR, 10.12.1981:1

The Greens are similarly split. Here, the cleavages are between the so-called "fundamentalists" and "realists". Should they remain a movement or become a party? Should they rely on fundamental opposition or participate constructively in the parliamentary system? While the vast majority of the Green electorate allegedly consists of realists, both paths entail difficult questions. More importantly, could aims considered extremely urgent (such as halting the dying of forests, halting the arms race, stopping nuclear energy production) be realized by stressing protest rather than by participating in the implementation of constructive solutions? If the fundamentalists path were chosen, votes were likely lost –even though many fundamentalists would not regret that. The realists face the question to what extent participation might lead to cooptation, compromises and, ultimately, the loss of the so-called "green identity". More specifically, they would have to develop a coherent program, accept the professionalization and institutionalization of the party structure, the evolution of "prominent" leadership, and the assumption of positions of power in government.

The response of the labor leadership to the seemingly irresistible Green growth has been mixed and slow. Crucial seems the perception of whether the realists or fundamentalists dominate the party organs. DGB-Chairman Breit was willing to meet with the Bundestag caucus but not with the party's executive board. The caucus, Breit argued, showed signs of economic and social concepts that allowed to attempt a meaningful dialog. The board, on the other hand, did not appear to be legitimized to speak in behalf of the membership on any issue of importance (SZ, 17.10.84:5). The IGM expressed some interest in cooperation with the Greens (FR, 17.11.84:4), while the IG Chemie

	1964	1966	1968	1970	1972	1974	1976	1978	1980	1982
Total	407	384	367	396	408	455	407	409	405	
Winners	276	199	207	241	244	321	290	270	241	
% Won	67.8%	51.8%	56.4%	60.9%	59.8%	70.5%	71.3%	66.0	59.5%	64.5%
House	354	333	323	336	362	389	365	344	361	
Winners	237	181	186	203	217	270	262	238	224	
% Won	66.9%	54.4%	57.6%	60.4%	59.9%	69.4%	71.8%	69.2	62.0%	
Senate	31	22	27	31	29	33	28	30	32	
Winners	25	9	15	19	16	25	19	12	11	
% Won	80.6%	40.9%	55.6%	61.3%	55.2%	75.8%	67.9%	40.0%	34.4%	
Governors	22	29	17	29	17	33	14	35	12	
Winners	14	9	6	19	11	26	9	20	6	
% Won	63.6%	31.0%	35.3%	65.5%	64.7%	78.8%	64.3%	57.1%	50.0%	

Source: COPE Research Department (November 1980)
1982: US News & World Report, October 17, 1983

Table 6-2 : COPE Endorsements and Success Rates 1964-1980, 1982

	1972	1974	1976	1978	1980	1982
Total	13	17	18	34	38	7o
Winners	7	13	1o	18	23	
% Won	54%	76%	56%	53%	61%	
Money spent[1] (dollar)	61300	75000		79000	262000	9oo,ooo
% for winning candidates	69%	50%		52%	44%	
House	9	12	14	21	28	
Winners	6	9	9	12	18	
Senate	2	3	2	7	8	
Winners	1	2	1	3	2	
Governors	2	2	2	6	2	
Winners	o	2	o	4	2	

[1] money spent on and contributed to candidates but not funds raised for candidates

[2] total budget figure estimate

Source: LCV Election Reports 1972, 1974, 1976, 1978, 198o
1982: Symonds(1982:141)

Table 6-3 : League of Conservation Voters Support for National and Gubernatorial Election Candidates 1972 - 1982

Chairman would prefer a SPD—CDU coalition over one involving the Greens (FR, 20.11.84:1). Following the cancellation of the Hessian toleration agreement the chairman of the Hessian DGB district blamed the Greens for "anti—workers politics" which in turn was criticized by the Hessian teachers' union (GEW) as unjustified (FR, 3.12.84:18).

In the long run, the LER may well depend on how compatible the SPD and Greens will be. Functioning alliances in city halls or state governments might be the best means to diffuse mutual distrust and prejudices among voters, members and officials. Failing alliances will further the image of irresponsibility held by critics of the Greens and that of entrenchement and establishment ascribed to the SPD. If blue—collar workers see red—green successes in issues like unemployment or social justice, their tilt to the CDU might actually be reversed. The Greens would continue to reach out for the young, ecopax voters, i.e. those strata, the SPD has increasingly lost. Even though the red—green honeymoon in Hessia has come to an end for the time being over an issue not included in the cooperation agreement, both sides have expressed their interest in further cooperation. In the state elections of Berlin, Saarland, North—Rhine— Westphalia and Lower Saxony coming up in 1985 and 1986, even formal coalitions are a distinct possibility. Locally, various forms of red—green pacts have been instituted in many places and with varying success (e.g. Spiegel, 29.3.1982; Spiegel, No. 41, 1984). The more the environmental movement loses its protean character and becomes a predictable political ally, the easier should it be establish an ongoing and institutionalized relationship with organized labor.

In the US, labor and environmentalists have successfully participated in electoral politics. The candidate who decides to run for office usually depends on the support of interest groups. The support takes many forms but the two most essential ones are money and people. While the Federal Election Campaign Acts limited certain kinds of campaign financing, interest groups are still allowed (if not encouraged) to provide money for campaigns. There are no limitations on personal activities in congressional election campaigns. Traditionally, American labor has been a big spender in federal elections, has actively supported the candidates of its choosing, and has mustered considerable manpower in the campaigns. At its peak in 1974, labor made half of all Political Action Committee (PAC) contributions to Congressional candidates (Jacobson, 1980:230). It has been contended, however, that "labor's true strength lies not in its campaign war chests but in the volunteers it can muster to handle the strenuous precinct work, with all the drudgery of registering voters and getting them to the polls" (Alexander, 1976:107). In terms of the success rates of those candidates supported by COPE, labor's overall efforts ought to be considered effective (Table 6—2). In each election year between 1964 and 1982, around 400 candidates have been endorsed and between 50% and 70% of those endorsed were also elected.

Environmentalists had only a small fraction of the money available that labor could spend. Labor PACs spent 6.3 M dollars in 1974 and $ 10.3 M in 1978 (Jacobson: 230) while the LCV spent $ 75,000 and $ 79,000 in those two years. Of course, the League could support far fewer candidates but —as Table 6—3 shows— this figure has considerably increased since 1972. On face value the success rate is comparable to that of labor.

Thus, electoral activities are a potential area of labor—environmentalist interaction. The question arises whether the interaction could mean cooperation, indifference or conflict. Do both sides see benefits from cooperation and to what extent do they support the same candidates? There are several developments that would suggest the benefits of such cooperation. First, the success rates of candidates supported both by labor and environmentalists have declined from the mid—1970s until 1980 but have slightly picked up in 1982 (see

146

Tables 6-2 and 6-3). While this is not apparent in the LCV data, it was clearly stated in its 1980 election report: "There is no question that this is the worst election we have experienced since the league was formed in 1970". Thus, concerted electoral actions might help to counter this trend.

Second, contributions to Congressional candidates from other than labor PACs have increased dramatically since 1974. The share of labor PACs dropped from 50% in 1974 to 29% in 1978, while corporate PACs increased their share from 20% to 28% and trade/ membership/ health PACs from 18% to 33% (Jacobson: 230). By 1982, labor's share had further declined to merely 20% of all PACs' spending —despite the fact that in absolute terms union contributions had more than doubled since 1974 (Congressional Quarterly, Aug. 28, 1982:2112). Labor's influence has declined accordingly. An old saying has it that labor can elect but it can't collect. At its peak in 1975, more than 220 members of Congress scored 80% or higher on the key roll-call votes the AFL-CIO identified each year as its top priorities. This figure had dropped to around 140 in 1981 (ibid.). Another indication for labor's shrunken influence might be the fact that by 1978 labor had less than 50 full-time lobbyists on Capitol Hill while business could bring 400 together at 24-hours notice (SteelLabor, Nov.1978:20). On the other hand, the environmentalist lobbying power in Congress has grown enormously from 2-3 registered lobbyists in the late 1960s to more than 80 in 1982 (Symonds, 1982).

Third, if one compares the candidates supported or endorsed by both COPE and LCV, one finds a considerable overlap. Table 6-4 lists the number of candidates supported by LCV who were endorsed or opposed by COPE. Only 17 of the 120 candidates which the League supported in the five election years 1972 to 1980 were opposed by COPE while 83 had the support of both movements. These figures confirm the results of the analysis of Congressional ratings and suggest that electoral politics might, indeed, be a forum for further cooperation [3].

6.3 The Influence of Labor and Environmentalists in Energy Politics

6.3.1 FRG

In general, organized labor assumed a factor of order role within the SPD and in electoral politics but was a countervailing power regarding social legislation, civil liberties or co-determination. Regarding energy politics, however, the DGB and most of its unions were clearly a factor of order. They supported in principle the same long-term, supply-oriented energy policies (with respect to energy demand projections, energy R&D policies, siting policies, price subsidies, the nuclear fuel cycle, etc.) as the federal government and industry. They also went along with the SPD/FDP government in supporting certain energy conservation measures while advocating nuclear power —even though a less expansive approach than the CDU/CSU. Only in the last few years have the unions seriously turned to alternative ways of energy production and consumption for being both environmentally desirable and useful for employment.

In energy politics, the corporatist mode of interest intermediation was particularly prevalent and the network of formal and informal ties was dense linking labor, industry, the governments and parties. One such linkage was the works councils that —as noted in Chapter 5— often sought to square union policy on nuclear power with the interests of their enterprises.

A second linkage was the presence of labor leaders on the supervisory boards of the industry. In the coal industry, in particular and contrary to other sectors, labor's influence has been nominally equal to management's because the "Montanmitbestimmung" has applied here since the early 1950s. Further, in the electric utility industry, local and regional governments usually sit on the supervisory

	1972	1974	1976	1978	1980
Total					
supported by LCV	13	17	18	34	38
and also endorsed by COPE	9	13	11	22	28
but opposed by COPE	3	3	5	3	3
House					
supported by LCV	9	12	14	21	28
-and endorsed by COPE	6	11	11	13	22
-but opposed by COPE	2	1	3	2	3
Senate					
supported by LCV	2	3	2	7	8
-and endorsed by COPE	2	1	0	6	6
-but opposed by COPE	0	1	2	0	0
Governors					
supported by LCV	2	2	2	6	2
-and endorsed by COPE	1	1	0	3	0
-but opposed by COPE	1	1	0	1	0

Sources: COPE Research Department (Nov.1980)
LCV Election Reports 1972-1980

Table 6-4: Comparison of LCV and COPE Support for Congression
and Gubernatorial Candidates 1972-1980

boards as well as labor leaders. They are often the major shareholders and wield corresponding control.

The high degree of public (i.e. state) control and involvement in energy matters formed a third channel of influence for labor. This is a consequence of the energy resource base of the country and its geographic— political distribution. The only major indigeneous source of energy in the FRG is coal and the deposits are centered in the Ruhr area, which traditionally has been a stronghold of the SPD. Until the early 1970s, energy policy in the FRG was essentially coal policy —a fact that has added to labor's influence in energy policy—making. The German coal industry was in a severe crisis in the 1950s and could only survive with the aid of substantial financial subsidies and legal assistance from the governments in Bonn and North—Rhine Westfalia. In the 1960s, the bulk of the surviving coal industry was consolidated into the Ruhrkohle AG, a holding company in which the coal companies, the IGBE and the governments cooperated closely (Meyer— Renschhausen, 1977). In the consolidation process, employment in coal mining dropped from 600,000 in 1958 to 250,000 in 1970 (Atomenergie und Arbeitsplaetze, 1977:29). It was not the least the influence of the IGBE, so observers noted, that helped to master the coal crisis without serious social conflict. Recognizing the extent of the coming crisis, the IGBE changed from a "mining" to a "mining and energy" union. Hence it became an advocate of nuclear energy which it expected would both complement and substitute coal and thus save the remaining employment in coal mining and create new employment in what was considered a new modern industry.

The German energy law has granted exclusive rights over the distribution of electricity in a given region to so—called "compound utilities". There are eight such compounds in the FRG that amount to regional monopolies and give these utilities considerable influence in energy matters. The electric utilities in the FRG both decide on nuclear power plant investments and are the major user of German coal. Besides energetically promoting the expansion of nuclear power, the utilities have agreed to burn large quantities of German coal (as long as its price is held competitive by an elaborate system of subsidies) and thus guarantee the survival of the industry in the medium term. Much less energetically did they pursue the "de—centralized" energy systems advocated by environmentalists. In part, they might have thought these systems not to be competitive with (highly subsidized) coal and nuclear energy. Others have claimed that also the monopoly situation has slowed decentralized electricity and heat production and cogeneration [4].

Given the semi—public nature of the utility industry, all three channels of union influence, of course, are brought to bear. The unions, therefore, have carried the German nuclear program as have the government and industry from its beginnings in the 1950s when the support for this new source was virtually unanimous, and have felt committed since. No wonder that the unions have also supported advanced reactor designs such as the high—temperature gas reactor (HTGR) which, in addition, bears the promise of effective coal gasification and liquefaction. These techniques, their advocates believe, will assure the viability of the German coal industry in the long run. It is quite understandable, therefore, that the IGBE (in stark contrast to the UMW in the US) and those parts in the OTV representing utility workers belong to the staunchest supporters of both nuclear energy and large coal—fired plants, in general; and in particular have flexed their political muscle to aid the breeder and HTGR projects threatened by cancellation due to huge cost overruns (e.g. SZ, 7.1.1982; FAZ, 12.2.82; SZ, 14.6.82:8).

Environmentalists, among them numerous labor union members, have cited the closely interlocked relationship between the unions, government and the energy industry as a major reason for the official energy policies of the unions. They have cited several examples of high union officials who are also members on the supervisory board of energy (incl. component manufacturing) companies such as the Ruhrkohle AG, VEBA, Preussische Elektrizitatswerke, Siemens, RWE, NWK, etc. The perhaps most notable example is the president of the IGBE, Adolf Schmidt. He is also a member of the SPD in the Bundestag, a vice—president and spokesman on energy matters of the SPD Bundestag caucus, the first vice—president of the Ruhrkohle AG, and vice—president of VEBA (Strohm, 1981:967f). Environmentalists have lacked anything even remotely resembling labor's access to energy policy—making and institutional/political clout. Therefore, explaining the labor— environmentalist conflict as one between a factor—of—order and a countervailing power as a consequence of the political and constitutional framework seems particularly appropriate in regard to energy matters.

6.3.2 United States

The different general political frameworks, and the state— economy relationships in particular, have also affected energy policy making in the two countries, the roles labor and environmentalists played in it, and thus the LER.

The American government has been less interventionist and the state—economy relationship less corporatist than in the FRG —in general as well as with respect to energy politics. As a case in point, the first message on national energy policy to Congress ever submitted by an American president was sent as late as 1971 —"one of Richard Nixon's many unprecedented acts" wrote Bupp (1977:285). This and subsequent proposals of the Nixon— Ford era like Project Independence, the Energy Independence Authority, or Senator Jackson's National Energy Production Board as well as, one might add, Carter's National Energy Plans all faced stiff criticism behind which was a "combination of fear and pessimism about the ability of government to shape events" (op.cit.:292). Shonfield's observation —elucidated below— applies to the energy debate in the US as well: compared to private enterprise, public initiative is given a subordinate role, unless there is a manifest national emergency. While the proponents of the various government energy proposals sought to recall war mobilization efforts and "corporatist" "heroic periods" like the first New Deal years (Shonfield:308) where government and business cooperated actively with one another in the pursuit of agreed economic objectives, the opponents of these proposals included the "major industrial actors and environmentalists at the same time" albeit for different reasons (Bupp:291). Thus, the situation in the US was distinctly different from the German one, where the "global steering" mechanisms mentioned by Alemann involving government, business and labor were applied with little dispute to the economy, in general, and energy in particular.

In the US, interventions by the state tended to be more haphazard and piecemeal than in the FRG. This might be explained by the lack of the aggregating and integrating function of the type of party to be found in a Parliamentary system. Instead, the judiciary played a central role. Shonfield argued that since the New Deal, there was a rival to the "corporatist" vision of the type of collaboration between government and business that emphasized "public supervision, of an essentially judicial character, of the activities of private enterprise" (p.310). He saw a "large slice of American government ... farmed out in pieces" (p.322) to the judiciary that neither knows nor is expected to care about long term policies. "It is the principle of 'anti—planning' deliberately elevated into a way of life" (ibid.). The Humphrey— Hawkins legislation which nominally sought to introduce longer— term planning with respect to employment, in the final outcome lacked the teeth to accomplish its initial objectives. It is supervision rather than collaboration, Bupp (p.293) argued similarly, that has been the dominant element on the public policy response to the US energy problem. In the process of establishing standards and regulations for the burning of fossil fuels and concerning nuclear energy usage, the affected parties and interests have not cooperated if, indeed, they were not openly antagonistic (Bupp:297,313). The US Light Water Reactor program, for example, which was often applauded as a model of successful joint government- industry research and development, Bupp argued, was in fact just the opposite. The AEC reactor development program assumed that the uncoordinated actions of private companies would guarantee that all necessary support services would somehow become automatically available as soon as an effective reactor had been designed. But there was no coordination of the development of the entire system. Bupp concluded that "there was, in short, no planning" (p.320).

Environmentalists have been both critics and beneficiaries of the anti-planning characteristics of the policy process. Environmentalists For Full Employment (EFFE), for example, but also labor unions, criticized the lack of coordination of energy and employment planning. EFFE contended that existing policies had treated energy and employment as separate problems and, therefore, had been decisively misdirected. The government had not been interested in examining the employment impacts of different energy options.

> Labor Department — had been paying attention to the complex relationships between these two vital public policy areas. Even though the old Energy Research and Development Administration (ERDA) had a Division of Manpower Assessment, and the Labor Department a Division for Occupation Outlook, federal policy makers simply had skipped over this area. When pressed, they repeated the claims of the major energy industries: that the key to employment is ever-increasing energy production (particularly electricity production via coal and nuclear power). No analyses had been done to verify such claims. And we could find no one in the Administration who seemed to care. Thus, we were not surprised when Secretary of Labor Marshall, and then- Secretary of Energy Schlesinger, testified before the Energy Subcommittee of the Joint Economic Committee in the spring of 1978 that DOL had not even participated in the preparation of NEP I. Nor were we surprised when Secretary Marshall suggested that even if the DOL had been requested to provide advice on the labor-energy connection, the Department would have had a great deal of difficulty doing so [5].

At that testimony, EFFE also gave an example of the way the DOE perceived the unemployment issue. Quoting from the National Energy Plan II:

> The unemployment rate is almost by definition a shortrun concept. An individual is unemployed when he or she is looking for work, but cannot find a suitable job at that moment. In the long run, an individual will adjust to this situation by either working, e.g. by acquiring suitable job skills, or taking a lesser job; or by not working, e.g. retiring, living on welfare, etc. In either instance, the worker is no longer unemployed. Unemployment, in short, is a disequilibrium phenomenon where workers are between one of two possible equilibria, namely, working or non-working. (in: op.cit.:4)

EFFE sarcastically concluded, that the nation had "currently ... more than 10 millions of its citizens dangling between these two equilibria" (ibid.). The economic "theory", EFFE argued, which apparently prevails among officials is that employment has no business being a criterion for energy policy formulation.

However, environmentalists profitted vastly from the other "anti-planning" characteristic: the judiciary. Besides the better access opportunities to the legislators and the electoral process as compared to the FRG, the American environmental movement has, in particular, used the courts. That was facilitated by the availability of class action suits, built-in statutory opportunities for public scrutiny [6], a tradition of public control in US common law, and the existence of the National Environmental Policy Act [7] combined with the financial and organizational power of the large national environmental organizations. Symonds (1982) has pointed to the increased professionalization of the new "green giant" in Washington. Not only have the environmental groups introduced word processing and computerized data banks into their daily operations, but the NRDC, the Environmental Defense Fund, NWF and the Sierra Club alone employ about 50 lawyers. The regulatory process for nuclear energy, the burning of coal, or oil exploration has been highly complex and has provided many handles for intervenors. In that context, the fundamental constitutional purpose of public involvement came to bear: As Bupp pointed out, the belief in the necessity of protecting the rights of individuals from arbitrary acts of the government is deeply ingrained in the US, and, one should add, is much stronger than in the FRG.

William Futrell, formerly president of the Sierra Club, stressed that citizen suits have been very central in enforcing environmental laws since official authority alone has proved insufficient. Environmental intervenors, said Futrell, have come to the conclusion that in order to be successful "the study of the thing (air, water pollution, etc.,HS) itself was not so important as the study of the governmental institution" involved (Speech at the Amerika Haus, Berlin, 12.3.80). In the 1970s, more than 5,000 environmental law suits were brought to federal courts. More than 1500 of them resulted in court decisions many of which were favorable to environmentalists.

While the American political framework provided for more environmentalist involvement than the German political scene, the opposite was true with respect to labor in general and regarding energy politics. To be sure, US unions have been engaged in energy politics (as the previous chapters have indicated) but their engagement was not part of a long-term coordination with government and business as in the Federal Republic and was far more piecemeal: The UAW consulted on an ad-hoc basis with the auto-industry on emission regulations; the tri-partite working group of government, steel industry and USWA representatives was formed in response to a complex but still single issue; the Nuclear Power Construction Stabilization Agreement between nuclear power plant contractors and the building and construction unions, that sought to assure the uninhibited construction of nuclear power plants, reportedly entailed substantial concessions by the unions to industry regarding work-rules and working hours (c.f. Section 7.4.2) and was concluded in spite of deep conflicts on Labor Law Reform or the Humphrey- Hawkins legislation between labor and business.

On the other hand, the energy industry in the US is less publicly owned than in the FRG. It is therefore less subject to public (i.e. state) control and thus less open to labor's influence qua politics. Given the more diversified American energy sources, government involvement on a scale such as in German coal mining is hardly conceivable. Further, the electric utility industry in the US is less oligopolistic than in the FRG or, to repeat Schmitter, has not been granted "deliberate representational monopolies" within their regions "in exchange for observing certain controls" by the state. In other words, the US energy industry/ state relationship is less corporatist than in the FRG. In addition, because workers' co-determination rights or its equivalents do not exist, US labor had no channels of influence comparable to the German works councils or representation on the supervisory boards of energy companies. Also, while American labor's influence in the Democratic party might not be smaller than that of German unions in the SPD, US party positions have been less relevant for policy than in the FRG. Finally, given the greater diversity of the American labor movement compared to the German movement, "deviant" union positions on energy therefore were more frequent.

6.4 The LER and Deregulation and Reindustrialization Under the Reagan Administration

A popular goal of the Reagan candidacy was "to get the government off people's backs". Reductions of government regulations were one way of achieving this. Reagan had promised in his campaign that "there are tens of thousands of ... regulations I would like to see eliminated" (cited by Lash:19). Another way of making the state less interventionist was to reduce taxes both for individuals and corporations. The idea was that a lesser tax burden would stimulate the economy and entrepreneurial talents, and thus help to "reindustrialize" the country.

Of course, it is easy to point to the inconsistency and inadequacy of the Reagan version of reduced state interventions. The growth rates of the defense budget, the high interest rates and the huge budget deficits certainly mean a more interventionist state in the long term than under Reagan's predecessor. Furthermore, "less government" per se is not a reasonable social goal. Labor laws, employment programs, energy policy, welfare programs, and occupational and environmental regulations have all been attempts to respond to the inadequacies of the free market in favor of disenfranchised constituent groups. The government was mandated to force the economy to internalize external cost, to include public goods in its microeconomic calculation, and to enhance the information and participation rights of the economically weak.

Thus, in theory, both environmentalists and labor unions must be considered victims of changing state—economy relations along Reagan lines. Doing away with environmental regulations means, of course, as a rule less protection. Similarly, fewer and less enforced OSH rules, union organizing rules opened to undue management interference, curtailments of the right to strike, high unemployment or cut—backs of social programs are all contrary to long—held union beliefs and interests. Still, parts of Reagan's concepts had considerable sympathies in labor. Not only did more than 40% of the union members vote for Reagan in 1980, with several unions endorsing him as a candidate, some of his policies also seemed to promise jobs to one union or the other.

Therefore, both groups being victims (in theory) was not enough to guarantee common interests in real politics. Indeed, the possible effects on the LER of changing state— economy relations are quite complex. One key issue was the low rate of productivity growth in the US during the 1970s. When Reagan took office, one could expect that if labor was required to choose, and accepts this choice as a valid one, between environmental cutbacks and reduced wages in order to improve productivity, it would tend to choose the former. In that case, labor—environmentalist conflicts would likely have grown. Further, regardless of the productivity issue, reduced environmental regulations, in principle, could have been expected to encourage (energy) production and facility construction and, thus, appease the employment starved building trades while further increasing the potential of environmentalist resistance. "Reindustrialization" fostered by deregulation made it likely that —at least in the short term— new jobs would be created, and thus would be welcomed by the unions. Moreover, support from government agencies that had helped labor—environmentalist rapprochement in the past could be expected to be significantly reduced.

As it turned out, in actual politics labor and environmentalists indeed perceived themselves as victims rather than beneficiaries of "Reaganomics". As a whole, labor has not accepted the aforementioned choice between wages and the environment as a valid one. More accurately, the choice was often posed as one of either agreeing to painful wage concessions or facing the shut—down of entire plants. In collective bargaining, the environment usually tended to be a minor point, if it came up at all. As noted (c.f. Section 3.2.2.1), in Steel the stretch—out was hardly used but major wage concessions were extracted from the union. Business as a common enemy had already been a tangible motif for labor—environmentalists cooperation in the past. Regarding deregulation and collective bargaining, this image has become more powerful, albeit not predominant, during the Reagan years.

Congress must block efforts to dismantle or weaken federal regulatory agencies and federal laws and regulations which were established to protect consumers, workers, the environment and the general public from unfair, monopolistic, and anti—social business practices.

The power of big corporations and big financial institutions is getting bigger and bigger through mergers and takeovers and expansion of foreign operations, as well as through the pro—big—business policies of the Reagan Administration. Corporate power and corporate misconduct must be brought under control (AFL—CIO, 1983:94).

Labor, moreover, has harshly criticized the Administration's budgetary policies. Instead of creating relief for those hit hardest by the recession, the AFL—CIO (1983:81) argued, the Reagan Administration budget cuts strike at key economic and social programs:

—Job training and employment funds are to be cut.

—Unemployment compensation funds are reduced.

—Trade Adjustment Assistance is to be killed.

—Education, student loans, compensatory education for the disadvantaged, vocational and adult education were cut.

—Housing programs for low— and moderate—income families suffer deferrals, stretchouts and cutbacks.

—Federal employee pay and retirement benefits are sacrificed.

—Aid for the poor is cut in Medicaid, food stamps, child nutrition.

—Aid to families with dependent children and low—income energy assistance are cut.

—Medicare and other health services take cuts.

—Revenue sharing with state and local governments is further tampered with.

—Railroad retirement increases are postponed.

—Mass transit and other transportation programs are reduced again.

—Legal services for the poor are killed.

—Mine safety and health inspectors are cut.

—Environmental protection funds are drastically reduced.

Yet labor's criticism was more fundamental, proposing an alternative to the government's purist free—enterprise, anti—planning mentality. For the short term, the AFL—CIO proposed an economic program that would provide jobs for the unemployed and increase opportunities for the poor. It was to create 900,000 jobs in 1983 and 1.8 million in 1984 by expanding public services, building planned public works, constructing and rehabilitating low-cost housing, training and job placement of youth, and assisting displaced workers (op. cit.:83). In addition, those out of work would receive extended unemployment insurance, mortgage and rent payment relief, and health care. This program would cost 68.5 billion dollars but was proposed be financed by closing tax loopholes particularly favoring the wealthy and by reducing the growth rates of defense spending. The program, according to the AFL-CIO, would have increased the federal deficit slightly in the near term, but would have reduced the deficit by about $150 billion in 1986, not counting the indirect effects resulting from putting people back to work.

For "long term revitalization", the AFL-CIO called for a more interventionist state embarking on a reindustrialization program. Labor co-chaired a study group on industrial policy comprised of business, labor and government leaders (Center for National Policy, 1984). The group concluded that despite the recovery from recession, further improvements in productivity, employment and growth were needed. The underlying structural problems remained, and the next economic downturn could be expected to cut even more deeply. The government was called, in addition to exercising sound fiscal and monetary policies, to deal more effectively with the large budget deficits, high interest rates and the overly strong dollar. The government, the report argued, has often relied on its broad array of policy instruments affecting industry "incoherently and haphazardly", while the industrial policies of other nations were frequently more coordinated and explicit. Besides a less adversarial relationship among government, business and labor, a new approach to industrial policy was needed with the goal of competitiveness in world-markets. What was found to be particularly lacking was "an effective process for making policy decisions". The institutional framework for public policy ought to be improved. Specifically, the Group proposed:

*An Industrial Development Board, composed of government, labor and business, to advise the President and develop cooperative strategies promoting industrial growth.

*Creation of an Industrial Finance Administration to provide financial assistance as part of a development strategy by the Board.

*An expanded commitment to technological research and development.

The debate on industrial policy has encompassed many more groups than the traditional Big Three of Government, Business and Labor. A study by the AFL-CIO Industrial Union Department (1984) titled "Deindustrialization and the Two Tier Society" was, among others, endorsed by the National Organization for Women, the National Urban League, the Wilderness Society, the Congressional Black Caucus, the National Association for the Advancement of Colored People, and the Sierra Club. Among other issues, the study touched upon the environmental stake of an industrial policy.

The study traces the erosion of America's industrial base and points to the mismatch that has developed between the jobs lost and those being created.

Millions of relatively well-paying production jobs in manufacturing and construction have been eliminated, while the overwhelming bulk of employment created in the expanding service industries has been concentrated in jobs with very low incomes and little realistic opportunity for upward mobility. Conversely, the highly paid layer of managers, engineers and professionals at the top has been strengthened, but only slightly. As a result, the once solid middle tier of American jobs has been undermined (p.v).

Wthout a healthy industry, the study stressed, full employment will remain out of reach. Only an adequate supply of good middle—income jobs will allow the existing income gaps for minorities and women. Only a healthy, competitive industrial base will allow to sustain and expand public investments in infrastructure. While, at first glance, deindustrialization might benefit the environment, since major sources of pollution would be eliminated, reindustralization is also in the environmental interest for three reasons:

(1) Failure to modernize will result in increasing obsolescence and low profitability which, if past experience is followed, will lead to noncompliance with environmental laws and mounting political pressure to relax standards.

(2) The alternative to greater US production is a larger share for foreign producers. This would be harmful to the environment abroad where environmental standards are generally weaker.

(3) Regional imbalances in the US in terms of pollution levels and unemployment rates would be excacerbated.

Given these employment, environmental and social equity considerations, the study concluded, "a conscious focussing of policy —an industrial policy—" was needed that would seek to strengthen the American industrial base "as if people mattered". Industrial policy will—formation and decision—making, designed for overcoming failures of the market place and sustaining socially desirable industrial development, "must provide ample channels for input and participation, not only for labor, business, and government, but also for other ... concerned public interests" (op.cit.:vii).

NOTES

[1] Counted as votes considered in common are only the same votes, i.e., votes on the same bill but on different amendments are not included in that count.) The voting analysis also reveals the areas of common interest and of conflict. On several of the votes that LCV and COPE had both considered they disagreed on what constitutes the "correct" outcome. These votes were on the SST, bottle bills, Clinch River breeder development, and water projects. They agreed on anti—pollution, OSH and bills controlling energy companies.

[2] The first such case occurred in Hamburg after the June 1982 elections. Prior to the elections, the SPD was in government with a 69 to 51 seats majority over the CDU. In the 1982 elections, the CDU obtained 56, the SPD 55 and the "Green Alternative List" (GAL) 9 seats. Thus, given the stated unwillingness of the two large parties to form a great coalition, the key to the government now lay with the GAL. As a first sign of support for the SPD, the GAL voted with the SPD in order to turn down a no—confidence vote introduced by the CDU seeking the resignation of the SPD governor. While both SPD and GAL refused to form a coalition, the two sides have entered into a series of talks on the question whether and under what conditions the GAL would support a SPD minority government (e.g. SZ, 5.7.1982:1,2; 6.7.82: 1,2,4; 7.7.82:7; 8.7.82:3; 10./11.7.82:1,2,4; Spiegel, No.28, 1982:20—22).

[3] The 1980 Senatorial election campaign in Iowa is a case in point. Both, LCV and COPE supported or endorsed the incumbent Senator Culver. In addition, he scored 100% "correct" on UAW's and 93% on AFSCME's voting scores. Culver's opponent, Rep. Grassley, on the other hand, scored 9% with AFSCME, zero with UAW, and 17% with COPE. Environmental Action gave Grassley its "Filthy Five" award for getting the most money from what it considered were the worst five corporations. Out of $150,000 spent by LCV on the 1980 elections, $97,000 were spent for Culver (LCV, 1980 Election Report: 5ff). When the League entered the race only five months before the election, Culver was 17 points behind in the polls. The League's canvassing and grass roots efforts reached over 200,000 voters in Iowa. It opened offices in four cities and, in addition, used two mobile offices. The canvass was very effective in boosting voter turnout and to help Culver win the cities, the LCV claimed.

> Culver won all the cities we canvassed most intensively. Altogether they gave him 57% of their vote and a 40,000 vote margin over Grassley. In the urban counties that we did not canvass, Culver got only 45.6% of the vote, losing to Grassley. And Grassley clobbered Culver in the rural areas. But here, too, the canvass seems to have had some effect; Culver got 45% of the vote in the 19 rural counties that we canvassed, and only 38% of the vote in the 63 rural counties that we did not canvass. Altogether Culver got 19,000 more votes than Grassley in the 25 counties where we did some canvassing. (LCV, Election Report 1980:5,6)

The leading state officer of each of the major environmental organizations in Iowa —the Izaak Walton League, National Audubon Society, Sierra Club, and NWF— all supported Culver publicly. This was the first time that any of these environmental leaders had been willing to get involved in a political campaign. Culver's opponent was so alarmed by the League's campaign that he called it the "League of Conservation Vultures" and, after the election, acknowledged the effectiveness of its campaign. Culver lost by 46% to 54%.
The League does not mention any cooperation with labor during the campaign. It was the only non—party organization making independent expenditures to help Culver. Of course, there is no way of knowing whether a joint labor—environmentalist campaign would have helped Culver win. Culver was badly hurt by economic and right-wing, right-to-life issues. Grassley kept repeating that Culver was a big spender who was responsible for inflation and unemployment. Culver stood to his liberal economic policies, not denying that he was a spender and questioning the wisdom to balance the federal budget. These views were very much in labor's tradition. Grassley, on the other hand, was hurt by his environmental positions. The League distributed EFFE's book on Jobs, Energy and the Environment to people who expressed the most concerns about jobs. Culver was not defeated because of his views on either labor or environmental issues. Joint labor—environmentalist efforts, on the other hand, could have exposed more successfully Grassley's very poor labor and environmental records. Thus, Culver could have benefitted from Grassley's labor and environmental views and the race might have been very polarized ideologically on Culver's terms —and not, as it was, on Grassley's.

[4] Groner, 1979:114; SZ, 8.11.1977:22; Spiegel, 9.10.1978:60ff, 14.3.1977: 90–98, 28.3.1977:54ff; FR, 15.1.1980, 8.5.1979.

[5] Testimony of Clifford J.Aron, EFFE, before the Employment

[6] Two important federal laws have provided "unprecedented access to political and governmental institutions": the Freedom of Information (FOI) Act and the Administrative Procedure Act (APA) (Fanning, 1975:39). FOI laid down a general rule that all written federal information, with certain exceptions, must be made available to the public. APA has defined and prescribed procedures for two types of formal agency proceedings: adjudication and rule making. An adjudication is a formal process in which an agency's decision must be made on the record of a hearing similar to a trial. APA allows to submit evidence, rebut opposing evidence, and cross – examine opposing witnesses. APA does not require open, public hearings but court decisions have ruled against exclusive participation rights. Rule making is the agency process for formulating, amending or repealing a rule. APA requires a federal agency to give advance notice of rule making with a preamble of non—technical language, and allows at least 30 days of public review between the notice and the adoption of the rule. Alleged violations of APA are a basis for court review (Fanning, 1975:51f).

The Clean Air Amendments (CAA) of 1970 and the Federal Water Pollution Control Act Amendments of 1972 provided strong legal tools for pollution control. Fanning (p. 57) described the provisions for citizen information and participation of the 1970 clean air act as perhaps its greatest distinction from its predecessors. In Section 114, the CAA allowed EPA to require states and individual air polluters to monitor emissions, keep records, and submit periodic reports. Based an the FOI Act, most such records and reports are public information. Under Section 304, any citizen could bring suit against any person or corporation alleged to be violating an emission standard or other limitation applicable under the act. Both acts allowed citizens to sue the administrator of EPA for failure to perform an action required of him by the acts. The CAA, further, empowered the courts to award the costs of litigation to citizen plaintiffs. Environmental groups have frequently invoked the act, and have, for instance, achieved a landmark ruling by the Supreme Court in 1973 barring "significant deterioration" of air quality in areas which had had cleaner air than pollution standards spelled out as permissible. The clean water legislation directed EPA to provide for, encourage and assist public participation in developing, revising and enforcing all regulations, standards, effluent limits, plans and programs under the act. EPA regulations emphasized public hearings with sufficient advance notice being mailed to interested persons or groups, convenience of location and time of hearing, and availability of both advance material and records of the hearings (Fanning, p.61).

[7] The single most important piece of legislation giving environmental groups a formal role has probably been the National Environmental Policy Act (NEPA) of 1969. NEPA obligated the federal government to use "all practicable means consistent with other essential considerations of national policy" to ensure that "each generation of Americans will have a safe, healthful, productive and aesthetically and culturally pleasing" environment (quoted in Enloe, 1978: 148). Most importantly, NEPA required all federal agencies or recipients of federal funds to submit "Environmental Impact Statements" (EIS) detailing the probable effects on the environment of any project including the effects of possible alternatives. The EIS explicitly provided for public review, comment and legal action. The public review —concluded Andrews (1976:154)— with its opportunities for ad—hoc involvement

and legal action turned out to be the most effective mechanism —particularly, since the judiciary was responsive to environmental concerns. One landmark court ruling as a result of a citizen generated law suit based on NEPA was the Calvert Cliffs decision of 1972 requiring the Atomic Energy Commission to deal with the environmental impacts of nuclear power plant as well as radiological problems (Nelkin, 1978:7).

7 Explanation 5: The Role of Ideology and the LER

Ideology as used in this chapter shall not mean a well–defined theory. Rather, it refers to basic attitudes or world–views of labor and environmental groupings regarding their own role vis–a–vis the state, how the state–economy relationship should be organized, or –more general– how political life should be conducted. Of course, as already indicated in the preceding chapter, the ideological positions are interrelated with the political conditions and practices of a country.

7.1 Ideological Explanations of the LER

Most commonly, an ideological distinction between the left and right has been applied to the LER. Environmentalists have been accused of pursuing "petit– bourgeois" interests which go counter to the economic interests of the workers and union members. Since the average environmentalist is wealthier than the average union member, has a great distance to the blue–collar workplace, and tends to live in better and cleaner neighborhoods –this argument goes–, environmentalist concerns necessarily contradict those of the union membership that is interested in higher incomes, full employment, more social justice and secure and safe jobs. Therefore, in ideological terms, the labor–environmentalist conflicts have been explained along a socio–economic left– right dimension.

However, this explanation has severe shortcomings. In the US, the left–right distinction has generally been less politically salient than in Europe but labor–environmentalist conflicts have nevertheless existed. But also in Europe, at least since WWII, the left–right conflict patterns have eroded. Lerner and Gorden (1969:201) presented empirical evidence –in a chapter titled "Reshaping Old Values"– that formerly socialist ideas, that traditionally carried the left–right distinction farthest, have become widely accepted even among "capitalists and other rightists". In their view, the left–right distinction has become obsolete.

The political spectrum of post-war Europe has moved leftward. In the process, much that was distinctively Left in prewar Europe is now in the center and equally 'available' to partisans ... on either side of the spectrum. The process seems analogous the the leftward shift of prewar American politics under the New Deal... The interpenetration of ideologies in Europe today has been summarized succinctly by Andre Malraux: 'The Left is no longer on the left, the Right is no longer on the right, and the Center is no longer in the middle.'

The German unions themselves have abandoned many ideological tenets reminiscent of their socialist origins which defined issues in left—right terms. While, on paper, they still advocate the nationalization of the means of production, for all practical purposes, they have abandoned this goal. Moreover, the unions have drawn a separating line from communists inside and outside their organizations. Not only have unions (like the IGBSE) performed communist purges and sought to exclude or limit the visibility of communist members, but the DGB indeed decided by a formal vote that communism was not one of the major roots of the West German union movement [1].
    The left—right split hypothesis also does not hold up if one examines the positions of environmentalists. To be sure, parts of the environmental movement have taken stands on some issues close to the political Right [2], but the more visible and representative part of the environmental movement around the Greens and the citizen groups is clearly closer to what is usually labelled the political Left (e.g. SZ, 24.3.80:1, FAZ, 3.9.84:11). Not only have ecological groups in recent elections drawn most of their votes from the traditional SPD electorate (c.f. Table 7—1), but labor and environmentalists have expressed remarkably similar key political objectives [3].
    For all these reasons it seems doubtful that ideological influences on the LER have mainly been manifest along a left— right dimension. I contend that shifts in Inglehart's (1971, 1977 and 1979) terms from "materialist" to "post-materialist" values and from "Old" to "New" politics explain the ideological basis of the labor—environmentalist conflicts in the Federal Republic better than left—right patterns. The rise of environmentalism indeed has been described as one prime example of the shift to post materialist values while labor has continued to embrace above all materialist values. Old politics, i.e. the struggle along the socio— economic left—right dimension, this argument goes, are overlayed by New politics in which the lines of conflict are drawn among new actors in generational or lifestyle terms (Kmieciak, 1976; Eppler, 1977; Inglehart, 1971 and 1977; Kaase, Klingemann, 1979; Ronsch, 1980; Rosenau, Holsti, 1981).
    There are several features characterizing these shifts. While changes along the first dimension traditionally are sought by workers, "new politics" concerns are mainly voiced by a considerable and outspoken middle—class based minority espousing post—materialist values. Further, the shift to post—materialism, Inglehart conjectured, is accompanied by a shift in political skills from traditional "elite directed" to new "elite challenging" activities: Elite— directed politics is "largely a matter of elites mobilizing mass support through established organizations such as political parties, labor unions, religious institutions" while elite— challenging politics give the public an increasingly important role in making specific decisions rather than merely leaving a choice between two or more sets of decision makers (Inglehart, 1977:7). Albeit using different terms, Eppler (1977:36) argued similarly that "today, most conflicts in the FRG are those between structural conservatives and value conservatives". Structural conservatives have their ideological roots in turn of the century liberalism, equate growth and progress, believe in technocratic solutions, or say freedom and mean privileges. Value conservatism, Eppler writes, is rooted in the European Christian

conservative tradition and above all seeks to preserve our natural living conditions. It understands freedom as the chance and call for responsible solidarity. Environmental degradation, urban decay, increased differentiation and monotony at work, fighting crime by demanding more police, opposition to abortion laws, all correspond to or have grown out of the structural conservative mode of thought. The labor movement, Eppler stated at the first meeting expressly convening labor and environmental leaders held in Mullheim in 1978, is both value conservative and "structurally revolutionary". Well before the Greens succeeded on the party landscape, he predicted that the 1980s will either be determined by a majority of the structural conservatives or by an alliance between labor and the ecological movement (Stuttgarter Nachrichten, 2.10.1978).

7.2 The Ideological Basis of German Labor and Environmentalism

In presenting the evidence for the saliency of these shifts, I will start out with the ideological basis of German labor. German labor's "double function" of being both a factor of order and countervailing power —as Grebing observed in the last chapter— squares well with the theory that a transition from Old to New Politics is occurring. In each mode, almost by definition, labor played a different role. In Old Politics, labor was generally a countervailing power against business and the state. In New Politics, labor regarding certain issues has become a factor of order aligned with business and the state against new political actors —one of them being the environmental movement.

Characteristic features of the post-WWII West German labor movement were the readiness for political engagement, the commitment to "social partnership", its deliberately unified structure (the principle of "Einheitsgewerkschaft"), and the principle of Industrial Unionism. These features grew out of the historical experience of German labor and had ramifications for the LER.

The unions have assumed in their practice as well as ideologically a clearly political role within the economic and Constitutional order of the FRG. The Basic Program of the DGB (1980:28) states: "From the very beginning, it was the goal of the labor unions ... to fight for a social order which would make the pursuit of happiness possible for everybody." Today —the DGB is proud to say— important traditional demands of the labor movement have become incorporated as basic rights in democratic constitutions and have been accepted as such by the public. The labor unions are, so the Basic Program says, "the decisive integrational factor of democracy and the indispensable force for the economy and society to advance democratically" (op.cit:30; FR, 14.3.81:1). The unions themselves are committed to this dual role. On the one hand, the labor unions clearly support this democratic state (Leminsky, 2'81:88). On the other hand, they see themselves as "self-help and fighting organizations" protecting their members against the consequences of being economically and socially disadvantaged. The Basic Program stresses that "the protective and the formative function of the unions is an inseparable entity".

The principle of unity and the concept of industrial unionism were important implements for realizing both functions. Under industrial unionism, the workers of an industry or firm are represented by one and only one union. Industrial unionism was meant to counteract the split of the labor movement into various professional and occupational groupings. Unitary unionism was to prevent the labor movement from being divided along party lines. Both principles, not present in the labor movement when the Nazis came to power, were seen as a prerequisite both to keep labor strong and to preserve the democratic order of the newly formed Federal Republic.

In the formative years of the FRG and the DGB, labor's leaders opted to become both an active and constructive political force in the new state while holding onto nominally socialist goals such as seeking the nationalization of the means of production. In reality, the growing prosperity in the country and the important political role organized labor was able to play soon led labor to embrace the "social market economy" and "social partnership" as attainable ends rather than transitory stages on the road to socialism. Mommsen (1981:84) noted that the labor unions have turned to view co—determination based on parity as an alternative, and no longer as a preliminary stage, to nationalizing the capitalist enterprises. What Lasswell has called the process of "restriction by partial incorporation", i.e. subverting the traditional commitments of the ideological partisans and obliging them to seek a new pragmatic consensus (Lerner, Gorden:242), was applicable to the German union movement. Parts of labor, furthermore, have expressly affirmed factor of order functions. Georg Leber (1980:69f), who was president of the IGBSE and later became Minister of Transportation and Minister of Defense, wrote:

> Business organizations and labor unions have factor of order functions of vast and fundamental importance —regardless of possibly substantial differences in particular issue areas. They are jointly responsible in fulfilling these functions and —on the basis of our free society— are expected to jointly derive rules and procedures that govern the systems of industrial relations in the various economic sector guided by the interest of society as a whole.

Organized labor ideologically affirmed the existing order in such a way that at times it joined those treating an upcoming new movement like environmentalism as a potential threat to this order.

Moreover, the Einheitsgewerkschaft— principle has been adapted to fit the necessities of a central ally of a major political party. While it sought to achieve unity of labor across party cleavages, it has also been invoked to maintain the status— quo within the house of labor and in terms of the unions' general political role. While the DGB and the individual unions tend to have a perfunctory CDU member on the executive boards, their ideology and leadership is overwhelmingly social democratic. Friedhelm Fahrtmann, the former head of the Economic and Social Science Institute (WSI) of the DGB and presently SPD Secretary of Labor in the state of North Rhine Westfalia, indeed asserted that the unions for all practical purposes are social—democratic party unions (FR 16.3.81:3). When the SPD was still the party in power, a newspaper editorial put it succinctly:

> Some unions today can rightly be labelled "Chancellor—Unions" with the caveat that this label will only apply as long as the government is headed by a Social Democrat of the Helmut Schmidt type. Among these unions are the IGBE, the IGBSE ... and also the IGCPK. Their top officials bask in the power of this chancellor and feel proud and satisfied to be able to stabilize his power (ibid.).

While the Einheitsgewerkschaft principle sought to achieve unity of labor across party cleavages, it has also been invoked to maintain the status—quo within labor. As noted in Chapter 5, the unions have occasionally appealed to the notion of Einheitsgewerkschaften in order to curtail controversial debates and to bring deviant groups within the labor movement in line with official union policy. In the extreme, the appeal for unity indeed was used as a justification to expel critics (e.g. Mez, Wilke, 1977; FR, 23.6.1980:23).

I now turn to the ideological and value base of German environmentalism. The two aspects postulated by Inglehart's theory are also observable in reality. In three countries at two points in time, environmentalists were distinctly more post—materialist than the general population (Kessel, 1984:18f). The Green voters were found to value highly orientations such as solidarity, social justice, holding together, trust and friendship (FAZ, 3.9.84:2). The post— materialist aspect is evident by the priority given to ecological politics: Ecological politics, the Greens (1980:2) stated, "give priority to maintaining the natural living conditions for our and the future generations and are guided by peoples' needs and creative capabilities". However, most environmentalists would probably disagree if the term "post— materialist" were taken verbatim. The Greens feel also committed to "social" politics: the changes necessitated by the "ecological crisis", they emphasize, are not to be carried out on the backs of the working people, the disadvantaged and disabled. As Chapter 3 already indicated, many of the policies on employment, energy, economic growth, housing, transportation, etc. forwarded by environmentalists were guided by manifest materialist considerations. Indeed, at least on the programmatic level, there was considerable overlap on these issues between labor and environmentalists. Thus, post— materialist traits in environmentalist ideology must not be equated with aloofness toward practical concerns.

The second aspect, what Inglehart called "elite challenging" as opposed to traditional "elite directed" activities, has both been more appropriate as a label and is a very crucial characteristic of the labor—environmentalist conflict in the FRG. Since it has been little discussed so far, I will treat it at some length.

The saliency of environmental protection has gone hand in hand with the dissatisfaction, if not frustration, of those struggling for a cleaner environment with the way the political system has treated the issue. Indeed, an "environmental movement" hardly would have come into being, had it not been necessary to challenge the political and economic elites into taking environmental issues seriously. Thus, a linkage of environmentalism and the "elite challenging" aspect is by no means surprising.

When environmental parties began to enter the political scene in the FRG, opinion surveys found the public rather frustrated with the environmental policies of the established political parties. In 1978, around 80% of the German public considered environmental protection a difficult but resolvable problem, and 23% did not see acceptable approaches coming from the established parties. They expected remedies from extra parliamentary ad—hoc groups. Only 11% agreed to the statement that joining and working in an existing political party would enhance environmental protection. Fifty—three percent favored the proposition that citizen groups obtain rights to participate in environmental decisions (Fietkau, 1979:105). Also substantial was the potential support expressed for an environmental party (40%), even though that declined the more the possible negative effects from such a party were considered. The young, however, particularly engaged in elite challenging activities and increasingly supported ecological parties (as is indicated in Table 7—1 listing those states in which the Greens entered parliament). "Green voting" among the young has been approaching 25%.

Not only the impetus to become engaged in a group not belonging to the traditional political actors, but also the kinds of activities one engaged in were "elite challenging". The occupation of construction sites, massive demonstrations, urban squatting, or different forms of civil disobedience became common. For the activists and sympathisers, these activities had originally been chosen because they promised to be effective, but soon led to the conviction that the authorities were always on the side of the "enemy". Therefore, positions on whatever cause and opposition to state power became inextricably intertwined. In fact, opposition to law and order have become a common denominator of various causes.

The forms of politics and the issues proper thus have become closely linked for environmentalists (and other causes). "Grass—root

Previous Election

	Year	Total Population				Age 18 – 25			
		CDU	SPD	FDP	"Greens"[1]	CDU	SPD	FDP	"Greens"[1]
Bremen	1975	33.6	48.2	13.5	----	19.3	52.7	14.4	----
Baden-Württemberg	1976	56.7	33.3	7.8	----	46.8	41.5	8.2	----
Berlin	1979	44.4	42.7	8.1	ca. 4	31.0	43.1	9.2	14.4
Niedersachsen	1978	48.7	42.2	4.2	3.9	37.1	46.0	3.8	11.2
Hamburg	1978	37.6	51.5	4.8	4.5	21.6	48.6	6.8	18.3

Recent Election

Year	Total Population				Age 18 – 25			
	CDU	SPD	FDP	"Greens"[1]	CDU	SPD	FDP	"Greens"[1]
1979	32.0	48.7	11.1	5.4	16.9	50.5	10.3	19.9
1980	53.4	32.5	8.3	5.3	40.2	36.2	6.9	15.7
1981	48.0	38.8	5.6	7.2	32.2	36.4	5.6	24.3
1982	50.7	36.5	5.9	6.5	40.8	33.3	5.2	20.3
1982	43.2	42.8	4.8	7.7	29.8	38.7	3.3	26.0

1) various "Green" or "Alternative" Lists

Sources: Statistische Jahrbücher; Die Zeit, 1.10.82:35

Table 7-1: Federal Republic of Germany Election Results for states having the "Greens" in Parliament. Most Recent Election and Preceding Election, Total Population and Age 18-25

democracy" ("Basisdemokratie") and non—violence are the two other guiding principles (besides "ecological" and "social" politics) the Greens have adopted. They oppose "the spreading bureaucracy rendering private citizens helpless; the increasing arbitrariness and misuse of power of the economic and state apparatuses" and support the use of various forms of non—violent resistance (Die Grunen, 1980). Indeed, democratic practices and civil rights have become a major issue for the Greens in election campaigns.

There is also empirical evidence from public opinion data that ecological attitudes and views on what are the proper and permissible ways of political conduct are closely linked. Fietkau (1981:4f) and Kessel (1984) observed that the ecological perspective was not restricted to a set of views on facts and thus not independent of more deep—seated attitudes and beliefs. Rather, it fit into a more general value pattern of social and political convictions. They found in attitude surveys in the US, Great Britain and the FRG that individuals with ecological values also tend to believe that society should not strive for wealth by knowingly incurring non—negligible risks and that society should provide many opportunities for citizen participation in political decisions rather than leave these decisions to those in responsible positions. This attitude is not found among the "average" union members and citizens. Among those, considerable resentment exists against unconventional political activities, especially among older people (e.g. Conradt, 1980:250). In that respect, the countervailing power role of the German environmental movement is perhaps most pronounced. The conflicts with labor's factor of order role therefore are not only political as discussed in Chapter 6 but also ideological. Fietkau noted, in fact, that the value patterns he observed square well with Inglehart's theory.

Thus, at stake are not merely environmental (or housing or defense or women's rights) policies but the legitimacy of the political system. While the overwhelming majority of Germans including those protesting affirm the system in principle as laid down by the Constitution, there is considerable dissatisfaction with how it is implemented. The perception of the character of the W.German political system has shifted particularly among those cohorts most likely to be engaged in the environmental movement (c.f. Chapter 4). A case in point is a poll repeatedly conducted between 1953 and 1976, inquiring whether "today in West Germany one can freely state his political opinion, or is it better to be careful?". Conradt (1980:241ff) reported that the share of those affirming the former increased to a high of 84% in 1971, but declined to 73% in late 1976 and probably further since. This negative attitude was most pronounced among the young and better educated [4]. The scepticism, Conradt argued, can be traced to opposition to "security checks" applied since 1972 to candidates of public employment (i.e. including teachers) by the government [5]. Critics of these practices see them in line with various attempts by the authorities to criminalize protest movements (including environmentalists) and to declare these protests to be inspired or directed against the Constitutional order of the country. The responses of the authorities to protests in general, and the security checks in particular, have led to "Staatsverdrossenheit", i.e. being fed up with the authorities, especially among the post—WWII generation.

These findings must be seen in the light of other pieces of evidence. Fietkau (1981:7) noted that more than twice as many environmentalists (22.4%) work in (often public) service jobs than the average person (9.7%). Thus, these groups tend to be particularly affected by infringements of the state on personal liberties, and for that reason alone can be expected to be more critical of the existing order than the average citizen.

Moreover, polls found that those politically most active have become increasingly dissatisfied with the existing political parties and that their distance to the political system has grown (FR, 11.3.81:4). Their activities have shifted from political parties to citizen groups

165

and other unorthodox initiatives. By no means do they all rally around ecological issues. But public opinion analysis has yielded "apparent correlations" of an individual's attitudes on defense issues, nuclear energy, urban squatting or security checks (Spiegel, 23.11.1981:57; also Fietkau, Kessel, 1982). In addition, several surveys and the findings of the Bundestag Enquete Commission on "Youth Protests and the Democratic State" have indicated that the alienation of the "young" with moral and cultural traditions, with the established political parties and society in general has become considerable (e.g. FR, 12.7.80:1; FR, 28.10.80:1; FR, 10.4.81:4; SZ, 4.5.82:5; Tagesspiegel, 12.5.82, FR, 1.9.82:4). In the unions, their waning attractiveness to the young was attributed to the same sentiments that caused young people flock to citizen groups, peace groups and the Greens (Buente, 1984). A survey in 1984 reportedly even found that a majority of the public favored the Greens being represented in Parliaments for two reasons: the Greens were valued for their mobilization against environmental degradation, and for their vivid opposition against those in established positions (FAZ, 3.9.84:11).

For all these reasons one can plausibly argue that the environmental organizations and activities are only one manifestation of a broader dissatisfaction in the Federal Republic. As Chapters 2 and 3 indicated this dissatisfaction has been expressed on a wide range of single issues. These single issue activities have increasingly built linkages to other groups and the aggregation of these activities comprise what Inglehart labelled New Politics. This is not to say that Old Politics are dead —the CDU victory in the 1983 federal elections attests to the contrary. However, New Politics have complemented the Old ones at the polls, in the streets and within established political actors such as in the SPD, the FDP, the unions or the churches.

7.3 The Effects of Ideologies and Values on the LER in the FRG

It appears quite plausible to apply Eppler's and Inglehart's concepts introduced earlier to the LER in the FRG. In Eppler's terms, post-materialism corresponds to "value" and materialism to "structural" conservatism. The conflict between the two movements, hence, lies neither strictly on a left–right axis nor on a materialist/ post-materialist axis. Watts (1979) pictured the framework of the traditional and new political debates in Figure 7–1. Furthermore, Figure 7–2 indicates the possible distribution of value preferences for labor and environmentalists. It suggests that labor's preferences are oriented along traditional lines while those of environmentalists follow the new dimensions. But a still vast overlap of concerns is indicated.

The overlay of two dimensions has confounded the LER in several ways. First, it makes a definition of what the issues in question are more difficult. If both sides viewed the issues on the same dimension and one could agree which questions ought to be asked, the debate would focus on facts and thus facilitate a constructive dialogue even if the two sides would often come up with different answers to the questions posed. But the absence of such a common basis has encouraged misunderstandings and often resulted in unfounded hostility.

Second, the existence of the two dimensions blurs the countervailing power/ factor of order distinction. If only a left–right perspective were taken, labor's factor of order role with respect to environmental, energy, or housing issues postulated by the New Politics framework would be pushed aside by the countervailing power role it has taken on social and equity issues. Environmentalism, on the other hand, indeed would become the fad of the more affluent and better educated as the left–right framework suggests while the "elite challenging" aspect of New Politics would be lost.

As a result, the conflicts between labor and environmentalists were as much over form as over substance. While there was some name-calling

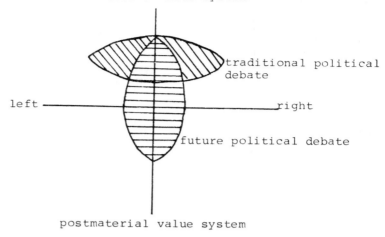

Figure 7-1 :   Frameworks of the traditional and future
              political debate (Watts, 1979)

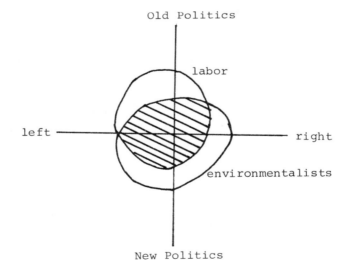

Figure 7-2 : Dimensions of labor and environmentalist
              political engagements

167

from the environmental side —the unions, for example, were labelled as "growth fetishists", "Atomfilz" or "optimists about progress" (Fortschrittsoptimisten)—, the established parties and the unions until recently sought to dismiss environmentalism without entering into a substantive debate.

In the mildest form, environmentalists were done away with as political dayflies, dreamers, romanticists and utopians. A commentator on the aforementioned Muellheim meeting of labor representatives and environmentalists noted that the main obstacle to an "integrative dialogue" was the fact that the citizen groups "demand entirely new solutions that radically inquire about the causes of the critical deformations of nature and society thereby taking off into the clear skies of theoretical considerations". On the other side, he argued, are the politicians and labor unionists "caught in the thickets of practical life whose outlook is not free enough to visualize solutions to the practical difficulties" (Badische Zeitung, 3.10.1978).

Moreover, environmentalists were accused of adhering to Spenglerian "cultural pessimism" (e.g. Vorwaerts, 5.10.78; Stuttgarter Nachrichten, 2.10.78) but, as Chapter 2 already noted, were also defamed as cover–ups for terrorists, communists, subversives and criminals who used environmental concerns merely as a pretense for undermining the constitutional democratic order of the country. For Hessian's SPD Prime Minister and former (construction) union leader Borner, at one time the Greens even put themselves in the proximity of fascism because they allegedly challenge the parliamentary system and threaten the state. (SZ, 16.8.1982:2; Der Spiegel, 33/1982:36). Similarly, CDU politicians repeatedly accused the Greens of resorting to fascistoid methods —at other occasions, the same politicians blamed them of receiving funds from East Germany.

Before the environmental movement developed its party leg, a standard criticism saw environmentalists break the "groundrules of parliamentary democracy", i.e. environmentalists did not express their grievances through the political parties as they should have done but relied primarily on extra–parliamentary activities. Again, the debate focused on form rather than on substance. When large demonstrations, occupations of construction sites, urban squatting, etc. were discussed, the "problem of violence" or the formal violations of the law, were the main concerns rather than the question why these actions were taking place. Nor was there much discussion on how appropriate and applicable "the law" was in the particular circumstances (e.g. Tagesspiegel, 10.8.82). Such questions, however, were central concerns of the protestors whose "elite–challenging" sentiments of course were reenforced by the feeling that the debate was deliberately put on an abstract and artificial level while there was virtually a "non–debate" on what they thought were the real salient issues.

To be sure, there were attempts to engage in "dialogues" with environmentalists and other protest groups but, in general, they were not accepted as sincere. It was another sympton of the elite–challenging character of New Politics that environmentalists soon suspected that these "dialogues" —where they occured at all— were primarily meant to quell protest rather than freely exchange views (e.g. FR, 12.2.82:14).

As a whole, however, formal discussions and meetings with participants from both labor and environmentalists were rare. The only significant government sponsored attempt to provide such a forum was the Working Group on Environmental Matters (Arbeitsgemeinschaft fur Umweltfragen) but this did not lead to constructive labor–environmentalist interactions [6]. Moreover, union halls often remained closed to critics from within the unions and from outside (e.g. Sarrazin, 1982:37). The above–mentioned Aktionskreis Leben, a forum of critics within the unions of official energy policies, for example, usually was not given access to union facilities. Environmentalists within and outside the unions were depicted as political and ideological outsiders without further explanation. As outsiders and political 'immatures' unwilling to play by the political groundrules, they were not to be taken seriously since substantive discussions with them would anyway be useless. Thus, the circle for rationalizing the avoidance of contacts was closed.

When environmentalism had successfully consolidated into a political party, the line of arguments again changed. At center stage moved the question whether the Greens possessed, in fact, the ability to engage in politics ("Politikfaehigkeit"). As noted in the last chapter, the distrust of the party to institutionalization and professionalization, incoherent party platform positions, the "rotation" of Green representatives in the legislatures after two years in order to prevent the formation of an entrenched party elite, the often tedious decision-making process by the party "base" —they all nurtured the party image of inpredictability and unrealibility. Nevertheless, situations of political stalemate between the SPD and the CDU such as in Hessia induced politicians to perform dramatic role reversals: Less than two years after putting the Greens close to fascism, the same SPD Prime Minister concluded the first "red—green" alliance. In other states, the Greens were attacked for hesitating to seek formal coalitions with the SPD. The CDU glittered as well with astonishing rhetorical reversals: the criticism shifted from blaming the environmental movement for not engaging in party politics, to warnings of a looming "red— green chaos", to chastizing —after the red—green alliance in Hessia had failed— the supposedly lacking ability or willingness of the Greens to assume political responsibility. Labor leadership, as noted, was split. The majority advocated a cautious exchange of views with selected parts of the Greens and condoned SPD/Green alliances, while several unions prefered SPD/CDU coalitions.

7.4 The Ideology of American Labor and the LER

Richard Grossman of EFFE was the first who suggested to me that the split among American unions toward environmental and energy issues follows roughly along old AFL versus CIO lines (Interview May 1979). Similarly, Logan and Nelkin (1980:8) have argued that the different positions the American unions have taken toward nuclear power are to some extent a reflection of the history and structure of organized labor in the US. Therefore, this section will briefly touch on the historical and ideological experiences of US labor. Especially, it will examine the distinguishing traits of "social" and "business" union traditions and how they have possibly affected the LER.

7.4.1 "Social" and "Business" Unionism: General Remarks

American unions operated mainly on the model of "business unionism". Piore (1978:2) called its essential characteristic "the effort to appeal to workers on narrow, particularistic grounds, eschewing any claim to represent other interests outside the immediate work. As such it is distinguished from broader, more general appeals to workers as consumers, citizens, members of a broader social class or of an ethnic or racial grouping". The second characteristic of a business union, according to Piore, is the sharp distinction between economic and political activity. Economic activities are meant to occur between a union body and the employer, i.e. mostly in the form of collective bargaining, and are separate from the pursuit of goals through pressures on governmental bodies. A third characteristic is the belief in being non—ideological, in Piore's (1978:3) words, in the ability "to define itself in opposition to philosophies and ideologies in which issues of work and the economy are seen in terms of a transformative vision of the socio—economic system such as socialism or communism".

And a fourth aspect is an extreme distrust of "intellectuals".

However, an important faction of American labor has considerably deviated from the business union model. It has been inclined to see labor's interests in the context of larger political, social and ideological questions. This perspective has brought some unions and their leaders in conflict with mainstream union policy in a number of areas including energy and environmental issues. Sidney Lens (1959) called this perspective "social unionism". It is characterized by a far less accomodating approach to management than business unionism and a tendency to define the problems of labor in terms of social class. Social unions mean less to be institutions providing services to the membership but rather vehicles to give workers greater power at the workplace, their community and in general politics. Therefore, they are committed to organize the unorganized and to seek alliances with other constituencies. Their agenda includes issues of health, safety, working conditions, civil rights, etc in addition to economic benefits (Logan, Nelkin, 1980:8).

Grossman's proposition restated will become the central argument in this section: The differences within American organized labor with respect to environmentalism have at their ideological foundation the difference between the traditions of business unionism and social unionism. The more a union has adhered to social unionism, the likelier it is that it has cooperated with environmentalism. The reverse applies for business unionism: Important exceptions notwithstanding, business unionism is stronger in the old AFL unions while the former CIO unions have tended toward social unionism.

Most characteristics of business unionism can already be found in the AFL tradition. McConnell described the AFL as an organization based on craft unions espousing trade autonomy. It insisted on economic rather than political action and was devoted to a "voluntaristic" laissez-faire tradition that opposed any meddling of government in union matters as well as actions involving the law and politics. It distrusted intellectual approaches to the labor movement, believed in action through local government while rigidly opposing national government actions (pp.80–86).

Some anecdotal remarks may elucidate the mode of thinking prevalent in the old AFL in the 1920s and 1930s. Labor lobbyist Edelman (1974:56) described in his autobiography that the AFL of the 1920s was no place for social objectives. The attitude was prevalent that a labor union should confine itself to attending to the welfare of its due-paying members. Before the depression, the concept of the labor movement was still the guild tradition of a group of skilled craftsmen banding together to protect their own economic interests. The old building trade leaders (up to the 1930s) had been always "to a man opposed to public housing and to women's rights". In the same vein, "the bumbling leaders of the old guard (the AFL International presidents, HS) saw no reason at all to concern themselves with the problems of labor abroad". Further, at the 1920 convention, AFL President Samuel Gompers had opposed the nationalization of the railroads because, in his opinion, the workers would then be enslaved by government authority (Kramer, 1962:15). Incredible as it may sound today, organized labor opposed legislation providing for old age, health and unemployment insurance until the 1930s. Although the Great Depression had already laid-off millions of workers for years, the AFL leadership thought unemployment was none of the government's business (McConnell,1967:83). In 1935, the formation of AFSCME was made more difficult than necessary since the AFL leadership at that time was not determined to organize the public service.

The lesser parochialism of social unionism has its roots in the formative years of its major unions in the 1930s. The Great Depression led to unprecedented government intervention in the economic life of the US. With the election of a Democratic president in 1932, the government began to actively support economic expansion and job creation, and thus "to lay the groundwork for an informal alliance with organized labor" (Hildebrand, 1979:121). The advent of industrial unions and a broadening of social objectives were mutually reenforcing. The unions in place had been able to meet to a large degree the interests of the old skilled craft workers by controlling access to the craft and the setting of wages within the craft. One immediate consequence of the then prevailing traditional union voluntarism, Herding and Sabel (1979:369f) argued, had been "to leave the semi—skilled and unskilled workers... in a subordinate and vulnerable position". However, the traditional exlusionary policies could not work for the new species of an industrial worker whose basic needs of having a job, earning enough, having decent housing, etc. could not be satisfied by collective bargaining agreements between the union and the employer alone. Thus, the newly forming unions had the task of tackling a wide range of social objectives which made political engagement a must. As a rule, Herding and Sabel stated further, only reform legislation could guarantee basic job rights, including the right of the union to do collective bargaining, to these workers. Political discourse in the union movement was in the 1930s largely limited to the CIO unions (p.371).

The AFL craft unions were bitterly antagonistic to industrial unionism. In 1940, both the AFL and business urged the repeal of the Wagner Act since they considered it too advantageous for the CIO (Hildebrandt, 1979:22). Grant McConnell (1967:306f) termed their hostility as doctrinaire and rigid but also rational on two grounds. First, industrial unionism meant a change in the constituency foundation which in any organization is profoundly disruptive —especially so to the security of its leadership. Second, organizations with small constituencies and limited objectives have very real tactical advantages: benefits for a few are more easily obtained than for many.

The prevalence of business unionism today does of course not mean that labor's attitudes toward political engagement and the state—economy relationship have remained unchanged since the 1920s and 30s. Voluntarism in the AFL days meant rejection of government involvement in the economy. Today's business unionism by all means believes in the government's presence in the economic sphere (Barton, 1974:516) and "organized labor stands firmly committed to the policies of the new welfare state" (Hildebrand, 1979:121). However, collective bargaining remains labor's "still central institution" whose "outlook remains dominated by an ethic of immediate ends" guided by "particular pragmatic objectives rather than the pursuit of overriding and unitary ideology" (Hildebrand: 121/122).

The business unionist outlook discouraged labor—environmentalist cooperation for several reasons. First, the appeal to workers on narrow, particularistic grounds will, of course, preclude contacts with environmentalism and other causes. If unions represent merely the work interests of their members, why should they be concerned about the negative effects of environmental pollution on their members in their role of citizens outside of the workplace? The American labor movement has been more concerned about hazards at the work environment than those for the natural environment. OSH has, in fact, been an increasing and non—controversial concern among the American unions including the building and construction trades. Furthermore, the work orientation helps local union bodies to play down the pollution stemming from facilities under their jurisdiction. Second, the separation of the economic from the political sphere with respect to the environment complements work particularism. Intervention by a union body against pollution in general would be in the political sphere, and the union would face it as a political and not as an economic problem. This might be different, if there are specific pollution sources in a union body's jurisdiction. Then economic and political considerations might merge but the union would still face the problem of whether to address the issue at all, and, if so, whether to rely on collective bargaining or political activities or both. Third, the claim of business unionism of being not ideological is probably the smallest barrier toward environmentalism. Most environmentalists probably share this belief themselves. Where environmental groups link environmental protection and systemic socio—economic transformation, as has occasionally happened, unions will likely be most suspicious and reserved. Finally, anti—intellectualism conceivably puts distance between unions and environmentalists and their programs and arguments. Intellectuals belong to environmental groups in disproportionally high numbers. Further, many ecological processes are fairly complex, abstract and do not allow for black—and—white solutions.

On the other hand, social unionism tended to favor labor—environmentalist cooperation. For social unions, environmental protection was a social end and considered worth while pursuing. These unions embraced less work particularism, complemented political and economic activities, and sometimes represented "intellectuals" such as teachers and maintained substantial highly educated staffs.

Thus, a paradox is apparent. On the one hand, labor—environmentalist cooperation in the US clearly involved social unions while there tended to be conflicts with business unions. On the other hand, German labor resembles more the social than the business union model but the LER in the FRG has been more conflictual than in the US. The answer to the paradox, I think, lies in the different ways in which the unions could relate their ideological propensities to political life. In the FRG, the unions could pursue many aims of social unionism as a factor of order; in the US, the labor movement —and especially the social unions— were in a countervailing power role politically and ideologically. The stronger countervailing power role of American labor, of course, increased its needs to look for political allies. Social unions both saw themselves more so in that role than business unions and were principally open to alliances with environmentalists.

7.4.2 "Social" and "Business" Unionism: Cases

This section presents the heritage and ideology of the International Union of Operating Engineers (IUOE) as a prototype of a building and construction union rooted in the business union tradition and then turns to the UAW as an example of social unionism. Subsequently, I will look at examples of the labor— management relations that have been distinctly different for the two types of unions and have affected the LER with respect to energy matters a good deal.

The IUOE was formed in 1896 and became a member of the AFL. Until 1940, it was strictly a craft union of stationary and operating engineers. By the mid 1960s, the building and construction industry had become its mainstay, and at present, three quarters of its members are in construction and one quarter are stationary engineers (interview Ted Reed, IUOE Director of Research, February 25,1981). Garth L. Mangum (1964), writing on the union's economic history described the IUOE as slow to depart from the old AFL traditions "of which it was an unusually orthodox example" (p.8). In the 1920s, the local unions had highly parochial views which "stemmed from the fact that each member was interested only in his own immediate employment" (p.68). A "more members — less jobs" philosophy prevailed among the membership at large (p.110). "The engineers have been as practical as the machines they operate. One could search the union's literature from 1896 to 1960 without finding a shred of discussion of an ideological nature. The engineers' union has had but one ideology —preservation of the craft, and one goal— improvement of the wages and working conditions of its members. It would be difficult to find a more orthodox example of business unionism" (p.60).

In the case of the IUOE, business unionism as an ideological cause for the conflicting relationship with environmental organizations was supplemented by the very work IUOE members perform. Mangum described technology as the key to the union's growth and development, the union having been "unusually sensitive to changes in the technology of motive power and the development of various types of machinery" (p.1). This fact might explain why the IUOE has felt particularly critical toward groups and values that sought environmental protection and were sceptical of technical progress. The mechanization of construction made possible projects such as the Hoover, Grand Coulee and Glen Canyon dams, the Tennessee Valley Authority, the Alcan Highway, the "Big Inch" pipeline, the St. Lawrence Seaway, etc. They made possible the growth of the IUOE, the membership of which rose from 58000 in 1940 to 302000 in 1959 (p.152). In that period, 11,000 pieces of road-building equipment all manned by operating engineers were used for the construction of the Alcan highway, 1284 airports and 1475 miles of "Big Inch" pipeline were constructed in the US. The atomic plants at Oak Ridge, Hanford and Los Alamos employed operating engineers in large numbers while residential building construction meant little work for operating engineers (p.162). Thus, exactly those types of construction projects which environmentalists later have bitterly opposed provided employment for IUOE members while the employment alternatives usually offered by environmentalists have not been in the union's jurisdiction.

The United Autoworkers is probably the union most renowned for being a social union ideologically distant from mainstream AFL-CIO tenets. The UAW started as an AFL autoworkers drive but joined the newly formed CIO in 1936. In its formative years, intense factional struggles often along ideological lines on organizing, collective bargaining, and National Labor Relations Board representation elections were frequent. Walter Reuther, who might be seen as a prototype "social unionist" had been a leader of the Socialist Party faction within the UAW and was elected International president in 1946. His leadership, which lasted until he died in an airplane accident in 1970, had a decisive influence on the UAW (Stieber, 1962:9).

The UAW displayed several of the features that distinguished social and business unionism and were also relevant for the LER: Closeness of community relations, emphasis on education, engagement in politics, high intellectual standards, reliance on generalist rather than particularistic approaches, recognition of the limits of collective bargaining. Reuther was convinced that the UAW could move ahead only with and not at the expense of the community. As a case in point, he emphatically stressed the importance of rooting environmental protection efforts in a solid local base, and the UAW repeatedly hosted and participated in activities seeking to strengthen the ties between various community based interest groups.

Similarly, the union gave high priority to political activities. At times, the union had strong sentiments in favor of a third party but mostly it was a driving force of the liberal left within the Democratic Party. In 1948, the UAW International Executive Board adopted "as its official political objective the formation ... of a genuine progressive political party" (in Stieber:37) but abandoned this plan after Truman's surprise election. In the next three decades since then, the UAW has been a major "progressive" force WITHIN the Democratic party. "No longer does one hear talk of a third party at Solidarity House", UAW headquarters in Detroit, noted Stieber (p.112). In October 78, UAW president Douglas A. Fraser called the organizations of the liberal left to Detroit "to consider formation of [a] new alliance aimed at transforming the American political system by making it more accountable, responsible and democratic" by transforming "the Democratic Party into a genuinely progressive people's party" (Boston Globe, 15 October 1978:A7; [7]).

In addition, there is little evidence of the anti-intellectualism ascribed to the AFL tradition and business unionism in the UAW.

Stieber (1962:93) reported that the UAW staff was probably the most diverse, talented and professional of any union in the US and, indeed, might be the most distinctive aspect of the union. Further, the UAW educational program was (at the time of Stieber's writing) considered by labor educators to be the best of any US union, in terms of both size and quality. Stieber also pointed out that the union had integrated its political among its other activities. For example, in 1967, it established a Department of Conservation and Resource Development and re-designated the Recreation Department to include Leisure-Time Activities.

The two following quotations summarize the obligation Reuther felt a union ought to have for the work, social and natural environment of its members and the larger polity:

> The UAW in its politics, programs and activities has recognized historically that service to its members requires not only progress in the area of collective bargaining but also progress within the community to build a better life for all citizens. Our members and their families are directly affected by the environment around them, whether inside the plant or outside the plant. The pollution of the air and of the water; the unwise waste of the natural resources are of concern to all of us. As the new technology creates the opportunity for an increasing measure of leisure time, the constructive use of that leisure time by our members and others in the community can make a significant contribution to building a better society and to assuring individual self-fulfillment. (UAW Administrative Letter (Aug.1,1967:1))

Reuther saw clear limits to labor's "still central institution -collective bargaining" (Hildebrand, 1979:121):

> I tell the membership of my union — there are 1,600,000 members of the UAW — I say to them: what good is getting higher pay, what good is it to get a shorter work week so you have more leisure time, or longer vacation periods , if the lakes you want to take your families to are polluted and you can't fish in them or swim in them or if the air is poisoned and if our cities are becoming big asphalt jungles, turning the green parks into parking lots? That's not the kind of world in which free people ought to live. Yet, that's the kind of world we are going to give them if we continue to neglect these basic problems. UAW members have a strong union, but they can't solve the problems of their living environment at the bargaining table. They must join with men and women of good will in the community so that together they can participate in generating a great citizens crusade to deal with the problems of clean water, to deal with the problems of improving our living environment. (Policies and Priorities for Progress: To Combat Air and Water Pollution, 25 Sept.68:18)

The perhaps most dramatic example of the UAW's deviance from AFL-CIO beliefs was the split between Meany and Reuther in 1967 when the UAW disaffiliated from the AFL-CIO. Reuther and Meany perhaps personified social and business unionism. A.H. Raskin wrote in the New York Times (Feb.6, 1967:28L) that their differences were most fundamental in foreign affairs where the AFL-CIO position under Meany "is almost indistinguishable from that of the American Legion on Vietnam and the cold war". On the domestic front, they had the same objectives in civil rights, the abolition of poverty, national economic planning and full employment —only the UAW was more committed to make these objectives become real. Edelman (1974:183ff) pointed to their differences on coexistence with communist nations, civil rights and anti—poverty programs, and what the function of a union ought to be. When Reuther worked with Martin Luther King on civil rights and anti—poverty programs, Meany tolerated the "flagrantly discriminatory practices of some of his most important unions, the building and construction trades" (ibid.). The two leaders' understanding of the functions of a union was wide apart. Reuther was passionately convinced that unions had to become an active social force by supporting action programs in poor neighborhoods not only financially but that they should also involve union members in them, setting up workshops and holding classes. Meany would agree, Edelman wrote, that such involvement was desirable, "even that his own building trades should be more socially minded but nothing could change his hard—core conviction that the first duty of a union is to its own dues—paying members".

Let me now turn to the relationship with management especially in the electric utility industry which was distinctly different for social and business unionism. The building and construction unions in the US have frequently joined forces with the utility and nuclear industry in order to promote power plant siting and construction. Unlike in the FRG where union leadership has criticized too apparent ties with the nuclear industry, the American construction unions collaborated freely with industry where common interests were perceived. The social unions, on the other hand, often were highly critical of industry practices at and off the workplace.

In April 1978, the AFL—CIO Building and Construction Trades Department and 16 major building trades unions (including IUOE, IBEW, as well as the Teamsters), and the four construction companies which have built more than 80% of the nuclear powers in the US signed, the 'Nuclear Power Construction Stabilization Agreement'. President Carter even witnessed the signing and announced the action ti the press (The Carpenter, June 1978:7). The agreement superseded any other collective bargaining agreement in the construction industry, and, in the eyes of critics of the agreement, meant that major concessions were made to the employers ("Tower of Babel", SOUTHERN EXPOSURE, Winter 1979) [8]. The employers, in turn, agreed to recognize the signatory International unions as the sole and exclusive collective bargaining representatives for its craft employees at a nuclear power plant job site.

Labor—industry collaboration has been frequent in IUOE's and IBEW's history. Mangum (1964:206f) reported in a summary of IUOE's history in the 1940 to 1958 period that "the respect of the employers was gained through internal discipline, knowledge of industry problems, and willingness to cooperate and even take the lead in solving these problems". Further, the IUOE has worked with the National Environmental Development Association which includes labor, industry and agricultural interests advocating "reasonable" environmental regulations (OE, 1/78:8). With respect to the IBEW, Mangum reported, that electrical contractors have had an "exceptionally close" relationship with the IBEW because they usually employed only electricians, the craft is well organized, and the contractors themselves, for the most part, have risen from the ranks of the unions (p.292).

Recent examples of labor—industry cooperation involved mostly power plant siting issues. In response to an environmentalist court suit against the Colstrip coal fired plant in Montana, the IUOE joined with the National Building Trades Department to intervene in court in favor of the plant construction (OE, April 1978:10). The journal "Nuclear Industry" paid compliments to the Texas AFL—CIO for its role in helping defeat the Austin referendum on nuclear power ("Tower of Babel", op.cit.). In the face of anti—nuclear power initiatives in 1976 in Colorado and Oregon, coalitions of business and labor formed opposing the initiatives. The IBEW Journal (Oct. 1976) stressed that "IBEW members and local unions are very active in this quest". Further, an

"Edison Electric Institute for the Electric Companies" advertisement
featured a picture of AFL–CIO Building and Construction Trades
Department president Robert A. Georgine posing in the AFL–CIO
headquarters announcing: "Millions of future jobs hang on building
nuclear power plants now" (EFFE, Labor– Nuclear Power Package, no
date). Many of the 15 general union presidents affiliated with
Georgine's department participate officially in assorted industry
created "jobs & energy" coalitions, such as Americans for Energy
Independence, the National Environmental Development Association, and
their various local counterparts (In These Times, 18.6. to 1.7.1980).
   The building and construction trades have tried to utilize their
good relations with the nuclear industry to fight attempts of business
to repeal important labor legislation. In a letter to the Board of
Directors of the Edison Electric Institute and to the president of the
Atomic Industrial Forum, building trades president Georgine reminded
the nuclear industry that without the presidents of the 17 building and
construction unions

> the social benefits of nuclear energy might never have been
> recognized by the AFL–CIO. Indeed, the vast resources of
> organized labor might easily have been added to those of many
> other liberal groups advocating a "non–nuclear" energy policy.
> (June 26,1979 letter, in: EFFE, Labor–Nuclear Power Packet)

He called the nuclear industry an "ally" and the nuclear energy sector
a "symbol of labor–management cooperation" but pointed out that the
attacks on labor legislation have made it difficult for him to defend
this concept.
   Yet, Georgine's appeal has neither lessened business efforts to
repeal labor legislation nor has the uselessness of the appeal changed
the cooperation between the building and construction trades and the
energy industry. The building trade unions reportedly cosponsored
Annual Energy Advocacy Conferences in 1979 and 1980 organized by the
right–wing Heritage Foundation and "its anti–union corporate allies"
(In These Times, op.cit.). Prodded by the building trades, even
AFL–CIO president Kirkland participated at the 1980 conference.
According to the conference brochure (which, critics pointed out, even
lacked a union label), the conference focused on nuclear power,
synthetic fuels, and advocacy skills. The conferences have sought to
initiate corporate backed pro– nuclear "citizen groups" imitating the
tactics of the anti–nuclear movement.

   The perception of right–wing business as the common adversary has
been an ingredient in those cases where labor and environmental
organizations have cooperated (c.f. Section 6.4). IAM president
Winpisinger has perhaps painted the constellation of power between
business, labor and environmental organizations in most dramatic terms:

> Trade unions are concerned with the lives, limbs, health and
> safety of their members, just as environmentalists are concerned
> for the lives, health and safety of the citizens at large.
>   This is no time for timidity. If the trade unions or the
> environmentalists, acting alone, can't successfully challenge the
> corporate bully, then we must make common cause and enjoin the
> monster together.
>   We must recognize that a basic alliance of trade unions and
> responsible environmentalists will have to lead the fight.
>   Trade union members must recognize that our corporate employers
> are not our benefactors, if they persist in poisoning, polluting
> and killing us on the job.
>   Responsible environmentalists must recognize that in this

society, 98 percent of the people can't survive without a job and income.

Together we must realize that a political economy that cannot or will not guarantee the right to employment for every American and the right to organize and bargain collectively for every worker, obviously such a system will not cleanup the workplace, will not keep dangerous products off the marketplace, or conserve and preserve the whole wide natural environment.

Together, we must realize the barriers to job security and a wholesome environment, are not economic or technological.

They are political. The barriers are questions of political power.

Who has the power?

Corporate America has a lock on our natural resources; is interlocked horizontally and vertically with all other segments of business and industry; has the money to monopolize our airwaves and the print media; and has the money to buy controlling interests in both major political parties. (Winpisinger, IAM president, Remarks to the Hawaii Conference on Jobs and the Environment, Honolulu, Nov.17, 1978, p.7)

To be sure, the radical form of Winpisinger's criticism is not echoed by the other industrial unions. It also might have turned-off some environmental organizations from participating in his Citizens Labor Energy Coalition. Further, the Sierra Club, for example, has addressed the business community on the question on how business and the environment can live together (McCloskey, 1977). But many share Winpisinger's view, as Chapter 3 has documented, that labor and environmentalists have common interests often opposed to those of business. Lobbying efforts in favor of labor, environmental, or occupational legislation have usually been opposed by groups close to business and right—wing organizations. Particularly in the 1980 elections, many liberal candidates close to both labor and environmentalists were defeated by candidates heavily backed by corporate and "new right" interests. In sum, the attitudes toward business as a potential ally or adversary, respectively, were different among social and business unions.

NOTES

[1] At the DGB convention in March 1981, the revision of the DGB Basic Program provoked a major debate on the question of whether communism belonged to the major roots of FRG unitary unionism. This was not the case, a clear majority voted, since unionism in the FRG has been molded by the experience made in the Weimar Republic and Nazi dictatorship. Present unionism, so the revised Basic Program, has its primary roots in the liberal— socialist and the christian— social labor movement traditions (FR 11.3.81:8, 14.3.81:3).

[2] Especially the older conservation groups and a predecessor organization of the green party ("Green Action Future"—GAZ) around the former CDU Bundestag member Herbert Gruhl (e.g. Gruhl, 1978; "The Green Manifest", GAZ, in: Chamer Zeitung 5.9.78; Gaertner, 1978, critique of Gruhl and the Green Manifest; also see FR, 12.8.82: 9,10).

[3] Similar to the DGB Basic Program, the BBU views the "profit—maximizing" Western market economies as well as the "production maximizing" East European centrally planned economies

as unsuited for economic and ecological goals. The BBU 'catalogue of demands' cited in Section 3.1 supports the full employment goal and qualitative growth, and warns of untempered automation as a major source of unemployment. The 1980 Federal Election Platform of the Greens included demands for the 35 hour work week without loss of pay (same goal as stated in the DGB Aktionsprogramm 1979:6); for disarmament (also DGB Basic Program, op. cit.:34); the break—up of giant corporations into better controllable smaller units (the DGB Basic Program calls for more effective controls of monopolies and cartels and for the nationalization of key industries (p.47)) to be supervised by "Economic and Cultural Councils" which parallels the old labor union demand of establishing "Economic and Social Councils"; or the banning of lock—outs in industrial conflicts (the DGB went to the German highest Constitutional Court in order to have lock—outs prohibited).

[4] While the aggregate decline was 6%, the drop among respondents under age 30 in 1976 was 15%. Among respondents under age 30 in 1976 with above average education who reported "frequent" engagements in political debates, only 51% believed that they can freely express themselves.

[5] These security checks have led to denials, dismissals and threats thereof if individuals were (suspected to be) affiliated or sympathetic to groups adjudged by the state or federal governments (but not the courts) to be against the "free, democratic order" of the land. Critics of the security checks have argued that the authorities have used their power to discriminate against undesirable political views and to define and adjudge arbitrarily what comprises "permissible" political thinking and what not.

[6] Judging from the minutes of the annual fora, the representatives of the interest groups have talked past each other; questions were hardly asked; at the 1977 forum titled "Citizen Action Groups — Citizen Participation", the labor representatives took the floor only once. A representative of the OTV told me that contacts with BBU representatives have been limited. While the BBU people have been very competent, a fruitful exchange of ideas has only occured on technical matters. As soon as discussions could have reached the public, they became useless (interview Mr. Hecht, OTV, 10.7.1981). Mathar (1977:147f) reported that AGU above all was intended as a forum for cooperation between the government, labor and the business community. Mathar referred to a meeting between DOI and DGB officials, in which both sides expressed reservations about citizen group presence in AGU. However, both sides resigned themselves to environmentalists participating: the DOI considered citizen group representation "unavoidable" and the DGB decided "to put aside the reservations".

[7] Also see "Building Coalitions: Unanswered Questions", Social Policy, Nov/Dez 78:32ff

[8] The agreement mandates that there are no strikes and lockouts of a for the duration of the project. Wages and benefits are to be adjusted periodically as decided by an explicitly created joint labor management committee and an umpire. There will be "significant flexibility on work processes and manning patterns" to reduce labor costs of construction and to speed up operations. Substantial provisions for rotating shifts, work on weekends, and lower than usual overtime pay were further included.

8 Summary and Conclusions

This inquiry into the relationship between organized labor and environmentalism (LER) in the United States and the Federal Republic of Germany was based on the assumption that reconciling employment and environmental protection problems was impossible if both interest groups would not tolerate (if not actively support) whatever the solutions to the problem would be. The argument was not that the two interests SHOULD cooperate. Rather, I wanted to explore whether and how they COULD cooperate, and what prevented them from doing so.

As a whole, and notable exceptions notwithstanding, the LER in the two countries has been conflictual in the period examined since the mid—1960s —particularly with respect to energy issues.

Five —not necessarily mutually exclusive— explanations for the LER were discussed. Briefly stated, these were:

1. Employment and environmental protection concerns are perceived as a built—in dichotomy and a conflictual LER is therefore inevitable.

2. The demographic and socio— economic base of organized labor and environmentalism is distinct and as a consequence there have been conflicts.

3. Internal decision—making procedures of labor often did not allow for a fair treatment of environmental positions, and thus have contributed to the conflicts.

4. The overall political—institutional framework has discouraged labor—environmentalist cooperation in the FRG but has partially encouraged cooperation in the US.

5. Closely related to the political—institutional frameworks, ideology has been a factor bearing on the LER. The commitment to

"social partnership" prevalent among the German unions underlied the conflicts as did "business unionism" in the US. Those American unions espousing "social unionism" have cooperated with environmentalism on a case by case basis.

In the following, with respect to each explanation, I will summarize the conclusions and state the questions which have been raised but not answered.

Explanation 1

The perception of a built—in dichotomy between employment and environmental protection as argued in Explanation 1 was undoubtedly the major reason for the labor—environmentalist conflicts in the past. Regarding energy, this view entailed the promotion of non—import—dependent, especially nuclear, supplies which were believed imperative for the economic viability of the industrial countries and thus indispensable for securing employment. This view was the conventional wisdom and those not sharing it faced an upward battle to prove their point. While those sharing the conventional view usually conceded that environmental protection measures ALSO created some employment, they saw the opportunity cost in terms of employment considerably higher than the benefits. Labor, in general, shared the conventional view while environmentalists were among the foremost challenging it.

Beginning in the second half of the 1970s, this view was increasingly questioned. Reduced or stagnating energy consumption, rapidly rising energy prices, high structural unemployment, Lovins' (1976) "Foreign Affairs" article, sensational pollution incidents, the Black Lake conference, and opposition to nuclear energy all lent credibility and urgency to the closer scrutiny of the built—in dichotomy argument. An alternative perspective postulating the principal compatibility of employment and a clean environment evolved in a mutually reenforcing process of political/ social acceptance and new empirical and theoretical data and analysis. It was beyond the scope of this essay to assess the respective merits of the built—in dichotomy argument and the counter— perspective. However, it is important to note that the counter— view has increasingly taken hold among both movements. As a result, the LER has in parts improved, spearheaded in the US by several industrial and service sector unions. If, as many argue, it will prove a misperception that employment and environmental protection are compatible, then the labor—environmentalist rapprochement observable in recent years was based on shaky grounds and will likely be reversed.

Thus, generally stated, where employment and environmental protection were believed irreconcilable, the LER was conflictual. On the other hand, the more the two concerns were held to be compatible, the better was the LER. Therefore, Explanation 1 was valid insofar, as indeed a causality was evident between how compatible employment and environmental protection were perceived, on the one hand, and the LER on the other. In other words, a cooperative LER was not conceivable among those who believe that employment and environmental protection are mutually exclusive goals. At the other extreme, those who believed employment and environmental protection measures to be mutually benefitial, often —but not necessarily— tended to cooperate with one another. Particularly in the FRG in recent years, the perception that environmental protection creates jobs has markedly increased among labor, but the LER has not correspondingly improved. There are, of course, a variety of middle positions. Explanation 1 is insufficient to deal with those nor, perhaps more importantly, does it address the question why the political actors have adopted the positions and policies they have.

Many questions pertaining to the perceptions of the interdependencies among employment, environmental protection and energy, and what that may have meant for the LER have remained unanswered. Indeed, more questions might have been raised than answered. How should the UAW's position toward auto emission and fuel efficiency requirements or the USWA's toward air quality be interpreted? Believers in Explanation 1 in both cases would see the unions give up environmentalist positions in order to save employment for the membership. Others might interpret the unions' behavior as compromising their anti- pollution commitments in the short term in favor of securing employment and environmental protection in the long run. An answer to the question of which of these interpretations is the more accurate one would require more in depth case studies than I was able to do.

Another question raised in this context concerns the "environmental blackmail" argument. Parts of both labor and environmentalists have accused industry of environmental blackmail, i.e., of seeking to avoid anti-pollution measures by falsely claiming that these measures would inevitably cost jobs. Not all threats of job losses for environmental reasons, of course, are blackmail. Again, this essay did not seek to judge which of these accusations were justified and which were not. The question is, how does one distinguish between environmental blackmail and legitimate arguments of management? An answer to this question would be especially important for assessing the built-in dichotomy argument, but also has some direct relevance for the LER. First, the environmental blackmail accusation has a strong ideological component and, as such, has been a unifying factor for labor and environmentalists. Second, it is clearly related to the demand for more transparency and public accountability of corporate decisions. This has been an old labor union demand and, in principle, is also echoed by most environmental organizations, even though there might be different views on how to achieve it. Again, case studies of union environmental policy decisions might help to approach the environmental blackmail question.

Moreover, several questions pertaining to the effects of the state of the economy on the LER (raised in Section 3.2) can only tentatively be answered: Did the reduced construction work accompanying economic decline aid or complicate the LER? To what extent was the cancellation or delay of various construction projects the result of environmental pressure or considerations? Did economic decline result in loosened environmental requirements? Did labor and environmentalists cooperate on some occasions because of common beliefs or mainly for tactical purposes?

A tentative answer for the FRG would be that both higher environmental consciousness (at the political, administrative and judicial level) and fiscal constraints have preempted several construction projects. Regarding the IGBSE, the economic decline in construction has helped to turn its attention to the job creating potential of environmental measures. This may lead to somewhat more openness toward the environmental movement, but will hardly move the union to now reject environmentally harmful construction projects.

If weakened standards (compared to those previously in effect) are any indication, economic decline in both countries had at most a marginal impact (such as the steel stretch-out in the US). However, some qualifications are in order. First, corresponding to the concept of opportunity cost, one might assume that economic decline has prevented reaping what could be called environmental "opportunity benefits". In other words, had the economy been stronger, environmental requirements might have been stricter from the outset. The resistence to strict measures may have been less effective and supporters of tight requirements might have more resources (e.g. unions like the Steel- and Autoworkers). Second, the "extremist" approach of the Reagan administration toward deregulation confounds this issue. It is quite conceivable that a more moderate strategy of environmental and OSH deregulatuion would have helped those who wanted to weaken existing statutes to succeed. Of course, the gutting of regulation has been "successful". But it seems inappropriate to "credit" the economic decline for this, because the general pro—business, pro—free market philosophy of the Administration seems to have been the driving factor for the onslaught on regulations.

The confusion of economic and political/ideological factors also effects the question about the motives of labor—environmentalist cooperation. Prior to the Reagan administration, environmental support for an issue like Labor Law Reform might in part have been given, because it was an issue very dear to labor but did not "cost" much organizationally or in terms of conceding their own positions. Similarly, some environmental groups in 1970s might have supported OSH—related matters only half—heartedly. That is, these groups agreed to the necessity of OSH protection but saw little substantive relevance for the natural environment. On the other hand, the OSH law would probably not have been enacted without the support of environmental and other groups outside of labor. Thus, tactical motives have probably played a role in some cases.

Yet, the environmental commitment of a union like the UAW, exemplified by convening the Black Lake Conference, seems —without doubt— be founded in basic beliefs rather than guided by tactics. Furthermore, common opposition to Reagan's environmental and OSH policies was guided by a genuine concern for both issues by many labor unions and environmentalists. To be sure, a group such as the Sierra Club was probably more concerned about "Poisons on the Job" than the NWF. But there is no question that the interlocks of physical issues and of policies have also increased the quality of labor— environmentalist cooperation.

In sum, the perception of the compatibility of employment and environmental protection, or lack thereof, is a necessary but not sufficient condition for the LER. Altogether, there is no definite answer on how economic well—being has effected the LER. While this leaves the question of the validity of the built—in dichotomy argument undecided, it suggests careful consideration of the other explanations. The issues addressed in the other explanations must be expected to bear both on the compatibility question and the LER directly.

Explanation 2

The demographic and socio— economic composition of the memberships of labor unions and environmental organizations has been different. However, the differences have not translated into significantly conflictual opinions regarding environmental, employment or energy issues proper. There was dissensus among population subgroups but the cleavages were less along traditional class lines. Rather, they followed occupational, educational and generational lines. The comparison of the memberships of the Sierra Club and the NWF, and the organizations' attitudes toward labor shows that the LER is not necessarily better when the respective memberships are more similar.

In conjunction with the findings in Chapter 7, two different factors seem relevant. First, higher income, higher socio— economic status, better educated people may be less parochial and have longer time horizons in their thinking, and therefore be more open to cooperation with people of other backgrounds. This supposition would explain the cooperation between public employees' unions, service unions and environmental organizations on the one hand, and the little cooperation involving the NWF or construction unions on the other. It does not explain the pro— environmental attitudes of UAW, USWA or IAM unless one attributes the environmental policies of these unions to their leadership that was shaped by social union traditions.

Second, it is not only the attitude on the environmental, employment, or energy ISSUE proper that is important for the LER but also the general attitude toward the WAY the issues and interests are treated in the political process. Inglehart's "post- materialists" and "elite challengers" are found particularly among strata characterized in educational and generational, but not class—based, terms. This factor was especially important in the FRG.

If it is correct to emphasize these two factors, then the LER might improve in the future under ceteris paribus conditions. Among labor in general, and within unions in particular, white collar and service sector employment and educational levels have increased while age has decreased. On the other hand, the environmentally cooperative industrial unions in the US have substantially lost members and their influence will likely decline. Moreover, tight budgets will limit public sector employment. Still, the former development outweights the latter in terms of sheer numbers.

Explanation 3

The decision making procedures in both American and German labor unions generally favored the positions advanced by the leadership. Regarding the LER, the procedural advantage of the leadership and apparatus particularly came to bear in the nuclear power controversy within the German unions. This is not to say that the labor unions would have adopted anti— nuclear policies had the intra— union opposition only had equal opportunities. (Pertinent union membership opinion data, unfortunately, were not available.) But the decision making as it was contributed to the labor—environmentalist conflicts in the FRG in several ways. First, the influence of work council members from the energy industry and power plant component manufacturing industry was so strong that the DGB sponsored the Dortmund rally, and reversed its original position linking nuclear power plant construction to the problems of the back—end of the fuel cycle. These two decisions were heavy burdens for the LER. The question remains as to what extent these decisions were necessary to prevent factions of the unions from leaving the DGB. How real was that threat? On the other hand, what were the costs of these decisions in terms of increased internal dissent, more social polarization, or a weakened SPD?

Second, union decision making contributed to the factor of order image of organized labor and exacerbated the countervailing power role of German environmentalism. If the labor unions, in conjunction with the SPD, had been a credible forum for environmental concerns, it likely would have channelized much environmental dissent in and outside of labor. But as it was, labor's overt and covert hostility to environmentalists (and of other interests such as in housing or the "peace movement") strengthened new organizational efforts and the elite— challenging activities and self—image of these critics.

Decision—making in the environmental movement must also briefly be addressed. The German movement, unlike its American counterpart, was characterized by its protean structure, which has often been blamed for discouraging contacts with other groups. The Greens becoming a focal point of environmentalism might change this, and cooperation with other "established" actors therefore become easier. On the other hand, this process would increase the electoral competition with the SPD, which in turn would pose a burden for the LER.

The ramifications of union decision making on the LER are less clear in the US. While the building and construction unions might have had less democratic features than, let's say, the UAW or AFSCME, the official positions of the former on environmental protection, energy policies or construction projects were likely shared by most of the membership. Thus, more membership rights probably would not have made a difference. In the case of the UAW, the opposite might even be the case, i.e., many of the liberal, including pro—environmental, views and policies of the leadership might be much less widely shared by the membership. However, the lack of membership attitude data does not allow for a less speculative statement.

What did benefit labor—environmentalist cooperation was the great heterogeneity within American labor. "Deviant" unions in the FRG were more strongly pressured to conform to Federation policies than in the US. The reasons for that lie mostly in the different histories, ideologies, and ways of political integration of the two labor movements.

Explanations 4 and 5

Chapters 6 and 7 sought to make the point that political—institutional and ideological factors were a central determinant for the LER. These factors were the corporatist mode of interest intermediation particularly in Germany, the considerable degree of political integration of German labor, the interlocked relationship of organized labor and the SPD, labor's commitment to the W.German "social market economy" and "social partnership", the changing party landscape, and the perceived lack of adequate representation of environmental interests by the traditional political actors. These elements came to bear particularly strongly in energy politics.

While, with respect to the other explanations, different conditions in the US and W.Germany seemed less important, the distinct political frameworks were significant. The American electoral system and Congress have been more open to the influence of interest groups but virtually closed to an environmental party; American labor was politically less integrated and environmentalism more so than their German counterparts; while American labor's ties to the Democratic party were about as strong as those between the German unions and the SPD, party programs and discipline were much less important in the US; divisions among American unions on issues as well as ideology were more pronounced; and corporatism in general, and with respect to energy politics in particular, was less strong than in the FRG. All these factors have been a strong influence on the LER in the two countries in the past and will likely remain so in the future.

In an earlier version of this book, one of the main questions regarding the future of the LER in the US concerned the effects of Reaganomics: Has it entailed more labor—environmentalist conflicts because, for instance, the goal to raise productivity increased the competition between higher wages and environmental protection; because government agencies have ceased to promote labor—environmentalist ties or because, to pick up an earlier question, the economic situation and thus the unemployment rate have worsened, and therefore the pressures to disregard the environment have grown? Or have the Reagan government and increased corporate power fostered labor—environmentalist cooperation because it has put both movements into the defensive? Based on the experience of the first three years of the Reagan administration, the LER clearly has improved. The "extremist" policies of the Administration regarding deregulation and social justice, and increasingly unfair corporate labor practices condoned by the Administration have furthered this process. Moreover, shifts on the environmental agenda in the areas of toxics and occupational safety and health, the declining importance of nuclear energy, and the positive impact of environmental measures on construction jobs will tend to improve the LER further.

Another issue is the future of American organized labor as such. Looking at labor as a whole, the unionization rate has declined from more than 30% in the 1950s to less than 20% at present. Moreover, labor's political muscle has lost strength, and, most importantly, union organizing has experienced great difficulties. Looking inside the house of labor, dramatic shifts of relative union and sector strengths can be observed: the large unions representing workers in the auto, steel, manufacturing or construction industries have lost membership while service and public employees' unions have been gaining.

How these developments will affect the LER is not obvious. Will what remains of unions (if the relative decline of the past 25 years continues) concentrate on defending professional privileges, as the old craft unions did, or will the unions perceive a greater need for political allies? Further, will government deficits continue to increase and thus public employees' unions begin to lose members? Will the recent trend continue and the state intervene less in the economy? In that case, both public employees' unions and environmentalists might find themselves in the same boat.

The relative decline of UAW, USWA or IAM on first sight, of course, will weaken labor—environmentalist cooperation. On the other hand, two of these three unions have been on the fringes of the labor movement. The UAW has, until recently, not been affiliated with the AFL—CIO. The IAM's anti—corporate stands made it somewhat of an outsider in the federation. Thus, the relative decline of these two pro— environmental unions might after all not significantly affect the overall policies of the AFL—CIO regarding environmentalism. It might be more important with respect to the direct relationship between environmentalism and these unions.

Unions have in the past cooperated when structural adjustments were inevitable. Individual unions have often considerably lost in membership but have survived as organizations (which they might not have done without cooperation). The coal mining (UMW, IGBE), railroad or longshoremen's unions have lost many members in the process (McConnell, 1967:328; Meyer— Renschhausen, 1977), while IAM and IUOE successfully expanded into other sectors. Environmental and consumption—oriented energy politics might, indeed, reduce the employment opportunities and thus the traditional membership base of a union such as the IUOE. But hardships for the membership and the organization as a whole could be mitigated by programs, as has happened in the past. Controled adjustment to structural changes might, in fact, insure the long—term viability and employment security of a union and its membership, which the continuation of present trends might not. Numerous collective bargaining agreements and legislation exist seeking to mediate the effects of job losses caused by changing technology, economic structure, or public policy (Millen, 1979). As a case in point, existing environmental legislation contains some protection provisions against employment losses due to environmental policies. The Clean Water Act requires the EPA to conduct a continuing investigation of potential employment losses or plant closings resulting from effluent limitations. The Redwood National Park Act amendments of 1978 provide protection to workers displaced by the expansion of the park. Thus, these experiences might be applicable to the energy sector as well and preempt an important source of past labor—environmentalist conflict —given the political will to provide such adjustment aid exists.

Still, there is also some food for thought about the possibility that in the long run, an entirely new pattern of labor— environmentalist relations might evolve. Two developments seem particularly important. First, recently concluded collective bargaining contracts established two—tier wage systems differentiating between the old employed and the newly employed. Moreover, the wage differentials between old, newly organized and unorganized industries tend to be substantial. If these trends continue, a split within the labor movement between older, skilled, fairly well—paid workers represented by the traditional industrial and building and construction unions, on the one hand, and younger, more recently organized, less well—paid members of public and service employees unions, on the other hand, is likely to occur. This split might be accompanied by a second development, i.e. cleavages within the Democratic party. As the race between the presidential candidates Hart and Mondale highlighted, the Democratic party is split along generational lines. It is conceivable that four or eight years from now, the traditional parts of both organized labor and the Democratic party may get aligned against their respective "younger" counterparts. Should that happen, the "younger" faction will tend to push what the social unions have done in the past

—the environment being one of the issues. Should this party wing succeed, the Democratic party might turn toward a European style labor party with a heavy dose of "life—style" (including environmental) issues on its agenda. Much of what in the past might have been termed labor— environmentalist cooperation, might then take place within this rejuvenated Democratic party.

In the FRG, the central political topics affecting the future of the LER will probably be the realignments of relative party strength; the evolution of the Greens and their relationship to the SPD; and the future of the extra—parliamentary movements, not only with respect to the environment, but also on other issues like security policies, housing, unemployment and social cuts, or women's rights. All these issues, of course, are interrelated.
The key question with respect to the future composition of the German party system will be whether SPD chairman Willy Brandt was right when he suggested that there will be no majority to the right of the SPD. If one extrapolates the election results of the last two years (since the CDU/FDP coalition government took over in Bonn), the FDP will have problems surpassing the 5% limit nationally and in most states, while the Greens will safely overcome this hurdle. Should that happen, the SPD and the Greens would have a numerical majority. Since absolute SPD majorities are unlikely in most states, some kind of Green participation in state government will be a reasonable option.
Yet, whether working SPD—Green alliances will in fact be feasible, will depend on more than a numbers' game. In both parties, profound resentments would have to be overcome. The Greens would have to establish their credibility that they can compromise, that issues agreed upon will not be overturned by future party conventions, and that they can muster competent leadership and professional staff. The opposition of so—called fundamentalists in the party to such developments would be substantial. In the SPD, the cleavages are between what could be called materialists, who are sceptical about the Greens, and post—materialists, who would give formal cooperation a try. Before the party's demise from government, the two wings might have been personified by Helmut Schmidt and Willy Brandt. The former caters to a traditional working class constituency and is close to older labor union membership and leadership. The latter wing appeals to the young, "ecopax"—minded clientele of the party, and many of its spokesmen have been engaged in the environmental and peace movements and have often been leaders of the Young Socialists, the party's youth organization.
Despite the (temporary?) failure of red—green cooperation in Hessia, the prospects for another try are not too bad. Not only has Hessia's Prime Minister Boerner, traditionally a party conservative, proven that political imperatives can claim converts quite quickly, but in two upcoming state elections, the SPD candidates for Prime Minister have already expressed their interests in alliances with the Greens. For both parties, the best way to counter the resentments against such a cooperation would probably be successful cooperation. (Paranthetically, the dilemma between "Systemopposition" and "Reformpartei" that the Greens are currently in, in some ways resembles the one the SPD faced in 1903 after very successful elections: Could the state be radically changed by reforms (Bernstein) or only by a revolution (Kautsky) (c.f. DIE ZEIT, 14.12.1984:1)?)
The LER, I believe, will be significantly shaped by the outcome of red—green parliamentary alliances or coalitions. If they succeed, they would substantially reduce the credibility problem labor has viz—a—viz the Greens. Programmatic statements would become more tangible and consistent, formal contacts would be facilitated, personal interactions would gain in continuity,and the activities of the "green" members within labor would become more respectable.
On the other hand, if alliances fail, both labor's scepticism would be reenforced and the fundamentalist tendencies within the Green party

would be strengthened. As a result, the consolidation the Greens **have** meant for the environmental movement will possibly be reversed. While the traditional citizen groups might well have become "obsolete by their successes" —as a newspaper headline claimed (DIE ZEIT, 7.12.84:5)— the formation of more permanent, better organized, less parochial citizen groups would be stimulated. Together with a wide range of other concerns, environmentalism would again concentrate on extra—parliamentary activities to the effect that polarization of society outside of the established channels of interest intermediation would increase. Unless labor rediscovers its countervailing power role —which is unlikely—, conflicts with environmentalism and other extra— Parliamentary movements will tend to rise. These conflicts will be less along the "jobs versus the environment" lines of the 1970s but will have life—style issues at their heart. At this point, an interesting affinity to traditionally conservative —and thus non—labor— concepts might take hold. Not demands addressed to the state, but self—help initiatives might be the ensuing "politics". As the above cited article sarcastically stated, the natural food store might be more important to the "environmental activist" than dioxine threats.

List of Abbreviations

AFL–CIO	American Federation of Labor-Congress of Industrial Organizations	Amerikanischer Gewerkschaftsdachverband
AFSCME	American Federation of State, County and Municipal Employees	Gewerkschaft des öffentlichen Dienstes, der Einzelstaaten, Kreise und Kommunen
AKL	Forum of critical labor union members	Aktionskreis Leben
B	Billion(s)	Milliarde(n)
BBU	Federation of Environmental Citizen Action Groups	Bund Bürgerinitiativen Umweltschutz
BUND	German Federation for Environmental and Nature Protection	Bund für Umwelt und Naturschutz Deutschland
CAA	Clean Air Act	Luftreinhaltegesetz
CDU	Christian Democratic Union (political party)	Christliche Demokratische Union
CEQ	Council of Environmental Quality	Rat für Umweltschutzfragen (dem US Präsidenten unterstellt)

CLEC	Citizen Labor Energy Coalition	Energiekoalition von Bürgern und Gewerkschaftern
COPE	Committee on Political Education	Politischer Arm des ⌐ AFL-CIO
CSU	Christian Social Union (affiliate of the CDU only in Bavaria)	Christlich Soziale Union
DOE	Department of Energy	Energieministerium
DOL	Department of Labor	Arbeitsministerium
DGB	German Federation of Labor	Deutscher Gewerkschaftsbund
EFFE	Environmentalists for Full Employment	Umweltschützer für Vollbeschäftigung
EPA	Environmental Protection Agency	Umweltschutzbehörde
FAZ	Frankfurter Allgemeine Zeitung	(daily newspaper)
FDP	Free Democratic Party	Freie Demokratische Partei
FOE	Friends of the Earth	Freunde der Erde
FR	Frankfurter Rundschau	(daily newspaper)
FRG	Federal Republic of Germany	Bundesrepublik Deutschland
GAL	Green-Alternative List (Green party in Hamburg)	Grün-Alternative Liste (in Hamburg)
GEW	Union for Teachers and Scientists	Gewerkschaft Erziehung und Wissenschaft
HBV	Union for Trade, Banks and Insurance	Gewerkschaft Handel, Banken, Versicherungen
IAM	International Association of Machinists	Maschinenarbeitergewerkschaft
IBEW	International Brotherhood of Electrical Workers	Gewerkschaft der Elektriker
IGBE	Industrial Union for Mining and Energy	Industriegewerkschaft Bergbau und Energie
IGBSE	Construction Workers Union	Industriegewerkschaft Bau, Steine, Erden

IGCPK	Chemical Workers Union	Industriegewerkschaft Chemie, Papier, Keramik
IGDP	Printers Union	Industriegewerkschaft Druck und Papier
IGM	Metal Workers Union	Industriegewerkschaft Metall
IUD	Industrial Union Department (of the AFL-CIO)	Abteilung für Industriegewerkschaften (im AFL-CIO)
IUOE	International Union of Operating Engineers	Gewerkschaft der Bauarbeiter
KWU	Power Plant Manufacturer	Kraftwerk Union
LCV	League of Conservation Voters	Vereinigung von Wählern für Umweltschutz
LER	Labor-Environmentalist Relationship	Beziehung zwischen Gewerkschaften und Umweltschützern
M	Million(s)	Million(en)
NAACP	National Association for the Advancement of Colored People	Bürgerrechtsvereinigung für Farbige
NRDC	Natural Resources Defense Council	Institut für Rohstoff- und Umweltfragen
NUL	National Urban League	Bürgerrechtsvereinigung für Minderheiten
NWF	National Wildlife Federation	Natur- und Tierschutzorganisation
OCAW	Union of Oil, Chemical, and Atomic Workers	Gewerkschaft der Öl-, Chemie- und Nukleararbeiter
OE	Operating Engineer (newspaper of the IUOE)	Zeitung der IUOE
OSHA	Occupational Safety and Health Act	Gesetz für Arbeitsschutz und -sicherheit
ÖTV	Public Employees Union	Gewerkschaft Öffentliche Dienste, Transport und Verkehr
PAC	Political Action Committee	Finanzielle Lobby hpsl. bei Wahlkämpfen
RWE	Largest electric utility company in Germany	Rheinisch-Westfälische Elektrizitätswerke

RWP	Regional Workshops Program	Arbeitskonferenzen auf lokaler und regionaler Ebene (von der UEC koordiniert)
SEIU	Service Employees International Union	Gewerkschaft im Dienstleistungsgewerbe
SPD	Social Democratic Party	Sozialdemokratische Partei Deutschlands
SZ	daily newspaper	Süddeutsche Zeitung
UAW	United Auto Workers	Automobilarbeitergewerkschaft
UEC	Urban Environment Conference	Vereinigung für Umweltschutz, Arbeitsschutz, Stadtentwicklung, Recht für Minderheiten, ...
UMW	United Mine Workers	Bergbaugewerkschaft
USWA	United Steel Workers of America	Stahlarbeitergewerkschaft
WDA	World of Labor (weekly newspaper of the DGB)	Welt der Arbeit
WSI	Social Science Institute (of the DGB)	Wirtschafts- und Sozialwissenschaftliches Institut (des DGB)

Bibliography

ACTWU, International Chemical Workers Union, Allied Industrial Workers, IAM, International Molders and Allied Workers Union, OCAW, USWA: Statement in Support of Clean Air. February 24, 1982.

AFL—CIO: man and his environment. Publication No. 143, January 1969.

AFL—CIO: Building and Construction Trades Department Conference. "Position Paper", 1979.

AFL—CIO: Industrial Union Department. Blueprint for a Working America Rebuilding Our Economy for the 1980's, 1980.

AFL—CIO: Committee on Political Education. National Survey of AFL—CIO Members, August 1980.

AFL—CIO: Executive Council Statement on The National Economy. Bal Harbour, Florida, February 16, 1981.

AFL—CIO: Report of the Executive Council to the 15th Convention. Hollywood, Florida, October 3, 1983.

AFL—CIO: Industrial Union Department: Deindustrialization and the Two Tier Society. Challenges for an Industrial Policy. Washington, D.C., 1984

Albracht, Gerd: Thema: Umweltschutz und Arbeitnehmerinteressen. IG Chemie, Papier, Keramik, Hauptverwaltung, HA VII, Abt. Umweltschutz, 1980.

Alemann, Ulrich von: Auf dem Weg zum industriellen Korporatismus? Entwicklungslinien der Arbeitsbeziehungen in der Bundesrepublik Deutschland und Grossbritannien. GMH 9'1979: 552—563.

Alemann, Ulrich von, Peter Mambrey: Gewerkschaften und Buergerinitiativen – Konkurrenz oder Kooperation? In: Hauff (Hrsg.), Band 9, Februar 1980.

Alexander, Herbert E.: Financing Politics. Money, Elections and Political Reform. Congressional Quarterly Press, Washington, 1976.

Andritzky, Walter, Ulla Wahl-Terlinden: Mitwirkung von Buergerinitiativen an der Umwelpolitik. Umweltbundesamt, Berichte 6/78, Erich Schmidt Verlag, Berlin 1978.

Askin, Steve: Labor's disenchantment with nuclear power. The honeymoon may be coming to an end. In: The Progressive (March 1981):43–45.

Atomenergie und Arbeitsplatze. Eine Auseinandersetzung mit den Thesen des DGB-Vorstandes und der Atomindustrie, Burgerinitiative Chemiekollegen gegen AKW, Mitglied der BUU-Hamburg, 1977(2).

Baring, Arnulf: Machtwechsel. Die Ära Brandt-Scheel. Deutsche Verlags Anstalt, Stuttgart, 1982.

Barton, Allen H.: Consensus and Conflict among American Leaders. POQ, Winter 1974–75: 507–530.

BBU: Forderungskatalog fuer ein oekologisches Gesamtkonzept in der BRD. Mitte 1979.

Benson, H.W.: Democratic Rights for Union Members. A guide to internal union democracy. Association for Union Democracy, Inc., 1979.

Berger, Suzanne: Interest Groups and the Governabilitiy of European Society. In: ITEMS, Social Science Research Council, Vol. 35, No. 4 (Dec. 1981), pp 63–68.

Bergmann, Joachim: Organisationsinterne Prozesse in kooperativen Gewerkschaften. In: Leviathan, 2/73 (Mai 1973): 242–253.

Bergmann, Joachim: Organisationsstruktur und innergewerkschaftliche Demokratie. In: Bergmann (Hrsg.), 1979: 210–239.

Bergmann, Joachim (Hrsg.): Beitraege zur Soziologie der Gewerkschaften. es 905, 1979.

Binswanger, H.C., H.Frisch, H.G. Nutzinger, B.Schefold, G.Scherhorn, U.E. Simonis, B.Struempel: Arbeit ohne Umweltzerstoerung. Strategien einer neuen Wirtschaftspolitik. S.Fischer Verlag, Frankfurt, 1983.

"Black Lake Conference": Summary of Conference Proceedings. Working for Environmental and Economic Justice and Jobs. A National Action Conference, May 2–6, 1976, at the Walter and May Reuther UAW Family Education Center, Onaway, Michigan.

Bloomgarden, Kathy: Managing the Environment: The Public's View. Public Opinion, Febr./March 1983: 47–51.

Borsdorf, Ulrich, Hemmer, Hans O., Leminsky, Gerhard, Markmann, Heinz (Hrsg.): Gewerkschaftliche Politik: Reform aus Solidaritat. Zum 60.Geburtstag von Heinz O.Vetter. Bund-Verlag, Koln, 1977.

Bunte, Frank: Sorgen um engagierten Nachswuchs in den Betrieben. Deutsches Allgemeines Sonntagsblatt, 16.9.1984:9.

Bupp, I.C.: Energy Policy Planning in the United States: Ideological

BTU's. In: Lindberg (Ed.), 1977: 285-324.

Buttel, Frederick H., William L. Flinn: Social Class and Mass Environmental Beliefs. A Reconsideration. In: Environment and Behavior, Vol. 10 , No. 3 (Sept. 1978): 433-450.

California Energy Commission: 1979 Biennial Report.

Center for National Policy: Restoring American Competitiveness. Proposals for an Industry Policy Washington, D.C., 1984.

CEQ (1980), DOE, EPA, USDA: Public Opinion on Environmental Issues. Results of a National Public Opinion Survey. US GPO, Washington D.C., 1980.

Chaffin, Tom: Environmentalists are Reaching Out. The Nation, October 9, 1982.

Chaikin, Sol C.: Trade, Investment and Deindustrialization: Myth and Reality. Foreign Affairs, Spring 1982: 836-851

Conradt, David P.: Changing German Political Culture. In: Almond, Gabriel A., Verba, Sidney (Eds.): The Civic Culture Revisited. Little, Brown & Co., Boston, 1980.

Cook, Alice H.: Union Democracy: Practice and Ideal. An Analysis of Four Large Local Unions. W.F. Humphrey Press, Inc., Geneva, New York, 1963.

Crozier, Michel J., Huntington, Samuel P., Watanuki, Joji: The Crisis of Democracy. Report on the Governability of Democracies to the Trilateral Commission. New York University Press, 1975.

Deutsch, Karl W., et al: Political Community and the North Atlantic Area. Princeton University Press, 1957.

DGB Umweltprogramm. DGB Bundesausschuss, 6. Maerz 1974.

DGB: Kernenergie und Umweltschutz. Stellungnahme des DGB-Bundesvorstandes vom 5. April 1977.

DGB: Vorschlaege des DGB zur Wiederherstellung der Vollbeschaeftigung. Duesseldorf, Juli 1977.

DGB: Grundsatzprogramm des DGB von 1963 und der Entwurf von 1979 im Vergleich. GMH 1'1980:28ff.

DGB: Stellungnahme zum Waldsterben. 1983.

DGB: Umweltschutz – Beschaeftigung – Wachstum. Thesen vorgelegt beim Umwelt Forum'83. Das Umweltgespraech, Arbeitsgemeinschaft fuer Umweltfragen e.V., Bonn, 1983.

Edelman, John W.: Labor Lobbyist. An Autobiography. Edited by Joseph Carter. The Bobbs-Merrill Co., Inc., Indianapolis, New York, 1974.

Edingshaus, Anne-Lydia: Wie unser Umweltbewusstsein gewachsen ist. In: Bild der Wissenschaft 4-1980: 101-113.

Environmental Action, Environmental Defense Fund, Environmental Policy Center, Friends of the Earth, National Audubon Society, National Parks and Conservation Association, Natural Resources Defense Council, Sierra Club, The Wilderness Society: The American Environment Under Attack: What Next?, March 1983.

Eppler, Erhard: Ende oder Wende. Von der Machbarkeit des Notwendigen. dtv, Munchen, 1977(2).

Ewringmann, Dieter, Klaus Zimmermann: Interessen und Widerstaende in der Umweltpolitik. Die Rolle der Unternehmen, Gewerkschaften und Gemeinden. IIUG II/77—12, Wissenschaftszentrum Berlin, 1977.

Fanning, Odom: man and his environment: citizen action. Harper & Row, New York, 1975.

Feldengut, Karl: Umweltschutz und Arbeitsplatze. WSI—Mitteilungen, 7/1979: 368—377.

Fietkau, Hans—Joachim: Umweltbewusstsein und Wahlverhalten. Zeitschrift fur Umweltpolitik, 1/1979: 93—112.

Fietkau, Hans—Joachim, Hans Kessel: Beitraege aus der Umfrageforschung zur Konzeptualisierung einer Strategie zur Hebung des Umweltbewusstseins. In: Fiekau, Kessel, 1979.

Fietkau, Hans—Joachim, Hans Kessel: Strategien zur Hebung des Umweltbewusstseins in der Bevoelkerung der Bundesrepublik Deutschland. Berlin: Wissenschaftszentrum Berlin, August 1979.

Fietkau:Umweltbewusstsein: Stand, Artikulationsformen und Veranderungsmoglichkeiten. IIUG/dp 81—6, Wissenschaftszentrum Berlin, 1981.

Fietkau, Kessel: Okologische Werte und gesellschaftlicher Protest. WZB—Mitteilungen, Nr.19—Aug.1982:15—18.

Fiorina, Morris P.: Public Opinion and Pollution: An Interpretive Survey. California Institute of Technology, Environmental Quality Laboratory, Memorandum No. 9, July 1973.

Giessen, Karl—Heinz: Die Gewerkschaften im Prozess der Volks— und Staatswillensbildung. Duncker & Humblot. Berlin. 1976.

Grebing, Helga: Gewerkschaften als Ordnungsfaktor oder Gegenmacht? GMH, 7'1973: 393—400.

Groner, Helmut: Wettbewerb in der Elektrizitatswirtschaft. Energiewirtschaft, 2'1979: 112—117.

Grunen, Die: Wahlplattform zur Bundestagswahl 1980. Bonn, Friedrich—Ebert—Allee 120.

Hagelstange, Thomas: Die Entwicklung der Mitgliedzahlen der DGB—Gewerkschaften 1950—1978. In: GMH, 11'79: 734—743.

Hallerbach, Joerg (Hrsg.): Die eigentliche Kernspaltung. Gewerkschaften und Buergerinitiativen im Streit um die Atomkraft. Sammlung Luchterhand. Darmstadt und Neuwied. April 1978.

Hauff, Volker (Hrsg.): Argumente in der Energiediskussion. Bd. 4/5: Energie, Wachstum, Arbeitsplaetze. Neckar—Verlag, Villingen, Dezember 1978.

Hauff, Volker (Hrsg.): Argumente in der Energiediskussion. Bd. 9 Buergerinitiativen in der Gesellschaft. Neckar—Verlag, Villingen, Februar 1980.

Herding, Richard, Charles Sabel: "Business Unions" in den USA. Eine Verteidigung gegen ihre falschen Feinde. In: Bergmann (Hrsg.),

1979: 363–387.

Hildebrand, George H.: American Unionism: An Historical and Analytical Survey. Addison–Wesley Publishing Co., 1979.

Hill, Christopher: A Theoretical Introduction. In: Wallace, Paterson (Eds.), 1978.

Hirschman, Albert O.: Exit, Voice and Loyalty – Responses to Decline in Firms, Organizations, and States. Harvard University Press, Cambridge, Mass., 1970.

Hoffmann–Lange, Ursula: Theoretical and Empirical Problems in the Definition and Selection of National Elites. Workshop on "Elite Interviewing", European Consortium for Political Research, Joint Sessions, University of Aarhus, 29March– 3 April 1982.

IAM, William Winpisinger: Testimony befor the Environment, Energy and National Resources Subcommittee of the Government Operations Committee, US House of Representatives, Washington D.C., June 14, 1978.

IAM, William Winpisinger: Remarks to the Hawaii Conference on Jobs and the Environment. Honolulu, November 17, 1978.

IAM, William W. Winpsinger: Speech to Energy Coalition Rally. Washington, D.C., May 6, 1979.

Indictment: The Case Against the Reagan Environmental Record. Friends of the Earth, Natural Resources Defense Council, The Wilderness Society, Sierra Club, National Audubon Society, Environmental Defense Fund, Environmental Policy Center, Environmental Action, Defenders of Wildlife, Solar Lobby, March 1982.

IGM Arbeitstagung: Aufgabe Zukunft – Qualitaet des Lebens. Bd. 4, "Umwelt". Oberhausen, 1972; eva, 1973.

IGM, Eugen Loderer: Energiepolitik und Gewerkschaften. IGM Arbeitstagung zur Energiepolitik. Frankfurt/Main, 9. Februar 1978.

Inglehart, Ronald: The Silent Revolution in Europe: Intergenerational Change in Post–Industrial Societies. APSR, Vol.65, No.4(Dec.1971): 991–1017.

Inglehart, Ronald: The Silent Revolution. Princeton University Press, 1977.

Inglehart, Ronald: Wertwandel und politisches Verhalten. In: Matthes (Hrsg.) (1979): 505–533.

Jackson, Anne, Angus Wright: Nature's Banner. Environmentalists have just begun to fight. The Progressive, October 1981.

Jacobson, Gary: Money in Congressional Elections. Yale University Press, 1980.

James, Edgar N.: Union Democracy and the LMRDA: Autocracy and Insurgency in National Union Elections. In: Harvard Civil Rights – Civil Liberties Law Review. Spring 1978: 247–356.

Kaase, Max, Klingemann, Hans: Sozialstruktur, Wertorientierung und Parteiensystem: Zum Problem der Interessenvermittlung in westlichen Demokratien. In: Matthes (Ed.), 1979: 534–573.

Kabelitz,   Klaus   R.:Umweltpolitik   als   Beschaftigungspolitik?
Wirtschaftsdienst, 1980/1: 36–43.

Kazis, Richard, Richard L.Grossman: Fear at Work. Job Blackmail, Labor
and the Environment. Pilgrim Press, N.Y., Fall 1982.

Kelleher, Catherine McArdle: Europe and Theater Nuclear Modernization.
International Security, Spring 1981: 150–168.

Kessel, Hans: Environmental Awareness in the Federal Republic of
Germany, England and the United States. Current Status and Changes.
Wissenschaftszentrum Berlin, IIES dp 84–4, 1984.

Klaus,   Barbara,   Karl   Th.   Stiller: Atomenergie   und
Gewerkschaftspolitik. AJZ Druck und Verlag GmbH, Bielefeld, 1979.

Kmieciak, Peter: Wertstrukturen und Wertwandel in der Bundesrepubliek
Deutschland. Kommission fuer wirtschaftlichen und sozialen Wandel
Bd. 135. Verlag Otto Schwarz & Co., Goettingen, 1976.

Kramer, Leo: Labor's Paradox. The American Federation of State,
County, and Municipal Employees, AFL–CIO. John Wiley and Sons,
Inc., New York, 1962.

Kuttner, Bob: Can Labor Lead?. The New Republic, March 12, 1984:
19–25.

Lash, Jonathan, et. al.:
A Season of Spoils. The Story of the Reagan Administration's Attack on
the Environment. Pantheon Books, N.Y., 1984.

League of Women Voters: Are Jobs Really the Price of a Clean
Environment?. current focus, Pub. No.400, 1977.

Leber, Georg: Vom Frieden. Deutscher Taschenbuch Verlag, Munchen,
August 1980.

Lehner, Franz: Ist die Hoffnung noch gruen? In: Psychologie heute,
November 1978: 46–55.

Lehner, Franz: Grenzen des Regierens. Eine Studie zur
Regierungsproblematik   hochindustrialisierter   Demokratien.
Athenaeum, 1979.

Leminsky, Gerhard: Wandel gewerkschaftlicher Strategien nach dem
2.Weltkrieg. Zwischen institutioneller Orientierung und Besinnung
auf die eigene Kraft. GMH, 2'1981: 86–92.

Lens, Sidney: The Crisis of American Labor. New York, Sagamore Press
(Cited by Logan, Nelkin, 1980).

Lerner, Daniel, Morton Gordon: Euratlantica. Changing Perspectives of
the European Elites. MIT Press, Cambridge (1969).

Levison, Andrew: The Full Employment Alternative. Coward, McCann &
Geoghegan, Inc., New York (1980).

Lindberg, Leon N. (ed.): The Energy Syndrome. Comparing National
Responses to the Energy Crisis. Lexington Books, Lexington, Mass.,
1977.

Logan, Rebecca, Dorothy Nelkin: Labor and Nuclear Power.. In:
Environment, Vol. 22, No. 2 (March 1980): 6–13,34.

Lovins, Amory: The Road Not Taken. Foreign Affairs, Fall 1976.

_____: Soft Energy Paths: Toward a Durable Peace. Friends of the Earth International, San Francisco, New York, Washington, 1977.

Lowi, Theodore J.: The End of Liberalism. Ideology, Policy and the Crisis of Public Authority. W.W.Norton&Co., New York, 1969.

Mangum, Garth L.: The Operating Engineers. The Economic History of a Trade Union. Harvard University Press, Cambridge, Mass., 1964.

Marchal, Peter: Gewerkschaften im Zielkonflikt. Gesellschaftsbild und Selbstverstandnis. Verlag BONN AKTUELL, Stuttgart, 1972 (Nov.).

Matthes, Joachim (Hrsg.): Sozialer Wandel in Westeuropa. Verhandlungen des 19. Deutschen Soziologentages, Berlin 1979. Campus, Frankfurt, 1979.

McCloskey, Michael: Business and the Environment: How They Can Live Together. Remarks to the Commonwealth Club, San Francisco, Sept.2, 1977.

Meissner, Werner, Hodl, Erich: Positive okonomische Aspekte des Umweltschutzes, Umweltbundesamt 3/1977, Berlin(West).

Meissner, Werner: Umweltschutzpolitik und Umweltschutzindustrie: Neue Beschaftigungsmoglichkeiten. In: Hauff (Ed.), Dez.1978.

_____: Umweltpolitik und Beschaftigung. Wirtschaftsdienst, 1979/VII: 330–335.

_____: Umweltpolitik und Beschaftigung. Bemerkungen zum Aufsatz von Kabelitz. Wirtschaftsdienst 1980/I: 44–45.

Meyer–Renschhausen, Martin: Energiepolitik in der BRD von 1950 bis heute. Pahl–Rugenstein Verlag, Koln, 1977.

Mez, Lutz, Manfred Wilke (Hrsg.): Der Atomfilz. Gewerkschaften und Atomkraft. Verlag Olle & Walter, Berlin, Mai 1978.

McConnell, Grant: Private Power and American Democracy. New York: Alfred A. Knopf, 1967 (2nd printing).

Millen, Bruce H.: Providing assistance to displaced workers. Monthly Labor Review, May 1979: 17–22.

Mitchell, Robert Cameron: The public speaks again: A new environmental survey. In: Resources, No. 60, September–November 1978: 1–6.

Mitchell, Robert Cameron: Silent Spring/Solid Majorities. In: Public Opinion, August/September 1979: 16–20,55.

Mommsen, Hans: Die Gewerkschaften und die Durchsetzung des Sozialstaats in Deutschland. GMH, 2'1981: 76–86.

NCAQ: Report of the National Commission on Air Quality: To Breathe Clean Air. US Government Printing Office, Washington, D.C., March 1981.

Nelkin, Dorothy: The Political Evolution of the Anti–Nuclear Movement in the United States. Program on Science, Technology and Society, Cornell University, January 24, 1978.

Nickel, Walter: Das Bild von der Gewerkschaft. In: Das Mitbestimmungsgespraech, Nr. 3, 1975:51–54.

Opinion Research Survey, Inc. (1980): National Survey of AFL—CIO Union Members. Prepared for Committee on Political Education, Washington, D.C., August 1980.

"PB 244 985": Consumer Attitudes and Behavior Resulting from Issues Surrounding the Energy Shortage, Highlight Report, Vol. VII, PB 244 985 (Microfiche), February 1975. Report from Opinion Research Corporation to the Federal Energy Administration, available from US Department of Commerce, NTIS.

"PB 244 989": General Public Attitudes and Behavior Regarding Energy Savings, Highlight Report, Vol. IX, April 1975 (Microfiche).

"PB—254 592": Public Attitudes and Behavior Regarding Energy Conservation: Detailed Tabulations by U.S., etc., May 1975 (Microfiche).

"PB—255 003": Public Attitudes and Behavior Regarding Energy Conservation: Detailed Tabulations by U.S., etc., June 1975 (Microfiche).

"PB—259 345": Public Attitudes and Behavior Regarding Energy Conservagtion: Detailed Tabulations by U.S., etc., December 1974 (Microfiche).

Perger, Werner A.: Die meisten Chancen hat die SPD als bessere CDU. Deutsches Allgemeines Sonntagsblatt, 23.9.1984:4.

Perlman, Mark: Democracy in the International Association of Machinists. John Wiley and Sons, Inc., New York, 1962.

Piore, Michael J.: Unions and Politics (draft). MIT, July 1978.

Radke, Olaf: Gewerkschaftliche Ueberlegungen zum Umweltschutz. In: GMH, 9'72: 562—568.

Riegert, Botho: Zum Stand und zur Entwicklung der energiepolitischen Diskussion im DGB. In: WSI Mitteilungen, 3/1980: 160—165.

Rönsch, Horst—Dieter: Die Grunen: Einmaliges Wahlrisiko oder soziale Bewegung?. GMH, 8'1980: 500—511.

Rosenau, James N., Holsti, Ole R.: American leadership in a shrinking world. The breakdown of consensus and the emergence of conflicting belief systems. A paper prepared for delivery at the Conference on Political Culture in the US in the 1970s: Continuity and Change, Goethe Universitat, Frankfurt, 15—20 June 1981.

Rothbaum, Melvin: The Government of the Oil, Chemical, and Atomic Workers Union. John Wiley and Sons, Inc., New York, 1962.

Sarrazin, Rainer: Entstehung und Entwicklung des "Aktionskreis Leben". Eine Fallstudie zum Verhaltnis von Anti—AKW—Bewegung und DGB—Gewerkschaften. Freie Universitat Berlin, Fachbereich Politische Wissenschaft, Diplomarbeit, Sommersemester 1982.

Scharpf, Fritz W.: Autonome Gewerkschaften und staatliche Wirtschaftspolitik: Probleme einer Verbaendegesetzgebung. Europaeische Verlagsanstalt, Koeln—Frankfurt, 1978.

Schmitter, Philippe C.: Still the century of corporatism? Review of Politics 36 (January 1974): 85—131.

Schmitter, Philippe C.: Modes of Interest Intermediation and Models of

Societal Change in Western Europe. Comparative Political Studies, April 1977.

Schmollinger, Horst W.: Zur politisch-gesellschaftlichen Beteiligung von Gewerkschaftsmitgliedern: Gewerkschafter in Parteien, Kirchen und Vereinen. In: Borsdorf, et al.(Eds.): 135-157.

Schumacher, Hans Guenter. In: Blaetter fuer deutsche und internationale Politik, 11'78: 1300-1323.

Seitenzahl, Rolf: Gewerkschaften zwischen Kooperation und Konflikt - von einer quantitativen Tarifpolitik zur umfassenden Verteilungspolitik. EVA, Frankfurt/Main, 1976.

Shonfield, Andrew: Modern Capitalism: The Changing Balance of Public and Private Power. Oxford, Oxford University Press, 1965.

Sierra Club: Natural Heritage Report No.4: Poisons on the Job: The Reagan Administration and American Workers. October 1982.

Simonis, Udo Ernst (Ed.): Oekonomie und Oekologie. Auswege aus einem Konflikt. Verlag C.F. Mueller, Karlsruhe, 1983.

Slaughter, Jane: Concessions and how to beat them. Labor Education and Research Project. Labor Notes, Detroit, 1983.

Steffani, Winfried: Congress and Bundestag. In: Andrew J. Milner (Ed.): Comparative Political Parties. Thomas Crowell Co., New York, 1969: 288-309.

Sternstein, Wolfgang: Die Grenzen der Macht - Das Lehrstueck Wyhl. In: GMH, 2'76: 76-85.

Stieber, Jack: Governing the UAW. John Wiley and Sons, Inc., New York and London, 1962.

Strohm, Holger: Friedlich in die Katastrophe. 1981.

Summers, Clyde W.: Worker Participation in the United States and the Federal Republic: A Comparative Study from an American Perspective. In: Recht der Arbeit, (Sept./Okt.) 1979: 257-266.

Symonds, William: Washington in the Grip of the Green Giant. Fortune, October 4, 1982: 137ff.

Tofaute, Hartmut: Ergebnisse der Umfrage des Deutschen Gewerkschaftsbundes zum Zukunftsinvestitionsprogramm der Bundesregierung. In: WSI-Mitteilungen, 8/1978: 462-469.

Trommer, Trutz: Die Grenzen von Buergerinitiativen (BI) als gesellschaftspolitischer Ansatz fuer Wirtschafts- und Sozialraete (WSR). (Zu dem Beitrag von Wolfgang Sternstein in Heft 2'76.) In: GMH, 5'1976: 288-294.

UAW, United Action for clear Water: Report of Papers Presented at Conference Held at Cobo Hall, November 6, 1965.

UAW: Resolution on Collective Bargaining in 1970. 22nd Constitutional Convention, April 21, 1970.

UAW: Statement of L.Woodcock, President UAW, before the Subcommittee on Air and Water Pollution of the Committee on Public Works. US Senate Hearings on Economic Impact of Environmental Control Requirements, June 28, 1971.

UAW, Leonard Woodcock: A National Energy Program. Remarks before The Economic Club of Chicago, February 20, 1974.

UAW, Leonard Woodcock: Statement before the Subcommittee on Environmental Pollution, Senate Committee on Public Works, May, 15, 1975, and appendices.

UAW: Testimony of H.Young, Special Consultant to the President, UAW, before the Subcommittee on Health and the Environment, House Energy and Commerce Committee, on Issues Relating to the Clean Air Act, September 22, 1981.

Ulman, Lloyd: The Government of the Steel Workers' Union John Wiley and Sons, Inc., New York and London, 1962.

Umweltgutachten 1978. BT-Drucksache 8/1938. Kurzfassung im Umweltbrief 17, 17. April 1978. BMI, Referat Oeffentlichkeitsarbeit, 1.1.3. Schadstoffwirkungen im Oekosystem.

Urban Environment Conference Inc.: Labor, Minorities and Environmentalists ... Together. Pamphlet published by UEC, 666 11th Street NW # 1001, Washington, D.C., 20001.

U.S. Government: Creating Jobs through Energy Policy. Hearings before the Subcommittee on Energy of the Joint Economic Committee. Congress of the United States, March 15 and 16, 1978. U.S. Government Printing Office, Washington, D.C., 1978.

USWA: Steelworkers Legislative Newsletter, July 15, 1980(a).

USWA: Steelworkers Legislative Newsletter, December 4, 1980(b). Van Liere, Kent D., Riley E. Dunlop: The Social Bases of Environmental Concern: A Review of Hypotheses, Explanations and Empirical Evidence. In: Public Opinion Quarterly, 1980: 181–197.

"Wahlstudie 1976". Repraesentative Bevoelkerungsumfrage, August 1976. Forschungsgruppe Wahlen e.V., Mannheim.

Wallace, William, Paterson, W.E. (Eds.): Foreign Policy Making in Western Europe. A Comparative Approach. Saxon House, 1978.

Wasserman, Harvey: Nukes and Jobs: Dismantling the Myths. New Age Magazine, June 1978: 32ff.

_____: Unionizing Ecotopia. Mother Jones, June 1978: 31–37.

Watts, Nicholas: Gesellschaftspolitische Bedingungen der Umweltbewegung im internationalen Vergleich. In: ZfP, Juni 1979: 170–177.

Weber, Juergen: Interessengruppen im politischen System der Bundesrepublik Deutschland. Bayerische Landeszentrale fuer politische Bildungsarbeit, A 52, Muenchen, 1976.

"Wohlfahrtssurvey", Christian Siara: Komponenten der Wohlfahrt in der Bundesrepublik Deutschland. Ergebnisse einer repraesentativen Bevoelkerungsumfrage im Juni 1978, Tabellenband.

ZDF Politbarometer (1979). Repraesentative Bevoelkerungsumfrage Juli 1979. Forschungsgruppe Wahlen e.V., Mannheim.

ZDF-Politbarometer (1980). Repraesentative Bevoelkerungsumfrage Februar 1980. Forschungsgruppe Wahlen e.V., Mannheim.